THE FILIBUSTER

Also by D. G. Bridson

AARON'S FIELD (Pendock Press)
THE CHRISTMAS CHILD (Falcon Press)
PROSPERO AND ARIEL (Gollancz)
THE QUEST OF GILGAMESH (Rampant Lions Press)

WYNDHAM LEWIS

The Filibuster

A STUDY OF THE POLITICAL IDEAS
OF WYNDHAM LEWIS

D. G. Bridson

CASSELL · LONDON

CASSELL & COMPANY LTD
35 Red Lion Square, London WC1R 4SJ
Sydney, Auckland
Toronto, Johannesburg

© D. G. Bridson 1972

All rights reserved. No part of this publication may be
reproduced, stored in a retrieval system, or transmitted,
in any form or by any means, electronic, mechanical,
photocopying, recording or otherwise, without the prior
permission of Cassell and Company Ltd.

First published 1972

I.S.B.N. 0 304 93860 2

Printed in Great Britain by
Northumberland Press Ltd, Gateshead

F.672

Contents

Foreword

The present study may be said to derive from two personal convictions: that Wyndham Lewis was one of the great creative geniuses of our time, and that his reputation as a creative writer has suffered from a certain distrust of his political thinking—as that, rightly or wrongly, has been understood. His case, in fact, would seem to be not unlike that of Milton, whose pamphleteering and activities in the cause of the Commonwealth delayed for many years after the Restoration a proper appreciation of his poetry. Milton's political ideas, on the other hand, were always known for what they were: Lewis's would seem to have been largely misinterpreted.

In an age so dominated by political antagonisms as our own, this was only to be expected; for Lewis wrote much which invited criticism in his time. He was loudly denounced as an apologist for Fascism, despite the fact that he refused to identify himself with the Fascist cause in Britain. In this he was at least unlike the twenty thousand of his contemporaries who joined the British Union of Fascists during the thirties. Even so, the label of crypto-Fascist—or Fascist fellow-traveller—has continued to be applied to him over the years.

One of the most likely reasons for this has been the comparative inaccessibility of his many political writings, most of which have never been reprinted and are now extremely difficult to find outside of the academic libraries. It is probably known to many readers that in *The Art of Being Ruled* he spoke out in support of Italian Fascism. It is probably remembered that he published two books about Hitler, that he condoned the Italian invasion of Abyssinia, and that he sided with Franco against the Republicans during the Spanish Civil War. It may even be known that he contributed (once) to Sir Oswald Mosley's *British Union Quarterly*. All this might seem, in itself, sufficient cause for Lewis's neglect by a generation which was engaged in a bitter war against Nazi and Italian Fascist militarism—to say nothing of a generation which had denounced that militarism from the outset. But before condemning Lewis for what he is *supposed* to have written, it is surely necessary to be clear in our minds as to what he wrote in fact. Even if one finds him sadly awry in his estimate of the dangers inherent in Nazism, the truth remains that he was far from being alone in his wrong judgment. And leaving his fellow-intellectuals out of the matter altogether, it is worth remembering that appreciation of the Fascist leaders, and even endorsements of Fascist policy, came at one time or another from prominent British statesmen who were later to be most resolute in defeating them. Quite obviously, the context in which any political opinion is expressed may often be no less important than the opinion itself. As this book is an attempt to show, this was no less true in Lewis's case than it has been in many others.

The tendency has been, among some of the critics who have considered Lewis's political philosophy, to regard it as an unchanging and consistent whole. This is to imply that he adhered throughout his life to hard and fast political beliefs that were never modified by events—or even dependent upon them. But as Ezra Pound has insisted, every man has the right to have his ideas examined one at a time: when the ideas are in process of changing, it is equally important that they should be examined phase by phase. And because Lewis was so concerned with events, the evolving pattern of his political ideas can only be studied as a graph in which the course of contemporary events provides one of the co-ordinates. The topicality and chronological order of his political writings, therefore, must be of particular interest—inspired as they were by the rapidly changing stresses in international affairs. In the same way, Lewis's occasional contributions to periodical literature must be compared with the larger works into which they were frequently tailored. To put Lewis's own simile to a different use, his occasional articles may sometimes even be thought of as the screen of destroyers with which he supported his capital ships. When they have anything useful to contribute, therefore, they have here been examined in their proper setting.

Many authorities have been cited already for some of the opinions which Lewis held: his political ideas have been related to innumerable sources with which he may or may not have been familiar. Most of the German nationalist writers discussed by R. d'Olier Butler[1] (to which attention has since been called by John R. Harrison[2]), Lewis had clearly never got around to reading, though he may have been aware of their theories at second hand. The same goes for the philosophical and journalistic apologists for Italian Fascism listed by Alastair Hamilton[3], though these were probably not known to Lewis at all. But while his initial interest in politics may well have been stimulated by his reading of the French neo-classicists, as Geoffrey Wagner had pointed out earlier[4], even that fact is relevant only insofar as Lewis himself quotes from them. What is perfectly clear is that most of Lewis's basic ideas and opinions derive from nothing so much as a strong personal conviction: some of them may be his partly by adoption—but they are his no less for that. What makes them important is not so much where they may be paralleled, as the fact that Lewis himself accepted them. What makes them significant is the use to which he put them, the sometimes faulty judgments which they encouraged him to make, and the way in which many of them were modified with time.

For the purposes of this study, therefore, only such sources as Lewis himself acknowledged have been regarded as relevant. Even then, it is the reason behind his acceptance of his sources which has seemed to be of most interest—where this can be guessed at or established. Where there is evidence in his own work to warrant it, therefore, the attempt has occasionally been made to suggest why he may have been attracted to some particular doctrine or theory. To that end, attention has been called to current events, political or social conditions, opinions being expressed by contemporaries, or even the circumstances of Lewis's private life at the time. By helping to explain the context, all these factors are important to any attempt at understanding how his thinking may have been shaped or influenced.

As already mentioned, the fact that most of Lewis's political books are out of print—or available only in excerpt—has made it difficult for many readers to decide what his political statement amounted to overall. The substance of what he said has been condensed and paraphrased and commented upon by many critics—for the most part fairly, but at times misleadingly. In any case, consistency was hardly Lewis's strong point, and his works abound with contradictions: he has even been accused of contradicting himself in the course of a single paragraph. This being so, it is easy enough to misrepresent him by selective quotation which fails to reflect the changing emphasis, the qualifications, the frequent reversals of opinion, and the continuous evolution of his ideas over some thirty years of writing. The changing, overall pattern of his political thinking is what the present study mainly tries to convey.

At least it has availed itself of generous permission to quote from Lewis's own text freely. In this it respects his maxim: 'It is best always to have the *ipsissima verba* of a writer whose views one is canvassing, or invoking.'[5] This is not merely the likeliest way to convey any view accurately, but also the personality behind it. 'There is a tone of voice, a manner of delivery, which only direct quotation can communicate, the importance of which cannot be exaggerated...' he explains elsewhere. Perhaps it is only fair to beg the reader's indulgence, as Lewis did himself, for the bumpy effect of 'bouncing one's way over bits of text enclosed in quotes'.[6] In the case of Lewis's more vigorous diatribes, this in itself can often be highly stimulating.

Not that much of his political prose was anything for which Lewis himself makes any great claims. He admits devoting ten times longer to writing a page of his fiction than he did to writing a page of polemic; he even admits that many of his lesser books, as writing, were 'extremely hurried'—if not actually 'slipshod'. One might possibly agree with him when he says that he 'accorded critical writing too much the status of informal letter-writing'. But however conversational, parenthetical, involved and even downright unsyntactical his political prose may sometimes be, there is a flavour to it which is quite inimitable. Nor am I forgetting T. S. Eliot's observation that all who write 'sympathetically or appreciatively' about Lewis 'tend to mimic his style'. It is easy enough—consciously or unconsciously—to *mimic* the inimitable: it is merely impossible to match it.

If I may be forgiven a note of personal explanation, it might be worth recording how and why this study came to be written at all.

In one of my earliest book reviews—*Wyndham Lewis, Pro and Con*[7]—I once gave a rather impertinent account of what I regarded as Lewis's tendency to smell out non-existent conspiracies (for example, in *Doom of Youth*), while at the same time paying the highest tribute I could to his genius as a creative writer. Three more of his polemical books were reviewed by me during the next two years—none of them, I am afraid, favourably. Reading those reviews again, I find little in them which I should wish to unsay, though I should now devote more space to praising the brilliance of Lewis's critical analyses in *Men Without Art*, and spend less time complaining about his habit of arguing 'from the particular to the general'.[8]

As a convinced Left-winger, I declined to read any of his purely political prose during the thirties, as I had no desire to qualify my great admiration for his creative work both as a writer and as a painter. From what I gathered as to his political alignment at the time, it seemed to me likely that any such reading might merely have had that silly result.

Indeed, while we had many mutual friends during the thirties, I never actually met up with Lewis until 1951, by which time he had virtually lost his sight. I have told elsewhere how I produced for the BBC Third Programme shortly afterwards a radio adaptation of *The Childermass*, and how this in turn led on to a radio production of the entire trilogy of *The Human Age*.[9] While he was writing that extraordinary work, and subsequently until his death in 1957, Lewis and I spent a lot of time together, and I think it would be true to say that we became good friends. But while I enjoyed the stimulation of regular talk with him on a variety of topics, politics were never among them. Feeling that they were a subject on which we were unlikely to agree, I suppose that we carefully avoided them: there were far too many other things to discuss without embarrassing each other.

In point of fact, it was only some twelve years after Lewis's death that I happened to acquire an almost complete collection of his political writings, and began to read my way through them in order of publication. While I found much in them with which I personally disagreed, I was surprised to find that most of them were far less antipathetic than my own Left-wing sympathies had led me to expect. What seemed perfectly clear to me was the fact that Lewis had been badly misjudged by many people (myself among them) who had simply not taken the trouble to read what he had written, or tried to understand the reasons which lay behind it when they did.

Despite our six years of friendship, indeed, *The Filibuster* is a book about a Wyndham Lewis that I simply did not know: it has accordingly proved easy enough to be perfectly honest in talking about him and his works. No doubt my commentary upon his works will suggest that our political viewpoints did not coincide. Nor am I convinced that his own was always a defensible one—in terms which I could completely accept. But agreement has nothing to do with understanding, and appreciation can grow quite sincerely without it. Now that they are of merely historical interest, it is easier to be dispassionate about the political issues of the twenties and thirties. And though objectivity in politics or political writing, as Lewis belatedly agreed, is almost impossible—at least it becomes a little more possible with time. For if time as a subject was hardly dear to Lewis's heart, it has its own advantages.

In his later years, Lewis himself admitted that in many of his 'purely topical books of political journalism', the views to which he committed himself 'often rest on no more than expediency'.[10] He also declared, in the light of experience, that given his time over again, he would not have troubled to write some of them at all. Even those two of them which seem to me the most misguided, were written primarily with a view to keeping Britain out of another disastrous war. They are not to be blamed merely because they failed in that purpose. Politics themselves have a way of failing in their purpose, unless they are content —in a politician's phrase—to confine themselves to exploring 'the art of the possible'. Perhaps it was Lewis's bad luck that he was always loth to accept such a compromise.

It remains to acknowledge my indebtedness to all who have

written earlier monographs or articles upon Lewis and his works. With some of them—Walter Allen, Michael Ayrton, C. J. Fox, John Gawsworth, Geoffrey Grigson, Hugh Kenner, Walter Michel, Hugh Gordon Porteus, the late W. K. Rose, T. G. Rosenthal and E. W. F. Tomlin—I have also had the benefit of discussing Lewis's work personally, at one time or another. Among the others whose books I have consulted, I am particularly beholden to Geoffrey Wagner's valuable Checklist of Lewis's writings. While reserving the right to differ from all my predecessors on points of opinion or interpretation, their conclusions have given me useful guidance in arriving at my own.

Most of all, I am grateful to Mrs Anne Wyndham Lewis for her kind permission to quote from Lewis's works throughout, and for much information provided. While she cannot be expected to excuse its shortcomings, or to agree with me in more than some of my views, at least I hope that she will approve of the spirit in which this study has been attempted.

D.G.B.

NOTES

1. *The Roots of National Socialism*, by R. d'O. Butler, 1941.
2. *The Reactionaries*, by John R. Harrison, 1966.
3. *The Appeal of Fascism*, by Alastair Hamilton, 1971.
4. *Wyndham Lewis: A Portrait of the Artist as the Enemy*, by Geoffrey Wagner, 1957.
5. *A C M*, p.200.
6. *W and A*, p.102.
7. *The New English Weekly*, 2.2.33.
8. *The Criterion*, January 1935.
9. *Agenda*. Wyndham Lewis Special Issue, Autumn–Winter 1969–70.
10. *R A*, p.221.

CHAPTER 1

That Notorious Machiavel

For a man who contrived to produce such an impressive body of creative and critical work, it is worth remembering that Wyndham Lewis was a comparatively tardy starter. Born in 1882, he was thirty-one before publication of his first separate work—a portfolio of drawings, *Timon of Athens*. A few of his stories and sketches had already appeared in the reviews, but he could not be said to have made his impact upon the public as a writer until a year later, when he dropped his explosive review *BLAST* like a puce bomb on the Georgian parlour floor.

BLAST No. 1 was published on 20 June 1914: the second and final number appeared in July the following year. Naturally enough, the war and his own enlistment in the Royal Artillery did much to delay Lewis's full recognition over the next year or two. Work of his appeared in *The Little Review*, the most important of which was subsequently reissued in pamphlet form. His novel *Tarr* was part-serialized in *The Egoist* and published as a book in July 1918, attracting a good deal of critical attention and some highly appreciative reviews. But the end of the war brought little immediate increase in Lewis's literary output. A pamphlet of art criticism, *The Caliph's Design*, was published in 1919, along with a further portfolio of *Fifteen Drawings*. A few articles for the reviews, and the editing of two numbers of his own review *The Tyro*, carried him on into 1922—when, at the age of forty, like Waring, he mysteriously vanished from the scene. In that year, and for the best of reasons, Lewis 'went underground' as he chose to put it—or rather more picturesquely, 'buried himself'. Apart from his odd appearance in

1

The Criterion, The Calendar of Modern Letters and elsewhere, little more was heard of him by the reading public for the next four years. On the other hand, a great deal of activity was going on subterraneously or behind locked doors. As early as 1923, there are references in Lewis's published correspondence to a 'little treatise' on which he is engaged, called *The Man of the World*. This work was designed to explore the relationship between modern man and society in terms of culture, government and social behaviour. In form, it was to combine critical analysis with philosophical and political speculation, the whole being bound together within a narrative framework. As a single concept, it was gargantuan, and Lewis devoted himself to the writing with an energy that must have been obsessive—if not indeed frenetic—working on at it month after month into the small hours of the morning. Under such a sustained onslaught, the work expanded rapidly, each new phase opening up new subjects for study and involving him in wider fields of research. Within a couple of years, it had become apparent even to Lewis himself that there was little chance of completing and publishing it as an entity—and indeed the work had soon begun to break up under its own impetus. Whole sections began to detach themselves centrifugally and move off into separate orbits. *The Man of the World* itself gradually ceased to exist, as Lewis found himself the centre of a whole system of related works bound together into a single group simply by the gravitational field of his own intellectual standpoint. Over the next six years or so, he was to publish seven of these works piecemeal—three of unusual length—apart from a bevy of ancillary pieces which enlivened his planetary system like so many asteroids and wandering comets. The narrative parts of the original structure are now discernible only in *The Apes of God* (1930), and perhaps in *The Childermass*, published in 1928 as the first part of an unfinished trilogy.

The order in which the other five works of the seven were published is confusing enough in itself. Excerpts from them were beginning to appear in the reviews as early as 1925, though there was a delay of anything up to six years before the last of them had been published in book form. Order of publication was no indication of the order of writing, and in many cases the titles were changed as expansion and revision went on. Some of them seem to have been written more or less simultaneously —with later additions confusing the chronology still more. It is not surprising, in the midst of all this activity, to find T. S. Eliot mildly reproving Lewis in a letter for his failure 'to concentrate on one book at a time' and urging him not to keep on planning 'eight or ten books at once'.

In March 1926, however, the first of the books appeared. This was *The Art of Being Ruled*, which was followed in 1927 by *The Lion and the Fox*, *Time and Western Man*, and two issues of Lewis's best remembered review, *The Enemy*—the second of which contained the major part of *Paleface*. From his premature burial, Lewis had obviously risen refreshed, and from then on he was to hammer away at his alarmed and mostly hostile contemporaries with an uninterrupted barrage of books until the outbreak of World War II. When that war had finally got itself declared, Lewis was on his way to America; and it was in the United States or in Canada that he was to remain virtually buried a second time, until peace restored him to London in 1945. From then on, until his death in 1957, the barrage was resumed.

It is worth remarking that 1926, the year of the General Strike, was a singularly apt one for Lewis's return to regular publication. As he saw it, the year marked the end of what he regarded as the post-war world. And though he did not choose to call it so until 1939, it also marked—for him—the beginning of a pre-war sequel. It was during those thirteen years of uneasy peace that most of Lewis's political writing was done—eleven 'political' books being written in addition to a dozen works of literature or literary criticism. Another was written during the war and published in Toronto: two more were published after his return to England in 1945. Fourteen primarily political works, therefore, will have to be considered in the present study —to say nothing of political sidelights in many others.

As we have noted, *The Art of Being Ruled* was published in the spring of 1926, but Lewis himself has explained that it should not be regarded as his 'first political book'—that distinction being reserved for *The Lion and the Fox*, which appeared some ten months later under a different imprint. This was obviously not Lewis's intention, for he goes on to excuse the fact by adding that its publication had been 'unavoidably post-poned' and that 'its true date is before, not after *The Art of Being Ruled*'.[1] This emerges clearly enough from a reading of the texts, and it is proper to consider the two books in their right order.

On its title-page, *The Lion and the Fox* bears the sub-title *The Rôle of the Hero in the Plays of Shakespeare*. According to Geoffrey Wagner, the manuscript bears an earlier sub-title *Or Shakespeare Unmasked*; but either way, the work would seem at first sight to be more literary than political. It describes itself in the text as an 'essay'—the essay being divided into an introduction and nine parts. Rather more accurately, the book comprises a series of essays, which range onwards from a lively analysis of the political and economic background of Tudor England and Renaissance Italy, to a consideration of Machiavelli and his influence, the true implications of Machiavellism, its treatment in Elizabethan drama, Shakespeare's conception of the tragic hero, his philosophical nihilism and probable political affinities, the Machiavellian overtones of his plays compared with those of Chapman (both being contrasted with the treatment of kindred themes by Cervantes), and the whole topped off with Renan's endorsement of Machiavellism in the Caliban of his *Drames Philosophiques*. For good measure, the book concludes with an appendix on *Shakespeare and Race*, in which good fun is made of both Renan's and Matthew Arnold's 'celtism'—and a brusque denial is tabled that Shakespeare had any trace of it.

As will be appreciated, 'essay' is a modest description for such a far-ranging and provocative work. *The Lion and the Fox* is shot through with original thinking on every subject that it takes up, one thought leading on to another in a wholly compulsive if not altogether logical sequence. It is Machiavelli's *Il Principe*, of course, which gives the book its title and sparks off the whole enquiry: 'Since he must know how to play the beast, a Prince must also be able to combine the roles of the fox and the lion; for the lion cannot save himself from traps and the fox cannot defend himself against wolves. A Prince therefore needs to be fox enough to avoid the snares and lion enough to frighten the wolves away. Those who are content merely to play the lion do not understand their own interests.'[2] Conversely, those who are able merely to play the fox will probably not be strong enough to hold on for very long to anything they may have been able to filch.

From a just understanding of the two disciplines—leonine and vulpine—Machiavelli had built up his whole theory of how to rule successfully, and live to tell the tale. Nor would anyone have been unduly shocked by the theory, if no more had been involved than ruthlessness of the usual political or commercial kind. But the Prince that Machiavelli was tutoring had to have rather more to his make-up than that. To begin with, he would probably be some usurper who had seized power for himself in the first place, and was interested in nothing so much as the easiest way to hang on to it. If that was the case, Machiavelli's answer was prompt assassination—the murder of all possible rivals or competitors or relatives who might be able to make common cause against him. The Prince was further advised to make himself feared rather than loved, and cruelty was firmly recommended as an instrument of policy. No obligation was put upon him to be trustworthy, or to act in any way which might prove inexpedient. Power was its own justification, and any Prince who enjoyed it could do no wrong—apart from letting it be taken away from him. For Machiavelli, politics were simply above morality: they had nothing whatever to do with the moral codes of humanity. In the world of politics, he believed, anything went: the end was always enough to justify the means.

All this has a depressingly familiar ring to it, and Machiavelli has clearly found many notable disciples in our time. So he did in his own time, not least of all in his native Italy. As we all know, his idea of the truly model ruler—the one to whose greater glory *Il Principe* had been written—was that paragon among Princes, Cesare Borgia. And the fact that even Cesare had failed to stay in power for long rather makes us wonder whether Machiavellian methods are quite infallible. On the other hand, it must be admitted that he was dead before he had had a chance to study the book: perhaps it might have taught him how to survive. As it was, circumstances beyond his control had contrived to depose him when no more than a few dozen of his friends, relatives and critics had been killed off in the course of duty. For this unfortunate fact, Machiavelli offers excuses:

the premature death of Cesare's father the Pope, and Cesare's own indisposition at a critical juncture.

The simple fact remains that as a ruler after the Machiavellian pattern, even a Borgia is liable to go down before a better application of the doctrine he is following. But when the doctrine is propounded so persuasively, how many rulers of Machiavelli's time could be expected to resist the temptation of trying it out for themselves? Tudor politics had been Machiavellian before the doctrine had ever been set forth: they continued to be still more so after it had been. So did the politics of the Valois rulers in France, ably abetted by the House of Guise and the fine Italianate hand of Catherine de' Medici. The Massacre of St Bartholomew's Day was not very long in finding its Marlowe; and by the time the rest of the Elizabethan dramatists had brought the art of rulership into the Bankside theatres, Machiavellism was accepted as part and parcel of the dramatic convention. All of which *The Lion and the Fox* points out with Lewisian gusto, much irony and a wealth of local colour.

There can be no doubt that Shakespeare himself was well versed in Machiavelli's doctrine, though *Il Principe* never appeared in English during his lifetime. But whether one agrees with Lewis's contention that Shakespeare ranked Machiavelli with Montaigne as 'one of his two main sources of philosophic inspiration'[3] is something that every reader will have to decide for himself. (Eliot, for example, prefers to link Shakespeare's 'Machiavellism' with the translated tragedies of Seneca.) After all, of the 395 references to Machiavelli which Lewis quotes Edward Meyer as having found in Elizabethan literature, only three mentions of Machiavelli himself are to be found in Shakespeare's plays. (Lewis might well have retorted that there is not even a *single* direct reference to Montaigne.) But the fact would seem to be that Shakespeare's 120 odd references to lions and thirty odd references to foxes, as such, mostly hark back directly to *Aesop* and *Reynard*—from which sources, of course, Machiavelli himself derived them.

Whatever he claims for Machiavelli as an influence upon Shakespeare's thinking, however, Lewis is not for a moment suggesting that Shakespeare was in any way condoning Machiavellism. For Shakespeare no less than for his contemporaries, 'that notorious Machiavel' was an object of popular detestation—an ogre whose doctrine was felt to be undermining all that was at the heart of Christian morality. Even those who followed his doctrine most flagrantly were always careful to denounce it—particularly so after *Il Principe* had been burned by the Jesuits, banned by the Inquisition and anathematized by the Council of Trent! After such an elaborate putting-down, not even a rabid *anti*-papist could be expected to stand forth as Machiavelli's disciple in the sixteenth century.

But whatever he thought of the Machiavellian ethic, like his fellow-practitioners Marston, Chapman, Webster, Tourneur, Massinger, Middleton and the rest, Shakespeare was willing enough to accept the Machiavellian counters for what they were worth dramatically. The lion and the fox are to be found at work in many of his plays—*Othello* being the one that first springs to mind. They are to be found at work in *Hamlet*, for that matter, in *Julius Caesar*, in *Macbeth* and in nearly all the Histories—*Richard III* presenting the most conspicuous foxiness of any, laid bare for all to see. But it is not in such obvious and well-known plays that Lewis is at pains to search out the Machiavellian overtones. It is rather in the political antipathies of *Coriolanus*, in the snarling vituperation and shabby-lionism of *Troilus and Cressida* and the self-pitying extravagances of *Timon of Athens* that he chooses to look for his hidden pointers. Nor does he seek them in actual words so much as in patterns of behaviour and attitudes of mind. (In the case of *Coriolanus*, he does not even trouble to call attention to Volumnia's explicit denunciation of the 'foxship' of Sicinius.) But an obsessive concern with Machiavellian philosophy is not what he is really looking for: it is rather Shakespeare's attitude to the world of power and action as manifested in his own contrived world of tragedy. His vaunted 'impersonality' also provides matter for study, his recurrent outbursts of misanthropy—and most of all, the nature of his political affinities. As for these last, Lewis is careful to point out that they are not in any way Machiavellian. What, then, does he deduce about Shakespeare's politics?

To begin with, he does *not* deduce (as many others have done) that Shakespeare's loyalties were feudal—that he tended to side with the ruler against the ruled. Contrary to the usual assumption, Lewis holds that Shakespeare was no more drawn to the militant authoritarianism of Coriolanus than he was to the 'fragments' whom Coriolanus despises—the rank-scented woollen vassals whom he regards himself as divinely ordained to rule unchallenged and to treat with open contempt. Admittedly, the abuse which Coriolanus heaps upon the mob has a sharp thwack to it which suggests a certain relish on the part of the poet. 'It would very nearly describe,' Lewis presumes, 'what Shakespeare probably felt about the London crowd of his time, and especially as he came in contact with it at the theatre. But from this to supposing that he discriminated between this crowd and that other small crowd to which Coriolanus belonged —the crowd that thronged the more expensive seats of the Bankside theatres—is a long step of snobbish unreason and self-deception that we have no right to assume Shakespeare at all likely to have taken.'[4]

Of all Shakespeare's major tragic characters, Coriolanus is the least likeable—and Lewis is probably right in affirming that Shakespeare was very careful to make him so. But whatever Shakespeare may have intended us to feel about him, Lewis leaves us in no doubt at all as to how *he* feels:

> The Coriolanus of Shakespeare seems to have the qualities and defects of the english public school boy, the really successful type of which has for its rationale a military or administrative objective, for which he is prepared by a castration of the imagination. Essentially also his training permits of no development: throughout life he remains the schoolboy he has been taught to be for ever, so that at sixty the same jolly, healthy face shall be there as at the beginning. No amount of physical courage can compensate for the defects of dullness and meanness inherent in such a system. And Coriolanus, who is crabbed, sullen and pompous, has none even of the features that redeem that.[5]

And just for good measure, a little further on:

> It is an astonishingly close picture of a particularly cheerless and unattractive snob, such as must have pullulated in the court of Elizabeth, and such as the english public-school and university system has produced ever since.[6]

Perhaps we should remind ourselves that Lewis himself spent

8

a couple of years at Rugby: the English university he managed to avoid entirely.

On which side of the dispute, therefore, between Coriolanus and the Roman citizens could Shakespeare's sympathies be said to lie? The short answer is—probably—on neither. This is by no means to say that he was indifferent to the issues involved. As one of the ruled himself, he had, after all, a stake in the argument. He was a man dependent upon his own efforts, but still more dependent upon the patronage of others—the so-called great ones and rulers of his world. To them, he was no more than a hireling—on a par with all the others who wore their livery. For most of them in return he may well have felt no more respect than did their valets. But it was their world rather than his own that he was in business to write about, and into that world—the world of the palace and the court—he duly introduced his tragic heroes. More to the point, any dignity which they may have lacked for him, he was at pains to supply in the tremendous poetry which he put into their mouths. As he must have known only too well, not one of them was capable of such utterance in real life.

Apart from their keen interest for him as 'characters', Lewis is of the opinion that Shakespeare had probably scant respect either for their position and dignity, or the events and destinies that they were hopeful of controlling:

> What was his attitude to the violent *action* in the depicting of which he was such a great specialist? What was his private opinion of the many kings and heroes it was his task to fit out for their *pathos*, with blank verse of the highest quality? Did he feel that without their doings there would be no blank verse, and so did he have a warm corner in his heart for them? Or, in the course of writing the series of warlike histories for which he is famous, must not a man of such a brilliant and free intelligence have arrived at Gibbon's conclusion—that history is a record of mankind's follies?[7]

For only one of his great men, Lewis believes—the Anthony of *Anthony and Cleopatra*—did Shakespeare show any discernible affection or respect. As for the rest, he accepted them as he found them—and made of them what only he could have done. But respect for their exalted social station or destiny?

As Lewis points out, the bitterness with which Hamlet is made to inveigh against 'the insolence of office', 'the oppressor's wrong' and the rest of it rather suggests that Shakespeare himself had a clear enough sense of what his verse was investing with a spurious dignity. Though his great men—and most of his little men—speak nothing but the purest poetry, 'there are no great poets, but only kings and princes, most often resembling Cesare Borgia more or less, throughout his many plays'.[8]

Summing his argument up, Lewis puts it this way: 'The view adopted here is that there is a great deal of evidence in Shakespeare's plays that he had the poorest opinion both of the action and the actors that he spent his life writing about.'[9] If the evidence proves anything at all, it would seem to prove that Shakespeare is on the side of the underdog—the ruled. His own voice, whenever it is heard at all clearly, is raised in defiance of unjust authority and in contempt for the raging ambitions that mean nothing to him. Lewis hears it even in the railing of Thersites and the cursing of Caliban. His comic spirit, on the other hand, is 'Puck-like and anarchic, and not at the service of reactionary superstition'.[10] He is even 'much more a bolshevik (using this little word popularly) than a figure of conservative romance'.[11] Finally, he is the 'executioner' of his tragic heroes, for whose suffering he may feel compassion, but of whose fall he is nevertheless the implacable instrument.

All tragedy is based ultimately upon failure—the failure of the hero to control his destiny and impose his will upon the world. And it is because of this that we see so clearly the difference between the Shakespearean hero and the Machiavellian. To Machiavelli, there is only the one true test for a hero—is he successful? Does he carve out his principality, destroy all opposition, and rule without interference? It was not because of his eventual failure that Cesare Borgia had appealed to him—there were mitigating reasons for that—but because he had hacked and strangled and poisoned his way to power and enjoyed it when it was his. Machiavelli would have been thoroughly in favour of Macbeth's short cut to a kingdom—and equally contemptuous of his failure to live with his conscience after he had won through to it. For Shakespeare, on the other hand, it was solely because he could be *given* a conscience that Macbeth acquired any meaning at all.

But if he was not unduly predisposed towards his lions, Shakespeare was no more predisposed towards his foxes. He accepted them as equally necessary to his purpose, and devoted no less of his art to making them live and breathe. He was indebted to Machiavelli for having invited action to channel itself into such convenient antipathies, but that was quite as far as it went. As for Machiavelli himself: 'This Italian was only interested in the founding of States, and he thought uniquely of power. The attention paid by Shakespeare to his doctrines would certainly not be that of one sharing this nasty obsession. What would attract him in Machiavelli would be the latter's exposure of the manner in which the thirst for power maddens men, and how ruling is in fact a disease.'[12]

If that is agreed, the despotic ruler is certainly at the mercy of his disorder—for nobody could be more hedged in by the love of it. Nor could anyone be more adroit than Shakespeare in tracing the ravages of the disease in the minds and hearts of his tragic heroes. To that extent again, then, he would seem to have been indebted to Machiavelli. For not only had he called attention to the disease as one with which any aspirant could easily infect himself: Machiavelli had done more than most to ensure that the disease became epidemic. More to the point, he had built up an avid audience for any dramatist who cared to devote himself to the study of it.

It might be worth remarking, as a footnote to his consideration of the fox in Shakespeare's plays, that Lewis had something highly significant to say about the most notorious of them all. It first appeared in an article *The Foxes' Case*, which was included in *The Calendar of Modern Letters* for October 1925 —over a year before *The Lion and the Fox* was published, though the book says it in a different context: 'Iago ... is for Shakespeare nothing but *Everyman*, the Judas of the *World*, the representative of the crowds round the crucifix, or of the ferocious crowds at the Corrida, or of the still more abject roman crowds at the mortuary games.'[13] In other words, Iago was one more denizen of the pit at Shakespeare's Bankside theatre....

So far, we have merely been considering what Lewis deduces as to Shakespeare's reaction to the role of the autocrat in his exercise of political power. But how did Lewis himself react to that role in *The Lion and the Fox*? First of all, it seems quite clear that he regarded himself as anything but a Machiavellian. The significant fact for him is not so much the cynicism of Machiavelli's opinions, as the candour with which he expresses them:

> Here was a political philosopher, trained in a small-scale imperialistic school amongst the little factious states of Italy, giving away the whole position of the ruler, and revealing even the very nature of all authority. The meaning of all political conquest, and the character of the people engaged in it, transpired with a startling simplicity in the pages of this pedant of crude 'power'. With Darwin's *Origin of Species*, it is a book that forces civilization to face about and confront the grinning shadow of its Past, and acknowledge the terrible nature of its true destiny. In his cold handbook of the *True Politic Method of Enslavement and Expropriation*, the real meaning of life by conquest and management, and almost the real meaning in a further analysis of life itself, was shown with that convincing simplicity, in a tone of engaging harmlessness, reminding you of Defoe's style of narration when a cutpurse is speaking.[14]

And Lewis goes on to compare Moll Flanders's account of how she first got her hands on a lady's watch with Machiavelli's account of how to hold on to power once it has been usurped.

It has often been pointed out—not least ably by Macaulay—that Machiavelli can hardly be blamed for the misdeeds of his disciples. Whatever the violent courses which he advocated in *Il Principe*, much more reasonable doctrine is to be found in his excellent *Discorsi*. In one of his letters he even denies that *Il Principe* had been written as an encouragement of tyranny and enslavement: he protests (perhaps a little lamely) that the book is rather a warning against them. Certainly, his own record as a servant of the Florentine Republic was unviolent and exemplary. Nor was he anyway responsible for the fall of that comparative democracy, or even involved in the anti-Medici conspiracy for which he was subsequently tortured on suspicion. It is quite possible that he secretly believed that only the rule of a ruthless autocrat, and one trained from the first in unscrupulous methods of government, could ever succeed in welding sixteenth century Italy into the single sovereign state that he longed to see established. That, after all, was the pious hope with which *Il Principe* concludes. In the event, it was some 350 years before that unity was finally achieved. But whether the cause of Italian unity was in any way helped by the doctrine of *Il Principe* is very much open to question. It might well be argued that the book had merely retarded unity—by encouraging petty princelings to the further fragmentation of a country already too much torn apart.

But whether Machiavelli should be held responsible for it or not, there can be no denying that his doctrine was to give rise to a great deal of human misery that the world could well have done without. That doctrine, after all, is an open excuse for all the autocratic rule, and the launching of every predatory war, that the world has had to suffer since first he set it down. And in *The Lion and the Fox*, it is this aspect of Machiavellism that Lewis underlines. As he points out, Machiavelli's Prince is concerned with power as an end in itself: what use he made of that power, once it had been assured, is a matter for him alone to decide. *Il Principe* certainly offers little enough by way of guidance in the matter of how to exercise power *well*: sufficient unto that particular text is the mere acquisition of power. But if the end is held to justify the means so completely—what exactly was the end? Autocratic ambition gratified and arrogance indulged would seem to be about the sum of it. For the autocrat himself, the end may well seem sufficient—at least, to begin with. But for how long will it remain so?

Lewis is careful to emphasize that precisely there lies one of the major dangers of Machiavellism: when the duplicity, the skulduggery and the mayhem have paid off—what then? 'The end is a pretence, success even is a fiction, since nothing accomplished and terminated is worth considering. It is not the end, it is the doing it, that is the reward of these as of all other activities.'[15] And certainly, the seizure and exercise of power is rarely enough in itself: all too often it is merely the start of an accelerating process. What had begun by seeeming to be an 'end' may become in time no more than another 'means'—and seizure of one degree of power promptly leads on to seizure of the next. In the case of a Bonaparte, it may well develop into a way of life. And unless that way of life runs finally up against its Waterloo, it may well go soldiering on indefinitely.

Though he cites Napoleon as a shining paragon of a later apostle of violence—Georges Sorel—in *The Lion and the Fox* Lewis chooses to consider a rather more modest disciple of the Machiavellian creed—Frederick the Great. He is chosen as being 'a pure Machiavel, half-way between the renaissance protoplast made in italian clay (and by way of being a *pastiche* of the antique) and the Machiavel of the present day'.[16] Just which 'Machiavel of the present day' Lewis had in mind, he leaves us to decide for ourselves.

What he has to say about Frederick, however, is no more enthusiastic than what he has to say about Machiavelli himself. But Frederick is far nearer to us in time than Cesare Borgia was. He played out his role of autocrat in sublime indifference to the opinions of Rousseau, and in earnest correspondence with Voltaire—against neither of whom, at this stage, Lewis has anything to urge. 'In the evolution of the Machiavellian type under modern conditions,' he confesses, 'Frederick the Great furnishes in a sense the furthest perfection that the type has yet attained. And he started most characteristically by writing a book against Machiavelli, in which he expressed his unlimited disgust and horror at this poisonous tract shamelessly extolling "rapacity, perfidy, arbitrary government, unjust wars". These are the things, of course, for which subsequently Frederick became famous.'[17]

The reason for the young Prince Frederick writing his *Anti-Machiavel* might not at first seem very hard to understand: there could be no better way, in the long run, of proving oneself a perfect Machiavellian. As Voltaire suggested, such a course might well have been thought up by the old fox himself—though on second thoughts, he rather doubted whether Frederick was intelligent enough to have thought it up in turn. In that case, he might even have written his *Anti-Machiavel* sincerely, before discovering the joys of kingship on the Machiavellian pattern.

But once he was fairly launched upon it, one has to agree with Lewis that he played the game like a master. The invasion of Silesia in defiance of solemn treaty was only the first instance of many in which he allowed opportunity and expediency to override all moral obligations—no doubt with tears in his eyes. As Macaulay agreed, this Anti-Machiavel was only too capable 'of violating his plighted faith, of robbing the ally whom he was bound to defend, and of plunging all Europe into a long, bloody, and desolating war; and all this for no end whatever, except that he might extend his dominions, and see his name in the gazettes'. The essay unfortunately does not concern itself with the partition of Poland....

But Lewis is far more forthright than Macaulay in his opinion of the first of the modern Prussians—no doubt because he knew all that Prussianism had unloosed upon Europe since Macaulay's essay had been written. In the light of what he was to be charged with supporting later, his summing-up of Frederick's impact as an authoritarian ruler is worth remembering:

> Launching one terrible war after another, he never ceased to inveigh against his unlucky star that forced him into these conflicts, which were odious to his pacific nature, he would affirm. He never for a moment dropped his mask of negligent detachment from such events, or at least he never allowed it to reveal the features and expression of the bird of prey. And he was spared, by the happy circumstances of the time and place, the necessity of poisoning people; and nothing but his actions, on a great impersonal scale, and with masses of slaughtered soldiers, towns and villages destroyed and so forth (things so big that no one ever, in any period, suspects that a *person* or persons can be responsible for them, unless his responsibility is theatrically advertised as in the case of Attila) could ever have enlightened anyone on the subject of the true significance of this hero....
>
> So the Solomon of the North, the antonine Frederick, is the ideal of a greater Machiavelli. He is the last *Machiavel* in history no doubt that will ever be seen, or at least of which history will be allowed to preserve a true portrait.[18]

There is a fine edge to that excoriation, as well as a shrewd sting in the tail-piece. The *last* Machiavel is probably beyond the ken of all history to come; but history has already recorded quite a few since *The Lion and the Fox* was written. As for those she will ultimately be 'allowed' to record—it is merely a question of who may happen to be around when the sanction is required. We have seen signal instances of Machiavellism writing its own history—and suppressing all the evidence at variance with its desired image. Such was the historiography of Stalinism—in the cause of which, testimony was seen to vanish from the record almost as fast as witnesses vanished off the face of the earth....

But Machiavellism does not always have to trouble itself in such a way: the record can be garbled even when *freely* written. Like every other Machiavel, Frederick himself has frequently been 'explained' in terms very different from those adopted by Lewis—or even by Macaulay. And a certain six-volume 'explanation' was doubtless in Lewis's mind when he took a calculated side-swipe in the direction of Ecclefechan: 'History *à la* Carlyle, written as though in anticipation of the Boy Scout Movement, with its exaltation of every brutal puppet that caught the blood-shot eye of that great sensationalist, is for the eternal infants' class merely. It would be pleasant to think that before long a more scientific type of history may be available.'[19]

The Lion and the Fox, as can be seen, leaves one with a very different impression of Lewis's political thinking—as of 1925— from that which we were persuaded to accept later. The tone of the book is distinctly liberal, and its attitude towards the concept of despotic rule is one of suspicion and antipathy. Like Shakespeare, Lewis may not have displayed any very deep sympathy for rude mechanicals as such, but certainly he betrayed no predilection at all for the autocrat who mechanically seeks to enslave and prey upon them. If *The Lion and the Fox* had been the first of his political books to come before the public, it would have 'placed' him politically as well to the left of centre. Or, as he put it himself some three years later, 'exceedingly remote from what is generally termed a "reactionary"'.[20]

There is certainly nothing in the book to suggest that he would ever emerge as other than a stern critic of the exploitation—to left or right of centre—of the many by the few. The book's scintillating analysis of the freebooting activities at the basis of Elizabethan expansionism, when 'management and defence passed into the hands of private persons or trading companies, after which piece of private enterprise 'the financial interests were supreme'; his calling attention to the 'housewifely marketing operations' which he sensed at the root of all imperialism since; his acid comment that 'many merchant princes are very emotional, and a keen sense of the service they are rendering the state by making money out of it is a well-known feature of their psychology'[21]—all suggested that he was far from being sympathetic to the financial imperialism of Britain in the twenties. All were sentiments, in fact, which might have been found (less pungently expressed) in the writings of the Fabians. Nor did Lewis's girding at the way 'the press is allowed the terrible licence that we see' suggest that the *freedom* of the press was anything less than of the first importance to him.

As to the advocacy of violence for political ends, he did not confine his strictures to Machiavelli. The predatory blond-beastery of Nietzsche he dismisses as contemptuously as the militant proletarianism of Sorel's *Réflexions sur la violence* whose 'phlebotomy' he compares unfavourably with Machiavelli's own on the grounds that the latter had insisted merely on 'the destruction of individuals rather than whole classes'.[22] As for the proletariat *qua* Proletariat, and those who have found the advancement of its rights a convenient leg-up for their own political ambitions, Lewis does not fail to remind us that Frederick himself pretended to make common cause with the common man. All too often, he hints, the supposed interests of the Proletariat—'that fierce, pitiable, harassed abstraction'—have been used as the smoke-screen behind which an oligarchy can operate as autocratically as any monarch.

All in all, *The Lion and the Fox* bears witness to a lively and enquiring mind at large in a field generally reserved for minds that are hermetically closed. It is a book which coruscates with original ideas—the ideas being linked, as already suggested, in sequences whose logic is not always quite demonstrable. For despite what he was later to say in disparagement of intuition, there is a fine intuitive quality to much of Lewis's intellectualism. Indeed, it is just this quality which differentiates all his liveliest writing from work which attempts no more than a careful by-play among incontrovertible facts. And one does not have to agree with him at all points to be stimulated by the galvanic impact even of Lewis's more unlikely theories.

In view of work that was to come, *The Lion and the Fox* is of the first importance, if only on account of the very different direction which Lewis's thinking appears to take later. For that reason alone, no doubt, he was later at pains to emphasize it as his first political book. Nor do we have to take Eliot's dictum that it was 'anti-political' too seriously. In context, this is merely offered in support of his contention that Lewis must always be regarded as a 'detached observer'—a very different thing, as he stresses, from a 'dispassionate' observer.[23]

It was precisely because of his 'detachment' that Lewis reserved the right to change his mind when he chose. And while the liberalism of *The Lion and the Fox* may appear to be unusual among his earlier books, it is not really so unusual as it seems. Apart from which, there is a great deal in the work which is symptomatic of his approach to any controversial subject. In much that he has to say there about the nature of government, there is already clear indication of his acuteness in uncovering hidden motivations. Machiavelli, he warns, is still 'the best textbook for much to-day being accomplished in the political field'.[24] And a truly remarkable mass of evidence in support of that thesis is assembled in the work which had (unluckily) been published nearly a year before—the key book of Lewis's earlier political thinking, *The Art of Being Ruled*.

NOTES

1. *R A*, p.160.
2. *Il Principe*, Chapter 18.
3. *R A*, p.162.
4. *L and F*, p.245.
5. Ibid., pp.202-3.
6. Ibid., p.241.
7. Ibid., p.161.
8. Ibid., p.162.
9. Ibid., p.161.
10. Ibid., p.14.
11. Ibid.
12. *R A*, p.160.
13. Op. cit., Vol. 2, No. 8, p.86 and *L and F*, pp.190-1.
14. *L and F*, p.76.
15. Ibid., p.107.
16. Ibid., p.102.
17. Ibid., p.102.
18. Ibid., pp.104-5.
19. Ibid., p.32.
20. *T and W M*, p.5.
21. *L and F*, p.30 et seq.
22. Ibid., p.96.
23. *The Lion and the Fox*, by T. S. Eliot. *Twentieth Century Verse, Wyndham Lewis Double Number*, Nov.–Dec. 1937. Unpaged.
24. *L and F*, p.201.

CHAPTER 2

The Ruler and the Ruled

In an appreciative review, J. W. N. Sullivan once declared: 'Mr. Wyndham Lewis is a man of innumerable ideas ... he can start more hares in a paragraph than most people can in a book.' As the statement appears among favourable notices of earlier work quoted at the end of *The Art of Being Ruled*, Lewis obviously took it as a compliment—as indeed it was. But where some people will talk about 'starting hares', others might occasionally prefer to talk about 'drawing red herrings'. And of all the herrings that were to bedevil Lewis for the rest of his life, the one that he drew—or started—in *The Art of Being Ruled* was among the most notorious. As it took the form of a hasty and ill-considered endorsement of Italian Fascism, however, perhaps one should think of it as a black herring. Either way, it smelt none too fragrant to many of his readers. 'I am not a communist,' he explains on page 27; 'if anything, I favour some form of *fascism* rather than communism.' And on page 369: 'for anglo-saxon countries as they are constituted to-day some modified form of fascism would probably be the best.'

In his later years, Eliot also was occasionally charged with 'Fascism' or 'anti-Semitism' or both—the charges generally being supported by the quoting of three or four of his more unfortunate pronouncements, invariably taken out of context. (If any of them was accidentally overlooked, Eliot would politely call his critic's attention to the fact.) And Lewis also must have become increasingly weary of citations like those quoted above from *The Art of Being Ruled*. Others could well be added to them, and frequently were. But one thing is worth getting clear from the outset: *The Art of Being Ruled* is certainly not a 434-page plea for Fascism in Britain: even less is it an analysis of Fascist doctrine or methods of government.

Where there are references to it in the book (and most of them are incidental) Fascism is regarded as an offshoot of Socialism—and generally equated with its Russian counterpart, Sovietism. There is one striking encomium of Italian Fascism, as it was known at the time the book was written (1925), but this, as will be suggested later on, may well have been something of an afterthought. Rather than discussing what *The Art of Being Ruled* is not about, however, it might be as well to consider what in fact it sets out to demonstrate.

Put at its briefest, it is an examination of certain trends in western democratic government, and an elaborate analysis of Socialist theory as exemplified in the writings of Marx, Fourier, Proudhon, Saint-Simon and others. It is concerned with the revolution in political thinking which has become a major factor of life in our time—our life in the seventies no less than life in the mid-twenties. From the outset, Lewis declares his opinion that while a revolutionary state of mind may have become 'instinctive', that is merely because the shifting frontiers of science have conditioned us to an acceptance of change. From that, it has become a tendency to suppose that any change is necessarily a change for the better—which Lewis, for one, is far from being persuaded is the case. But decisions as to what form political change may take, he insists, will not be decisions arrived at by the majority. The average man is in no sense politically minded, and the mass of people are 'as non-political as they are unscientific'. As Lewis sees it, there are two contending forces on the political scene: there are 'very many people, exerting great personal authority, who refuse so to regard politics and science as one and refuse to be revolutionary'. On the other hand: 'It is only the wealthy, intelligent, or educated who are revolutionary or combative'. And he concludes: 'The political battle to-day is between those political leaders who are "political animals", and those who are not (as prominent and successful men they are of course both "fighting animals").'[1]

In the course of the book, therefore, Lewis examines a few of the various forms that political change might take—it being underlined from the outset that 'any revolution to-day, just as it must be involved with science, must to some extent start from and be modelled on socialist practice. This applies as much to a fascist movement or putsch, as to anything else. Socialist theory is the school in which we all graduate. Mussolini was, to start with, a socialist agitator. And all *change* to-day is rooted in science: and in science and its imperative of change, all active political creeds meet and to some extent merge.'[2]

Finally, the book provides a careful assessment of the many expedients adopted (or adoptable) in the course of arresting revolutionary change by those to whom it is unwelcome. To such people, he maintains, 'democracy' is merely a means to an end—the end being the subjugation and exploitation of the majority by business and reactionary political interests.

By Lewis, indeed, who saw such expedients being resorted to on every side, some form of change in the political *status quo* was devoutly to be wished—provided that change resulted in improvement:

The european poor become poorer every day: whatever the reason may be for this, you cannot, unless you are a heartless fool, do nothing. And there is an immense instrument to your hand (in socialism), especially organized for the correcting of this terrible situation. As regards socialism, whatever brand you affect, yours is Hobson's choice: to-day you are compelled to be a socialist, at all events in anglo-saxon countries. In Italy fascismo provides you with a creditable alternative.[3]

As we have seen, in both the last two references to Fascism (and there are not all that many in the entire book) Lewis is clearly regarding it as a variant of the Socialism that he is discussing. We may well challenge that assumption, from later experience of Fascism in action. But if we regard some form of Collectivism as the final objective—and Sovietism or Fascism as merely two means of achieving it—we may be able to follow Lewis's argument with more equanimity. What he is interested to promote, in short, is a strong form of centralized government by which the economy of the country as a whole can be planned and controlled efficiently. The result of such government, he affirms, will necessarily be Socialism of some form or another.

It must be emphasized further that in his use of the word 'revolution', Lewis does not imply any form of armed uprising

—at least, not inevitably. He is careful to stress that the means by which he hopes to see revolution brought about 'is that of spiritual ascendency or persuasion, with the avoidance of all violence as an article of faith'.⁴ And so far as he is concerned, persuasion reduces itself to simple demonstration. This is the way it is, he suggests, and the question duly arises—is this the way that it ought to be? If not, then the alternatives are there to choose between.

The Art of Being Ruled is a long book, and a sizeable part of it is given up to Socialist philosophy and theory, in which Federalism is contrasted with Collectivism, Syndicalism with State-Socialism, and the doctrine of Proudhon with the doctrines of Rousseau and of Marx. A number of authorities are cited on both sides of every question—Fourier, Fouillée, Kautsky, Sorel, Suarès, Péguy, Bakunin, Lange, Leroy-Beaulieu and whoever not. For as Lewis is at pains to stress, Socialism also is a house of many mansions—or 'dwelling-places' as we are now invited to call them. It is also a doctrine beset with many contradictions:

> No one should attempt to defend socialism on the score of consistency or clearness. It is a living thing, a natural science, and not a philosophy. Regarded as anything else it makes nonsense. It is mixed up with a thousand warring racial needs and prejudices, and every sort of person for a century and a half has pulled its theory this way and that to suit his fancy. As a theory it is a rag-doll at the best, or, if you like, a gutta-percha baby. You cannot extract from the reading of the great revolutionary theorists any unanimity or agreement. They have only one thing in common, the religious fervour animating most of them. Their hearts agree, but all their minds agree to differ. And they have gradually come, in consequence, to regard their minds, and still more other people's, with dislike.⁵

This being so, the choice as to which particular order of Socialism should be adopted is one which Lewis does not trouble himself to decide: no doubt events will dictate the proper decision in due time. Nevertheless, one form of Socialism or another is what he is advocating: far more positively, he is also advocating a form of government which will impose it effectively. The only question is—government in what terms? And if he is disposed to say little in favour of democratic government on the western pattern, it is merely because he is painfully aware of the many anomalies which democratic government encouraged.

To begin with, he finds that the democratic ideal in government has always been essentially anarchic: it has always tended to deal with its problems piecemeal. It is fundamentally unstable, and it is not even representative. Its national shortcomings, furthermore, have been carried over into the government of Europe as a whole—which represents an agglomeration of the piecemeal anomalies bedevilling its individual nationalities. The vaunted 'independence' of these continue to make it impossible for Europe to be organized as a whole. 'And politically, organization is everything: talent, martial qualities, nothing.'[6]

For Lewis, in fact, the western democratic tradition was a disorderly failure, and the two-party parliamentary system had virtually lost all meaning. It had certainly failed to protect the peaceful development of Europe—to look no further—and had no solution to offer against its failure. His insistence upon the *oneness* of civilization, the need for humanity to bind itself into international unity—the 'One World' of H. G. Wells and Wendell Wilkie—is a recurring theme of Lewis's which will be considered in due course. Not merely the white race which he is concerned with in Europe, but the entire human race which he speaks for elsewhere, is an entity which he prefers to regard as indivisible—certainly, an entity which he believes it dangerous for politics to continue fragmenting indefinitely. Government for Lewis means government for the whole; and as such he feels that it calls for a far more just and emphatic exercise of power than he can find in the western democracy of the twenties.

For the parliamentary traditions of the time, he has nothing but contempt. While not so ludicrous as the ministerial leapfrog which passed for government in France (and had recently been responsible for the Fascist takeover in Italy) the shiftless vacillations and half-hearted reformism of Westminster did not appear to him to stand for anything notably better. And if the state of the national economy was to be taken as any indication of efficiency in government, industrial stagnation and crippling unemployment seemed to say little in favour of the British method. As Lewis saw it at the time: 'The parliamentary system is the great characteristic european institution that to-day has on all hands lost its meaning. There are no doubt worse things for the people than parliaments. But the humbug involved in such a transparently one-sided assembly makes it impossible to go on with it once a certain point of enlightenment or exasperation has been reached. All the liberal tricks are seen through and known now by heart. So, for better or for worse, parliamentary rule is finished.'[7]

The fact that parliamentary rule healthily persists in the western democracies half a century and a world war later does not entirely dispose of the question. Many of us in this particular democracy are currently aware of the fact that parliamentary rule *can* have its own anomalies. We agree to settle for it as being at least more acceptable than the two alternatives that we observe in the field. In other words, we accept it for lack of anything better. As it is, two-party democracy amounts to a simple compromise: government of the many in the interests of the slightly more. And while controversial policies continue to be rushed through parliament on the strength of a 'people's mandate'—which a marginal swing in public opinion can promptly reverse—it can hardly be otherwise. Indeed, since we do not enjoy proportional representation in Britain, 'slightly more' can well amount to 'considerably less' on an overall count of the votes cast. So who, in fact, is governing whom?

But it is not merely this kind of arbitrary anomaly to which Lewis is objecting in *The Art of Being Ruled*. He is taxing parliamentary rule—in 1925—with being hypocritical, inefficient, and dishonest in its aims and methods. Most of all, he is charging it with tolerating and seeking to perpetuate a deplorable degree of social injustice, with fostering imperialistic militarism, and with progressively forcing down wages and lowering standards in the interests of Big Business and private profits. He is charging it, in short, with ruling the many in the interests of the few—and with hypocritically pretending that it is doing exactly the opposite.

To anyone who remembers the times in which the book was written, the charges do not seem unduly exaggerated. Similar charges were regularly being made in the House of Commons. And indeed, if suddenly translated back into the social miasma of the mid-twenties, and faced with the arrogance of a privileged class, the subservience, under-nourishment and over-exploitation of all the rest, few people today would fail to indict the government of the time in a similar strain. After all, the calling of the General Strike two months after publication of Lewis's book was indicative of *something*.

It is at least a privilege of life under democracy to take one's government to task in public, and Lewis was happy to avail himself of the privilege. But as we have indicated, *The Art of Being Ruled* was far more than an attack upon mismanagement in office: it was an indictment of the whole democratic system. The book bluntly suggested that because of the inefficient and inequitable nature of the government enjoyed by the democratic bloc in Europe, such government would be better replaced by one more effective because more authoritarian. Lewis was certainly prepared to go along with Proudhon's assertion that government and authority are one—and that by abolishing authority, we abolish the effectiveness of government at the same time. If discipline is necessary to the creation of proper authority, authority is necessary to the proper exercise of power. And only by the proper exercise of power can government be just, constructive in programme, and effective. Or so he was firmly convinced.

It was Lewis's contention, in fact, that we should be well advised to examine the alternatives to two-party governmental rule, for the simple reason that such rule was already in process of breaking down. (It is perhaps worth remembering that with the formation of the first National Government in 1931, two-party rule was virtually to suspend itself. In the interests of national unity, it was to do so completely during the Second World War.) Certainly, as it appeared while *The Art of Being Ruled* was being written, the political scene in Britain was anything but reassuring. The first Labour Government had fallen the previous year after only nine months in office. The Tories had been returned to power in a landslide victory which followed publication of the (forged) Zinoviev letter and the 'Red Scare' which resulted. Winston Churchill, as Chancellor of the Exchequer, had brought the country's monetary system back onto the Gold Standard, and the unemployment figures had again risen above the million and a quarter mark. Industrial unrest was everywhere on the increase and a general cut in wages was threatened.

To begin with, then, Lewis insisted that the villain of the political scene was Toryism. He would equally have denounced Liberalism, if the Liberal Party had still been a meaningful factor in political life. As it was, Liberalism had already been replaced in effective opposition by Fabian Socialism, as exemplified in the policies and person of Ramsay MacDonald. But that, said Lewis, was hardly the answer to anything. Reformist or Fabian Socialism was itself already on the defensive: it was being forced relentlessly into the arms of Toryism by the newer radicalism of the extreme Left—which had stolen the Labour Party's thunder with a reformism that was far less insipid. The 'ultra-radical, desperate, ungentlemanly interloper', with which MacDonald's 'high respectability and professional scruples would not allow him to compete', of course, was Communism.[8] And so far as the record of Communism had gone to that time, Lewis had very little fault to find with it.

Like Italian Fascism, however, Communism was in no way committed to the principles of parliamentary government. No less than Jesuitism, it implied a strict and dedicated discipline: it also implied dictatorship—to begin with, a so-called 'Dictatorship of the Proletariat', which was in fact the dictatorship of a self-elected oligarchy of Communist Party administrators. And while he was in no doubts as to the true nature of oligarchical rule, Lewis was apparently prepared to accept it in the interests of better government. Indeed, he was prepared to affirm that the one went with the other. For no less than Italian Fascism, Communism in Russia could point to its achievements: 'What they have done in a short time in the way of organization must be the admiration of the world.'[9]

But whatever he came to think later about the respective autocracies of Russia and Italy, it is a singular fact—and no doubt a significant one—that in *The Art of Being Ruled*, Lewis carefully refrained from scrutinizing either of them. Indeed, the book gives absolutely no idea whatever of the administrative machinery at work in either country. Nothing whatever is said about the day to day realities of life under Communist rule; and the sudden two-page endorsement of life under Italian Fascism is uninformed and uninformative to an almost comical degree.

But as we have said, the book was not about Fascism.

What it is primarily concerned with is the philosophy of government as such and the techniques by which people can be persuaded to accept it. In other words, it is an invitation to all who are being ruled to examine the process as it affects them. More particularly, it is an incitement of all who are being ruled to recognize their exploitation for what it is—or at least, all those of them who can be expected to profit by reading the book at all. In this, Lewis's purpose is completely at variance with Machiavelli's, whose *Il Principe* is declaredly designed as a text-book for potential rulers. Being himself completely uninterested in ruling, Lewis, on the other hand, is passionately interested in the facts of being ruled as he understands them. Not having experience of these under either Communism or Fascism, however, he concentrates on the process of being ruled in Britain during the twenties. There are many things about the process which he dislikes; there are far more that exasperate him in the docility of most of the people he watches experiencing the process along with him. Unlike himself, they appear to be unaware of the fact that they are even *being* ruled: they certainly show no awareness of how they are being manipulated. Yet being manipulated—in the interests of some ulterior plan —they quite undoubtedly are, as Lewis is firmly persuaded.

The 'freedom' enjoyed under democracy, in short, is a concept which Lewis challenges from the start. Men are no more free under democratic rule, he asserts, than they are under any other. For while they may appear to be free from political persecution, they are anything but free from compulsion and indoctrination of a more insidious kind. Their thinking is carefully directed for them, their behaviour is carefully controlled. Individuality is broken down until their reactions are utterly predictable, and so can be channelled into group activity acceptable to a 'governing mercantile class' whose only aim is to exploit them. Choice is no longer free for them when it is rigorously predetermined in the interests of profitable standardization. 'The ideas of a time,' he declares, 'are like the clothes of a season: they are as arbitrary, as much imposed by some superior will which is seldom explicit. They are utilitarian and political, the instruments of smooth-running government. And to criticize them seriously, especially to-day, *for themselves,* would be as absurd as to criticize the fashion in loofahs, bath-mats, bath-salts, or geysers, in children's frocks or soft felt hats.'[10] Absurd, that is, for those more malleable than Lewis—who proceeds to criticize almost every idea of his time as a matter of course.

It is not his concern to be specific as to the true identity of the 'superior will' which he sees at work behind the body politic. As well seek to identify the *Zeitgeist* in personal terms: it is merely there, arbitrary and compulsive, moulding all opinion and directing all action. In general terms, Lewis equates it with the 'very many people, exerting great personal authority' whom he blames for most of the economic paralysis of his time. They may be regarded as the controlling influence behind Big Business, ably abetted by every government whose tenure of office depends upon a readiness to serve business interests faithfully. Such an identification would certainly have been acceptable to Communist analysis at the time.

There are two ways of looking at the evolution of a society: either it is a natural process in which the group will predominate; or, as in Lewis's view, it is a process in which sectional interests impose courses which the majority are induced to follow. In urging his view with the single-mindedness that he does, Lewis may sometimes be prone to smell out conscious conspiracies where none exist, a tendency already noticed. But it is dangerously complacent to ignore the possibility of conspiracy when it is at least shown to be plausible. And the great merit of *The Art of Being Ruled* is the cogency with which it calls attention to social trends that are highly significant—whether consciously engineered or not. Where Bertrand Russell has referred to the natural growth of a social system in Darwinian terms, for instance, Lewis is quick to take him up: 'There are, on the contrary, responsible human wills to-day, conscious and deliberate as formerly, and more powerful, responsible for all this mysterious natural growth that Mr. Russell compares to the irresponsible growth of a tree. The "pitiless" and "inhuman" character of nature has been overdone. We should have to look elsewhere, and nearer home, for "inhumanity".'[11]

The facts of poverty and inequitable distribution of wealth in the Britain of the twenties were undeniable: to a lesser extent, they are undeniable in the Britain of today. But are they an inevitable part of natural social growth, or are they condoned and made inevitable by interests that no less clearly benefit from them? Marx and Lewis were surely not eccentric in believing that they were. And if we agree that he was right in such a basic assumption, we shall be well advised to follow Lewis into some of his more debatable arguments. For upon his examination of the unlikely ways that the mass of people in a modern democracy are persuaded—or at least, encouraged—into convenient ways of thought depends his whole analysis of the methods by which 'benevolence' can rule no less effectively than rigorous autocracy. Effectively, be it noted, but certainly neither efficiently nor justly.

There are two fundamental ways in which the public can be manipulated by private interest: it can be confirmed in attitudes that are conducive to manipulation, or it can be induced to change its attitudes where others are likely to prove more amenable. And it is this possibility of changing or suggesting attitudes which Lewis is mainly concerned with clarifying.

There could be no doubt at all that change was very much in the air during the twenties. The terrible death-roll of the First World War, the emergence of the 'Modern Woman', the increased mobility of transport, the increase in newspaper readership and cinema attendance, the escalation of advertising and heightened pressure of publicity techniques, the growth of recording and the start of radio broadcasting, the rapid development of new industrial processes and consequent increase in cheap production—all had played their part in transforming pre-war habits of conservatism into post-war demands for novelty. If we can accept that war itself is a factor in Natural, Darwinian growth, it might be possible to accept this post-war proliferation of new behaviour patterns and new scientific techniques as being itself 'natural'—and so believe that a 'natural' demand had merely brought into being a 'natural' means of supply. But few of us could now accept that thesis any more than Lewis could in 1925: he was quite firmly convinced that —like all wars—World War I had been carefully engineered. Moreover, many people had benefited notably by the drawn-out course of that war. But in the event, the war had amounted to a revolution—'a gigantic episode in the russian revolution,' as Lewis wryly remarked. Transition into a post-war world had amounted to another revolution again: along with new scientific techniques it had brought in a new acceptance of the principle of change. The question therefore arose—how could this new demand for change be controlled? When change or revolution was in the air, if only as a philosophical concept, how could that concept be made to take unrevolutionary courses? 'How is it,' Lewis asks in reply, 'that the financier speaks the language of philosophy, and takes over the watchwords and fiercely re- formist temper of revolution? That is, of course, the key to our democratic society. It is the vulgarization of scientific and philo- sophic thought that provides him with his mighty excuse to enslave and change as he likes.'[12] Not merely his mighty ex- cuse, however: it has also provided him with the means. And from his consideration of the many ways that vulgarization has been relentlessly carried through—the inculcated contempt for intellect, the 'popularization' of science, the sudden apotheosis of the ordinary in the person of the 'little man'—Lewis goes on to discuss the process of giving the public what it wants. For what the public wants, the public will gladly buy—with money or with obedience: and what the public *thinks* it wants is what democratic government and business interests alike can profit by foisting off upon it.

Accordingly, the concept *What the Public Wants*, in Lewis's terminology, becomes a decisive factor in government and busi- ness policy. But it is hardly flattering to the public that its wants have been assessed so low. Not Machiavelli himself held the public in less esteem than the modern manipulators who have taught it to want so little in its own best interests. For with the means of suggestion, persuasion and 'education' at their disposal, they have taught it to want exactly what they are there to provide—and a cheap, nasty, shoddy substitute for excellence of any sort *that* has proved to be! 'As a result of the dogma of *What the Public Wants*, and the technical experi- ences of the publicist, a very cynical and unflattering view of what the Public *is* is widely held to-day. And, indeed, the con- temporary Public, corrupted and degraded into semi-imbecility by the operation of this terrible canon of press and publicity technique, by now confirms its pessimism. It has learnt to live up to, or down to, its detractor.'[13]

All this may be obvious enough, but the *nature* of what the public wants—on its own account, and without indoctrination —is what Lewis goes on to consider next. Apart from its consumer goods—all of them *new* and therefore necessarily *better* —the public is anxious to be reassured and to be left untroubled. It wants to be immunized against the necessity of thinking for itself, the need to make up its own mind, and all obligation to accept responsibility. In other words, it wants to withdraw from the problems of individuality, and to fall back upon the group rhythms and group responses of the herd. This wish to evade responsibility, as Lewis sees it, is one of the major factors in leaving the ruled at the disposition of the ruler—in a democracy no less than in an autocracy. If that wish can be encouraged in the public—which it can, only too easily—there is no limit to the ways in which the public can be dragooned. The habit of leaving the thinking to others is fostered by all the techniques of advertising; and no matter how blandly it urges the public to pick the cards for itself, the cards are always forced. What the public wants, it is the business of the salesman not merely to know, but also to dictate; and all such dictation is rightly held to be 'a great convenience to the customer'. If life can be made into a package-tour, then all the arrangements are at the discretion of the travel agent: you will only find yourself where he wants you to go, but at least you will be spared the anxiety of deciding where to go for yourself, and then of finding out how to get there. So long as they arrive at the seaside, children have always accepted that: why should not adults accept it too?

The truth is, as Lewis sees it, that people do not like to feel, think and suffer for themselves: 'They far prefer having it done for them. This position could actually be put in this way: they are not unlike the young man of Leghorn, on the whole, when first confronted with the major difficulties of life. If they could go back and *not be born*, they would. But the creative biologic life-instinct has them in its grip, and they have to go on. Now, at this moment any one who can show how they can at once live and not live, get through life, and get through it as a child gets through childhood, without responsibility, because so helpless, will be welcomed as a saviour.'[14]

Like all effective arguments, this is no doubt an over-simplification; but since he is applying it merely to the *majority* of the public—what we should now describe as the admass—it can be accepted as fair enough in its way. And in a democracy, Lewis would point out, it is the admass that elects the rulers—and the admass, accordingly, that answers for the whole.

He is not asserting that this yearning back after the irresponsibility of childhood is entirely the creation of mass-suggestion; there is unfortunately more to it than that: 'It is in freudian language, for instance, the desire of man to return into the womb from whence he came: a movement of retreat and discouragement—a part of the great strategy of defeat suggested to or evolved by our bankrupt society.... It is the diagnostic of a frantic longing to refresh, rejuvenate, and invigorate a life that, it is felt, has grown old and too unsimple, and lost its native direction.... It is, however, a "frantic longing" that is very thoroughly organized indeed. All the channels of publicity foster it. It is a part of the great, and I believe fecund, solution of the problem of "power".'[15]

For Lewis, in fact, there are only four 'freedoms' under democratic or any other rule. There is the irresponsible freedom encouraged in the neo-childhood of the human average; the irresponsible freedom enjoyed by wealth and power, in or out of office; the irresponsible freedom enjoyed by most women ('How enjoyable to be a slave! How divine to have a *master*!'); and there is the 'very rare freedom' of the intellectual who insists on thinking for himself—so long as the overriding cult of the human average allows him to do so.

But despite its encouragement of the human average to seek safety and reassurance in the herd, power can never allow the herd to develop an individuality of its own. As Lewis remarks in a long excursus on Rousseauism, the individual may be stronger than the group, but politically the group is stronger than the individual—unless he happens to be a ruler. If the group is not to represent a potential threat to authority, it must be divided against itself by an emphasis laid upon its various 'classes'. Quite apart from the social classes dear to the heart of Marxian dialectic, Lewis recognizes as 'classes' all such classifiable categories as age, sex, occupation, hobby, special prejudice or intelligence. (He might also have added sport and religion,

where these are not synonymous.) Within and around each of
these categories, 'wars' can be created—and everyone be encouraged to align himself on one side or the other. Apart from
the Marxian class-war, which Lewis does not trouble himself to
discuss, he finds the most significant to be the 'age-war', the
'sex-war' and the 'war of the brows'—all of which he discusses
at some length. In the promotion of all these wars, he sees a
conscious policy pursued by 'some superior will' with a view to
keeping the mass of average humanity in a state of happy confusion and happy subjection, while the wage-bill is being conveniently lowered for Big Business.

Whether one goes along with Lewis quite so far as this, his
theory is intriguing and at least persuasively argued. The fuller
implications of the age-war—crabbed age versus youth, or 'let's
give Youth its chance!'—can be left over for the moment, as he
returns to it more specifically in *Doom of Youth*, which we
shall be considering later on. In *The Art of Being Ruled*, he is
concerned rather with an analysis of the various ways that we
are encouraged to hark back nostalgically to our *lost* youth, as
already noticed. More particularly, he is concerned to show
how youth itself is urged never to grow up at all. The whole
process of doing so, the young are reminded, is beset with
difficulties: how much wiser to have no part of them! Growing
up means having to think, having to accept responsibility and
having to use your own judgment: why not leave all that to
the others and just keep on enjoying yourself as you did ever
since you left that silly old school? This, he argues, is the
message of the media: press, cinema, theatre, radio and publicity
are all at infinite pains to stop the young *growing-up*. This being
the case: 'Barrie's play, *Peter Pan*, is to our time what *Uncle
Tom's Cabin* was to the Civil War period in America. It gave
expression to a deep emotional current, of political origin.'[16]
Just precisely where this leaves Barrie—on the side of the hidden persuaders or in the forefront of their dupes—the reader is
once more left to decide for himself. If in fact Barrie was merely
trying to resolve his own emotional problems, what had created
those problems for him? Was it his mother, was it his hormones,
his stature, or the *Zeitgeist*? Even Lewis is prepared—with
qualifications—to concede ironically that the *Zeitgeist* can be
kind. . . .

33

The emergence of the sex-war in the twenties, on the other hand, is fact beyond all argument, whatever one thinks about the philosophy behind its full promotion. The concept of 'Modern Woman' could be traced back to Ibsen—if no further —but it was only with the struggle for women's suffrage at the turn of the century that she began to be recognized as a political force. With the outbreak of the First World War, the militant suffragette movement had voluntarily been called off in the interest of national unity. But as every suffragette realized, the war could completely change the role of women in any future society. In the industrial areas of the North, women of the working class had been at work in the factories since the start of the Industrial Revolution; but by channelling a vastly larger army of women into the munition factories, the war gave most of them their first experience of wage-earning outside the shops and domestic service. The social spectrum of those doing war-work was now far wider: no less important, the wages earned were considerably higher. And quite apart from work in the factories, a large number of women gained valuable administrative experience in business—as replacements for men called up to fight—and even in the Auxiliary Services as well.

In recognition of the part they were playing in the war effort, in February 1918 women had finally been given the vote. By the following year, the first woman had taken her seat in the House of Commons: two years later the first woman barrister had passed her final examinations and was ready to practise at the Bar. Work of nearly every kind was now open to them, and it became the done thing for women to take jobs in every field of social life. Previously, it had been unusual for women of the middle class—married women particularly—to think of earning an independent living: their place had been firmly in the home. With the twenties, all that had changed: every woman now began to see the possibility of a career before her. In a matter of a few years, her whole psychology had been changed—and her purchasing power increased. She had begun to drink and smoke in public, and to spend a great deal more on her clothes and personal pleasures. The fact was quickly reflected in the opening up of vast new business empires— cosmetics not being among the least of them.

With the belated emergence of the Modern Woman, there-

fore, the stage had finally been set in the twenties for inaugur-
ation of the sex-war. Modern Woman, after all, represented far
more than a mere market for consumer goods: a far more
active role was marked out for her to play in business and
industry. To begin with, Lewis declares, the family had always
been something of an anomaly in the modern state; and he
sees it already in course of being broken up by economic pressures and the sort of militantly feminist propaganda which
served more interests than those of the feminine sex. After all,
the break-up of the family would release a vast new body of
cheap labour. As it was, with the family supreme, far too many
women were still engaged upon tasks which could be performed
more economically under a communal system: the meals
cooked by a dozen housewives could be cooked in a canteen by
one—thus releasing the others for work elsewhere. Moreover,
the 'work elsewhere' was currently being done by men at a
higher wage than women could command. For that reason
alone, feminism was a reasonable cause for business interests to
support; and the sex-war was encouraged accordingly.

Whether one agrees with Lewis's conspiratorial theory or not,
it is a certain fact that it has taken half a century of women's
agitation even partially to redress that economic discrimination.
Women always *have* represented cheap labour to date, so to
that extent, Lewis had a perfectly sound case to put. But there
was a great deal more to the sex-war as he saw it than a simple
matter of economics. There was also a conscious policy on the
part of the State to undermine the dominant role of the male.
The picture that Lewis paints of the average male—'the little
father of the family squatting rather miserably in his shoddy,
uncomfortable castle'—is not a potentially dangerous one, it
might be thought. His role as a fighting man was over for the
time being, and there was no longer any premium put upon
heroism or militancy. Even when there was work there for him
to do, the price of his labour was little enough; and the gather-
ing threat of unemployment made it probable that he would
rest content with what he could get. Nevertheless, as head of
that rival institution the family, he represented a possible threat
to the authority of the State: at least, he might one day turn
himself into a tiny pocket of resistance. In the interests of
effective rule, therefore, it was advisable that the dominance of

his maleness should be eroded. Once woman had been raised to equal status with him, the average male would be less intractable—or rather, be even more tractable than he was already. Little as he enjoyed the role, and glad as he was to be relieved of the responsibility inherent in it, man as head of the family was still a dwindling symbol of authority. The real and ultimate aim of the sex-war was finally to deprive him of that authority. Or so Lewis's argument went....

Apart from anything else, woman is generally easier to rule than man. There is far more in her nature to identify her with the child: she could hardly have devoted herself so successfully to bringing up children if that had not been the case. Indeed, from the point of view of ruling power, the child and the woman can conveniently be equated. Women are even more credulous than men, and they are certainly more easy to influence. 'It is natural, therefore,' says Lewis, 'that a great political power, interested only in domination and in nothing else, would seize on them as its most readily manipulated tools. By flattery and coercion it would discipline their ignorance and weakness into an organized instrument of social and political domination.'[17]

As Lewis sees it, the very nature of rule creates a form of sexual relationship, in which the ruled represent the female principle and the ruler represents the male. Insofar as it implies a degree of rulership in itself, therefore, masculinity in the ruled is a tendency which the ruler must be expected to discourage: it can only represent a degree of potential opposition. But apart from the encouragement offered it to evade responsibility by persisting in or reverting to childhood, there is another way in which masculinity can be rendered less aggressive: it can be inverted.

In saying that the prosecution of Oscar Wilde in the nineties provided homosexuality with its first martyr, Lewis does not go so far as to suggest that the trial was staged with a view to *promoting* homosexuality! But he does suggest that homosexuality rapidly increased as a result of it. This was due in no small part to the charm of Wilde himself, whose plight awakened the chivalrous instincts of the public as though he had been 'a very attractive maiden in distress'. Certainly, the publicity which homosexuality enjoyed as a result of the trial must have invested it with a certain fashionable glamour for those with tendencies that way already. But the scruffy nature of most of the witnesses called could hardly have glamourized it for anyone else.

Nevertheless, no doubt Wilde's personality and the notoriety of the trial had played their part in 'the complete reversal of the erotic machinery' which Lewis notes as an increasing trend. As a result of that trend, he is even ready to find the heady delights of homosexuality being offered as an acceptable form of escapism to all such masculinity as the sex-war may have confused or defeated. After all, he suggests: 'For the smooth working of the industrial machine some degree of castration of the pugnacious, smally and uselessly, wastefully competitive, european male is necessary. He has been hypnotized (by snobbery—one of his weak points) into carrying out this operation himself.'[18]

If the industrial machine had in fact been guilty of any such hypnotism, it would have been as 'insidious and disgraceful' as Lewis protests. But if any such Machiavellian plan had been at work, one rather wonders why consenting adults found life made so difficult for them by the police over the next two generations! Admittedly, government is never averse to a certain amount of double-think; we find in our own time that smoking can be accepted in the interests of taxation while it is being roundly condemned on the grounds of national health. Male inversion in the twenties may conceivably have been regarded as sound in political theory while it was still being prosecuted in the courts as anti-social. On the surface, however, it seems rather unlikely!

But whether 'some superior will' could be credited with encouraging it or not, homosexuality was certainly very much on the increase when *The Art of Being Ruled* appeared. It was becoming fashionable, and it was becoming far more socially acceptable—so long as the police were not involved. To some extent, obviously, this could be regarded as an aftermath of the war: heroism's dwindling life-expectancy had rather cooled enthusiasm for it. Once the realities of modern warfare had been thoroughly understood, the young were proving rather less eager to have their richer dust compounded into a richer mud. The role of the elegant spectator was becoming more popular than that of the expendable protagonist. But apart from such an obvious reaction to the perils of masculinity, twentieth century youth had undoubtedly been unsettled psychologically by the changing status of women. Indeed, Lewis sees homosexuality as an essential by-product of the feminist movement. So far as his own analysis goes: 'The "homo" is the legitimate child of the "suffragette".'

But over and above the part it plays in hastening the disintegration of the family, its intensification of the cult of the childish, and its supporting role in the sex-war—Lewis also sees sex-inversion (or Shamanism, as he calls it) pressed into service in the war on the intellect. By its close affinities with feminine emotionalism and intuition, he sees it aligned against the logical discipline that he identifies with the masculine mind. In other words, he sees it as a cross-current in the Bergsonian 'flux' which he accuses of seeking to undermine the whole European intellectual tradition—a charge which will be considered in the next chapter. For although it is not to be held responsible for that attack, he sees the tendency to sex-inversion as one essentially helpful to those who are seeking, by vulgarization and all other means, to put paid to the intellectual as dangerously inimical to the standards of the admass average. 'A sort of war of revenge on the intellect is what, for some reason, thrives in the contemporary atmosphere,' he complains. And having gone to some lengths in exposing the reason for what he thinks the reason is, he concludes: 'So a revolution in favour of standards unfriendly to the intellect, and friendly to all that had been formerly subordinated to it, is the first and most evident result of sex-transformation. The "passions", "intuitions", all the features of the emotive life—with which women were formerly exclusively accommodated—are enthroned on all hands, in any place reached by social life; which is increasingly (in the decay of visible, public life) everywhere.'[19]

Without attempting to pursue all the other hares which start out of every chapter, or hoping to do anything like justice to the gusto with which he courses them, enough has now been quoted from *The Art of Being Ruled* to make Lewis's central argument reasonably clear. As an intellectual himself, he is asserting his right to practise and be heard in a society which he feels to be growing steadily more hostile to the serious creative artist. He is concerned about the way that the vast majority of his fellow-men are allowing themselves to be manœuvred into a state of apathetic submission to rule by an undeclared alliance of government and business interests. He is warning them against a carefully worked out policy by which all personal independence is being undermined, all opposition disarmed, and all intellectual integrity left at risk. It is not necessary to look around for the new Machiavel, he implies, for he operates today as a complex of power. It is merely necessary to realize, by studying how it operates, just what that complex is persuading you to become. It is necessary to understand that your vaunted independence is being progressively destroyed; and that whatever aims your rulers have for their own future, those aims are certainly not in the best interests of the ruled. If you are *content* to be ruled, on the other hand—ruled in a way that relieves you of all responsibilities, but in a way that leaves you open to limitless exploitation—then you have got the rulers that you deserve. You are in a fair way, under democracy, to suffering the political helotry that you fondly imagine is reserved only for those who are ruled by modern dictatorship. What is more to the point, you will be suffering it under the worst possible conditions—for two-party government is an outworn concept in a modern industrialized society. All such government is inefficient, it is hypocritical, and it is dangerously arbitrary.

Whether again one is convinced by this particular contention, Lewis has at least provided a set of useful pointers to several undoubted trends in the society of his time. He has shown how those trends are (conceivably) being encouraged, and he has warned that they are being encouraged for one sole purpose: the progressive lowering of wages, the depressing of the average standard of living, and the continued exploitation of the many in the interests of the few. It is certainly worth remembering that those were precisely the reasons behind the calling of the General Strike shortly after the book was published.

Whatever one feels about the machinations of Big Business, it is natural to wonder as one reads *The Art of Being Ruled* whether any *government* that Britain suffered during the twenties would have been capable of the sheer adroitness in political manipulation with which Lewis charges all of them. Lord Northcliffe undoubtedly would, his enormous circulations having been built up by dispensing *What the Public Wants*— at the same time fomenting war or political hysteria when it suited him, and deftly promoting The Battle of the Skirts (Long or Short) which has recently broken out again.... But Northcliffe, after all, had died a sick man, and were any of the politicos of the time astute enough to have indulged a similar thirst for power so successfully? Would Ramsay MacDonald and his colleagues, who failed to cope with even the Zinoviev Letter, have had the cunning to carry through such an overall strategy, much less to have evolved it? Would the Conservative Party under Bonar Law, or even the Coalition under Lloyd George? (In view of the way in which he master-minded the Abdication some years later, perhaps one would have to think twice about Stanley Baldwin....) But for the rest? The 1922 Committee? The hidden hand of Lord Milner and his disciples? The League of Nations' Union, the Press Barons, ICI and the Bishops in Convocation? Perhaps—though their aims and interests were not always entirely coincident. Such a Machiavellian exercise in the use of power as *The Art of Being Ruled* seeks to uncover would seem to be far more likely under Communism or Fascism than under the conflicting interests at work in western democracy.

It is this very assumption, however, that Lewis challenges:

Here we reach a point that must often have been observed by any one surveying at all intelligently the duel of communism and capitalism, of fascism and democracy; of the East and the West, for it is roughly that. It is a paradox of that situation that all *the frankness* is on one side, and that is not on the side of the West, of democracy. All the traditional obliquity and subterranean methods of the Orient are, in this duel, exhibited by the westerner and the democratic régime. It is *we* who are the Machiavels, compared to the sovietist or the fascist, who makes no disguise of his forcible intentions, whose *power* is not wrapped up in parliamentary humbug, who is not eternally engaged in pretences of benefaction; who does not say at every move in the game that he is making it for somebody else's good, that he is a vicar and a servant when he is a master. It is true that he promises happiness to the masses as a result of his iron rule. But *the iron* is not hidden, or camouflaged as christian charity. He says that *one* politics in a country, *one* indisputed government, will be for the good of the average man. And when these *one*-party states are centrally organized, as Italy is becoming, who can gainsay him?[20]

It should be remarked that Lewis had only been in Italy for a few days—at Venice in 1922, before the *advent* of Fascism—but that particular question was to be answered by the Italians themselves during World War II. It was also taken up, by all who insisted that political freedom was hardly worth exchanging for despotic government, whether efficiently centralized or not. Certainly, it was highly desirable to have the trains running on time—provided one was at liberty to catch them. But a large number of political prisoners in Italy and its islands were hardly in a position to do so under Fascism.

It was central to Lewis's argument, however, that political freedom was not what the bulk of the people wanted—under democracy or under dictatorship. Freedom, as Lewis saw it, was what most people only *think* they want. It was an eighteenth century abstraction which had been invented by the political theorists. As conceived and predicated by Rousseau, true freedom is the freedom of a solitary: most people, on the other hand, are essentially gregarious. As most people relish it, freedom—like the countryside—is something merely for the weekend. In daily life, it implies no more to them than a right to associate, a right to belong, and to seek safety and reassurance in group emotions, in class responses, or even in simply being one of a crowd. True freedom, on the other hand, implies the need to make one's own decisions, to stand on one's own against the rest, and the right *not* to belong. People admittedly like to believe they are free, and a wise ruler will constantly encourage them in that belief: they can be kept in subjection far more easily if he does. But that, after all, is done for them under dictatorship no less than under democracy: the iron hand, they are told, is there in defence of their freedom. But do the bulk of the people really care for a freedom which exacts rather more on their own part? Lewis is not persuaded that they do.

All that is necessary, he maintains, to confirm an electorate in a sense of general well being, is a course of regular indoctrination—by the educational system, by public pronouncement, by press, publicity and all other media. Granted that, the bulk of humanity is content to accept its freedom as it finds it—and that will amount to little more than a freedom to conform. Additional to this, the subject enjoys no more under democracy than the freedom to vote on either side of questions propounded by other people—a very different matter from posing the questions for oneself and getting the answers that one really wants. The right to heckle is hardly a substitute for the right to decide and administer policy.

This may appear to be somewhat cynical, but it must be clearly understood that in giving his considered opinion of the way things *are* in the political world, Lewis is by no means implying that this is the way things *ought* to be. On the contrary, he is underlining the fact that this is the way things ought *not* to be. In asserting that the majority of people exist quite happily under subjection, are not really anxious for independence even before indoctrination, and are generally indifferent to what he calls the 'most elementary' principles of freedom—he is merely stating facts as he sees them. Critical of the admass as it undoubtedly is, *The Art of Being Ruled* is written more in sorrow than in satisfaction. If he finds that the bulk of mankind can be irresponsible, that is unfortunate for them. If he finds that the bulk of mankind prefers to remain unenlightened, that is unfortunate for him: after all, his livelihood as a writer is dependent upon a sufficiency of enquiring readers. And perhaps it is significant that despite many highly enthusiastic reviews, the first (and only) edition of *The Art of Being Ruled* was not exhausted in Britain for over twenty years....

The question next arises as to whether the book, in fact, is *advocating* authoritarian rule? In a number of passages which could be quoted, it certainly is. Just what it was about authoritarian rule—as an intellectual concept—that appealed to Lewis so strongly, we shall also be considering in the next chapter. But in terms of practical politics, he holds that authoritarian rule is a more effective means of governing a modern industrial state efficiently, and so ensuring a wider and fairer distribution of the fruits of industry. Lewis accepts that most people are prepared to leave the business of ruling to others, in the same way that they are content to leave economic planning, rural development, law-making, theology, meteorology, invention, writing, painting, plumbing, sewage disposal and even slaughtering to others. In any case, he says, the process of government should be left to those who have an aptitude for it: such people should make no bones about the fact that they are in business to rule, and the only test of their right to do so should be the success or otherwise with which they rule in the public interest. He is saying, furthermore, that a form of Socialism is necessary to the modern industrial state, and that true Socialism is not on offer in the Britain of his time—at least, not by any of the political parties currently able to form a government. He is saying, finally, that such a form of Socialism is currently on offer elsewhere.

Is Lewis therefore advocating that Fascism on the Italian plan or Sovietism on the Russian plan should be imposed upon Britain? On the contrary, he is not advocating that *any* form of government should be 'imposed' upon Britain. He is inviting Britain to consider a reasonable form of Socialist rule which might be suitable to her needs—and which he for one is persuaded would be. The passage in which he does this is well worth quoting in full:

> If to-day you must be a socialist of some sort, what order of socialist are you going to be? For, evidently, you will say, 'socialist' means very different and indeed opposite things. I have said that in the abstract I believe the sovietic system to be the best. It has spectacularly broken with all the past of Europe: it looks to the East, which is spiritually so much greater and intellectually so much finer than Europe, for inspiration. It springs ostensibly from a desire to alleviate the lot of the poor and outcast, and not merely to set up a cast-iron, militarist-looking state. And yet for anglo-saxon countries as they are constituted to-day some modified form of fascism would probably be the best. The United States is, of course, in a unique position: and for the moment it is the only country in the world of which you can say it would not benefit by a revolution. And eventually, with its great potentialities, it may be able to evolve some novel form of government of its own.
>
> The only socialism that differs very much in principle from *fascismo* is reformist socialism, or the early nineteenth-century utopias, or, to a somewhat less extent, Proudhon. All marxian doctrine, all *étatisme* or collectivism, conforms very nearly in

practice to the fascist ideal. *Fascismo* is merely a spectacular marinettian flourish put on to the tail, or, if you like, the head, of marxism: that is, of course, fascism as interpreted by its founder, Mussolini. And that is the sort of socialism that this essay would indicate as the most suitable for anglo-saxon countries or colonies, with as much of sovietic proletarian sentiment as could be got into it without impairing its discipline, and as little coercion as is compatible with good sense. In short, to get some sort of peace to enable us to work, we should naturally seek the most powerful and stable authority that can be devised.[21]

Socialism expressed in those terms, with its inbuilt controls and restrictions, was roughly what was enjoyed by Britain under the Attlee Government of 1945—which Lewis described at the time as 'the best—or at least to start with the most promising—government it has ever known. No great compliment,' he adds, 'but, relatively, a mighty fact.'[22] (It did not satisfy him for very long, of course!)

Many people would certainly agree that some form of Socialism was badly needed in Britain during the twenties; but few could accept his assertion that Italian Fascism was very nearly akin to Marxian Socialism. As most people happened to realize at the time, Fascism was the antithesis of Marxian anything, and was currently engaged in liquidating both the Communist and Socialist Parties in Italy. Its support of Capitalism as a co-partner with Labour in the Corporate State was hardly an accident. And far from its being a 'marinettian flourish' put on Marxism, Fascism had been adjured by Marinetti himself to 'rid itself of all taint of Socialism' only the year before.

Whatever one thinks of Lewis's qualified endorsement of Fascism for the Anglo-Saxon, therefore, it was hardly likely to have resulted in any form of Socialism consonant with the usual understanding of the term. In any case, the very context of the suggestion is a trifle odd, coming as it does completely out of the blue in the eighty-second of his ninety-five chapters. Part XI of *The Art of Being Ruled*, in which it appears, is devoted to a comparison of the respective philosophies of Proudhon and Rousseau, to which it bears virtually no relation at all. The chapter is headed *Fascism as an Alternative*, but it is an alternative which is nowhere discussed in any detail. No attempt has been made to consider the governmental programme of

Italian Fascism—still less, the administrative machinery that went along with it. The nature of the Corporate State is nowhere analysed, the philosophy behind it nowhere contrasted with that behind any other form of Collectivism. Pareto, Gentile and the other supposed early theorists of Fascism are not even mentioned, let alone Rocco, Corradini or the other official Fascist apologists. Nor is the nature of the so-called 'reforms' which Mussolini is credited with having introduced. As for any comparison of the achievements of Fascism with the achievements of Turkey under Kemal—it is an interesting fact that the latter are not so much as referred to throughout the book. It is obvious that for Lewis, authoritarianism—and therefore Italian Fascism, the nearest form to hand—is merely an intellectual concept to be used as occasion serves.

In the single five-page chapter that he devotes to Fascism (the only one which even mentions it in the title) Lewis nevertheless comes up with a surprising eulogy for Fascism in action —though even that is introduced on a somewhat apologetic note: 'Mussolini is considered by many people as an unfortunately theatrical, grimacing personage, and is perhaps a little prejudicial to the régime of which he is the official figure-head. The power that he represents has, in its choice of a figure-head, showed, perhaps, bad taste. But in everything except taste it cannot be denied that it has chosen well.'[23] In ten years' time, therefore, the transformation of Italy would be complete—the new and better order of things being admittedly the creation of 'a tyrant, or dictator, with virtual powers of life and death'. Political assassination would have been at work (Matteotti had been killed already), imprisonment or exile would have been imposed on all who criticized the régime 'without ruffling the surface of opinion', the press having been completely gagged. But by way of compensation, 'all the humbug of a democratic suffrage, all the imbecility that is so wastefully manufactured, will henceforth be spared this happy people'.[24]

On the surface, this rather odd vision of eventual bliss would seem to be also an endorsement of force and violence in the best Machiavellian vein. But nowhere else in the book is the use of violence excused. Lewis's declared creed regarding 'the avoidance of all violence as an article of faith', as already noted. The use of violence, in any case, he feels to be utterly unnecessary in politics, where indoctrination can quickly achieve far more, and do so far less wastefully. Force is a 'passing and precarious thing' and as such, if for no other reason, its use is to be shunned. In the preservation of law and order, force may have to be employed by all forms of government: it is a last resort for civil authority everywhere. But that is a very different thing from the use of force as an instrument of policy; and for all the equanimity with which he could appear to accept its use in Italy and the Soviet Union, there is no suggestion that Lewis was prepared to accept the use of political force nearer home.

Just what prompted him to his ill-considered encomium of a political dictatorship which he had not even studied—still less, studied at first hand—it is difficult to say. Purely as a concept, no doubt he imagined it to be the lesser of two evils. The fact is, as he suggests in *The Lion and the Fox*, government of any kind seems to have had an ugly side for him. Having absolutely no interest in power himself, he accepts that strong government is 'quite indispensible' to a society in which the intellectual can hope to follow his vocation; but viewed dispassionately, he still finds government 'the most deadly machine of all those invented by men'.[25] One might be forgiven for feeling that *authoritarian* government in the Italy and Germany of the thirties would soon be proving itself precisely that.

In the twenties, on the other hand, the aggressively militant side of authoritarian government had not yet emerged in Europe. Neither Italy nor the Soviet Union had as yet indulged in *any* acts of military aggression. Kemal's war of liberation in Turkey had been bloody and terrible in its results for all those Greeks who suffered as a result of it. But that war had not been started by the Turks: it had been largely engineered by the western interests only too ready to sell their surplus arms to Venizelos for his irredentist gamble. And whatever one thinks about the highly ambiguous part played in the gamble by the British government, the fact that it had turned out so unluckily for the western powers could hardly be blamed upon Kemal. The sober fact remained that only a sudden climb-down by Britain and France had saved them from involving themselves in war against him—a war which might well have ended with the Soviet Union aligning itself against them in yet another general holocaust.

Coming as it did so soon after the end of World War I, this recent proof that war could still be an outcome of democratic politics was no doubt very much behind the onslaught launched against them by Lewis in *The Art of Being Ruled*. He declaredly held all war in the utmost detestation, having seen, as he caustically explained, quite enough of it on the Western Front in 1917. Whatever it may have achieved in the Middle Ages, he saw all modern wars as futile and unsuccessful 'for all but the private individuals who promote them, whichever side technically wins or loses'.[26] All modern wars, he insists, are *made* by the interests which benefit by them: wars do not merely 'happen'. A French scientist, Professor Richet, is taken sternly to task for even implying that mankind had ever embarked upon war in our time deliberately and of its own volition. 'To describe the carnage of the war as *willed* by the majority of men, in some sadic excess, is so stupid as to be almost *too* stupid. If you tickle the sole of the foot of a sane man he temporarily loses his reason. When excited, confused, worked up, drugged, and shrieked at by the magnate and his press for a few weeks, "Mankind" (*Homo Stultus*) becomes ferocious, that is all.'[27]

War fever can indeed be worked up by the popular press, and no doubt sells many extra copies. It can certainly sell many armaments, and makes healthy profits for those who deal in them—all which was something of a boring truism even by the thirties. It was much less of a truism when *The Art of Being Ruled* was published. The great efflux of anti-war books in Europe was not to start for another three years, when *Im Westen nichts Neues* and *Undertones of War* sounded a note which had been mostly forgotten in Britain since the war-poems of Siegfried Sassoon and Wilfred Owen. Lewis was to be sounding the note regularly for the rest of his writing life—sometimes unfortunately for himself.

War is the almost inevitable by-product of nationalism pushed to extremes, and Lewis was no nationalist. Rather than mere authoritarianism, it was a forward-looking *Inter*nationalism that *The Art of Being Ruled* was seeking to promote and urging upon its readers as humanity's one true hope of lasting peace. The national state itself was a concept that Lewis hoped to see abolished—swallowed up in a single World State and ruled by a single World Government. Whether that World Government emerged as capitalist or socialist, democratic or autocratic, was a matter of secondary importance to him, if not to Marx. His own preference, as we have seen, was for Socialism of one sort or another, but the first great need was for world unity to be achieved. In this belief he was at one with unlikely allies—the H. G. Wells of *The Open Conspiracy* and the Bertrand Russell of *Bolshevism and the West*—though he differed from both of them in his estimate as to how world unity could be brought about: 'That "single world-wide organization" that Mr. Russell desires, and that he truly considers is the only guarantee of peace on earth and the cessation of wars, is taking shape beneath his eyes—only, apparently with such unexpected rapidity that (looking for "gradualness") he cannot see it. That peace which, like anybody else, he desires, could be had to-morrow. By the agreement of the workers of the world, through their accredited representatives, to align themselves with the sovietic and fascist power, that unity would immediately be achieved. But if that is not done voluntarily, it will undoubtedly be achieved by compulsion and violence.'[28]

Compulsion and violence again? If so, Lewis protests, it will certainly not be sponsored by him—and he goes on to quote: ' "I believe that, owing to men's folly, a world-government will only be established by force," Mr. Russell says. More pacific than Mr. Russell, I believe it could be established without any force or violence at all.'[29]

It must be admitted that this is a strangely argued belief to come from anyone committed to the promotion of authoritarian rule—Italian or any other. If the 'workers of the world' were to align themselves with 'sovietic and fascist power', it seems highly unlikely that their 'accredited representatives' would be Fascist Party members! There is a strange suggestion of militant *democracy* about the imagined embassy, Socialists though the representatives would almost certainly be. When in the same paragraph, Lewis goes on to denounce 'the senseless bellicosity of the reactionary groups of the *Action Française* type' as calculated to result in 'far more violence, before long, than any one is able to measure', one really begins to wonder on which side of the argument—democratic or autocratic— Lewis is actually to be found. The fact is, of course, that he is committed to neither side—except as it advances the point he is trying to make at the time. As a concept, he is in favour of a strong, centralized rule; and as such he is prepared to accept Fascism for what it has to offer. It is at least a highly convenient stick to lay across democracy's libertarian back. In Italy, furthermore, it has not yet shown its bellicosity: it might even be persuaded to move—eventually—towards the founding of the World State. Democracy, on the other hand, shows no such tendency....

Either way, the note on which *The Art of Being Ruled* ends is completely in harmony with the passage just quoted. It is a plea for sanity in the ordering of world affairs, and one which is made above all to the rulers of the immediate future. It is certainly not in harmony with the (interpolated?) endorsement of violence on the Fascist plan which precedes it by twelve chapters. Once again, the passage deserves to be quoted in full:

> There seems no reason at present why this period of chaotic wastefulness should not be regarded as drawing to a close. In order to wind it up, further wars and revolutions may occur. But they are not any longer necessary. There is even no political excuse for them. There may soon therefore no longer be any reason for the despairing philosopher to enquire, 'Who made so soft and peaceable a creature, born to love mercy, meekness, so to rave, rage like wild beasts, and run on to their own destruction? How may Nature expostulate with mankind, "I made thee a harmless, quiet, a divine creature!", etc.'
>
> For we know quite well what makes such a soft and peaceable creature into a warrior—it is his rulers in the course of their competitive careers who effect this paradoxical transformation in their extremely soft subjects. If all competition were eliminated—both as between the small man and the big, and respectively between the several great ones of this earth—then this soft and peaceable, or 'mad, careless, and stupid' creature would be spared the gymnastics required to turn him into a man-eating tiger. It is also absurd, and even wicked, to attempt to turn him into a philosopher. He should be left alone and allowed to lead a peaceful, industrious, and pleasant life, for we all as men belong to each other.[30]

NOTES

1. *A of B R*, p.3.
2. Ibid., pp.4-5.
3. Ibid., p.341.
4. Ibid., p.415.
5. Ibid., p.317.
6. Ibid., p.68.
7. Ibid.
8. Ibid.
9. Ibid., p.75.
10. Ibid., p.419.
11. Ibid., p.42.
12. Ibid., pp.79-80.
13. Ibid., p.73.
14. Ibid., p.38.
15. Ibid., pp.180-1.
16. Ibid., p.185.
17. Ibid., pp. 206-7.
18. Ibid., p.272.
19. Ibid., p.242.
20. Ibid., pp.74-5.
21. Ibid., pp.369-70.
22. *R A*, p.172.
23. and 24. *A of B R*, p.370. Perhaps it is of some significance that in a review published by *The Calendar of Modern Letters* for January, 1926 (and therefore while *The Art of Being Ruled* was printing) Lewis offers Britain an alternative to 'such scowling condottieri as Mussolini' in the choice of a 'democratic' saviour. By such a course, 'the dictatorial power and the democratic tradition would mutually check each other'. One is surprised to find that a prototype suggested for such a saviour was Lord Beaverbrook! Or was this heavy irony? Op. cit., pp.361-2.
25. *R A*, p.191.
26. *A of B R*, p.46.
27. Ibid., p.83.
28. Ibid., p.49.
29. Ibid.
30. Ibid., p.425.

CHAPTER 3

The Hip and the Square

So far, we have considered Lewis's theories in *The Art of Being Ruled* only as they are applicable to everyday practical politics. Capitalism and Socialism, democracy and autocracy, even a hoped-for Internationalism—these are labels current in our own time: they relate to affairs as we understand them. But there are other matters thrown up by Lewis's argument—what we might call the intellectual overplus—which relate only to the possible nature of some *new* society of the future. And if he drew down wrath upon his head by his advocacy of authoritarian rule, he drew down even more for his vision of a future in which the governing class would have formed themselves into some sort of an élite and the mass of governed humanity would be left happily to its own devices.

If we consider the suggestion as Lewis explains it, on the other hand, it does not seem altogether improbable. For put in its simplest form, it is merely a suggestion that people will continue to do what they enjoy doing, rather than start attempting to do what they are quite incapable of doing. It amounts to a simple development of his *What the Public Wants* theorem, but it is a development in which the choice is made no less by the public itself than by its hidden persuaders. In fashionable jargon, it is merely a suggestion that sooner or later the vast majority of the public will become political drop-outs.

As Lewis sees it, the urge of the majority to live their lives in a way which suits them best is a constant irritation to the political idealist. And one can see that from the professional politician's point of view, any politics is better than no politics at all—at least, in a democracy. The *Don't Know* factor in the Opinion Polls has lost more General Elections than that of 1970, which it lost by making up its mind only at the last minute. If only people were interested in politics *all the time*, how much easier for the politician to arrange for them always to do what he wanted! And it is amusing how deeply the tendency to drop out—at least, politically—is resented at Westminster. The party leaders already insist on keeping their images bright by regular party political broadcasts, inflicted upon television audiences, without the option, at peak viewing times. Failure to vote at elections may soon be penalized—as it already is elsewhere. Whether or not the elector has a candidate to vote for whose policy he approves is neither here nor there: in a democracy no less than in an autocracy, votes will then have to be cast so that government may be seen to be popular.

One can understand the thinking behind such moral compulsion, without being altogether convinced by it. Vigilance, we are frequently told, is the price which must be paid for democracy. Without vigilance, even democratic governments may become either arbitrary or irresponsible: where vigilance is constant, they can be made to obey the will of the people. This is no doubt true up to a point, but as the issues become ever more complicated—will even the most vigilant people on earth be able to control decisions effectively?

T. S. Eliot once expressed the doubt whether the public was ever sufficiently well informed to have the right to an opinion. That is obviously the case with certain contemporary issues. The pros and cons of Britain's joining the Common Market are still in daily debate—and have been over the last few years. Yet is the average voter still in any position to assess the ultimate effect of Britain doing so? Evidence either way is of a complexity which confounds even the economists—and where doctors disagree, who among the rest of us can affirm? Certainly not the average voter, who has neither the time, the background knowledge, nor even the inclination to grapple with the problem in any way likely to be helpful. The pros and cons of Britain's participation in the European Space Programme were equally beyond the competence of most people to discuss. No government in its right mind would fight an election on any such technical issue: very few would refer it to the electorate for decision by referendum. Indeed, his complete distrust of a referendum in deciding even such matters as the abolition of capital punishment is a clear indication of how the professional politician views any prospect of decisions being taken out of his own hands. Vigilance by all means, provided that the *ultimate* decision invariably rests with him!

Government in the Space Age is hardly likely to bear much relation to government in the Age of Steam. The average man played little part in it then and he is quite certain to play still less in the government of the future. If he decides that to govern is his role in life, then he will be forced to train for it in the same way that he would be forced to train if his urge was to become a nuclear physicist. In an age of increasing specialization, only the qualified specialist is likely to get very far. And while the affairs of the borough council may still be right for the vote of the average man to influence (he will never control them), to saddle him with control of the thermo-nuclear bomb would hardly be in his own interests. Unlikely as the thought may seem, it is probably safer even in the hands of the politician —of whatever persuasion he may happen to be. At least the politician may be able to keep it out of the hands of the generals....

Lewis's prediction of a ruling caste of the future was made before the days of the thermo-nuclear bomb. But it was based upon a belief that scientific achievement, even in those far-off pre-nuclear days, had made it inevitable—just as it had made some form of World Government eventually certain. As already suggested, the complexities of national government are such that the man in the street has been virtually disqualified from taking any part in it. But matters have not rested there, for the decision-making even of government is today increasingly dependent upon the technical expertise of its 'advisers'.

Lewis's belief that the ruling class of the future would amount to a 'caste' may not be true of the rulers as we see them in the shop-window of parliament. There is nothing to prevent a pop-singer, TV personality, model or moron getting as far as that. But it is undoubtedly true of the bureaucrats without whose specialist guidance effective government would no longer be possible. Access to that bureaucratic caste is indeed by 'vocational tests on the american pattern' or by 'an examination system on chinese lines', as Lewis suggested that it might be.[1] It is already thirty years since James Burnham drew attention in *The Managerial Revolution* to the new caste of technocrats that is emerging; and in due course it may well take over the administrative machinery which it now serves. But is technical specialization enough in itself? Does government not demand a broader vision and wider experience than the technocrat normally commands?

Lewis was clearly of that opinion. He was also convinced that the failure of democratic government in his time was due in no small part to the amateurism of the politicians in power:

> In the democratic competitive system a certain type of energy of a not very valuable sort (except to its possessor) constantly carries men up into the ruling class. That has been happening ever since the establishment of the industrial system. The ruling class becomes more and more a collection of personalities with no tradition, no intellectual training except such as is involved in speculation in stocks and shares or business deals, no religious beliefs usually or any attachments at all in a wider system than that of the stock market or commerce. In a bureaucratic system, inevitably before long a different type of man to this chance jettison of the most brutal sort of success would be evolved. The *static* nature of the system would not be against it, but on the contrary for it, where the production of a valuable administrative *type* was concerned. The breezy elasticity of competitive commerce would not be there. Life would not be a 'lottery' any more. There would be no golden accidents, in which success was usually secured by the least desirable type of being. *Sheltered* from the coarsening rough-and-tumble of commercial life, developing freely a religious consciousness of the destinies of their caste, intellectually equipped in a way that no former european rulers have ever been, you would get (to place against the certain disadvantages of a too static system) an inbred and highly organized body of rulers. Access to this caste would be by way of examination, perhaps; at all events, by some other route than the brutal and unsatisfactory one of commercial success. They would form that necessary and versatile universal man above the specialist. That is of course at present in the nature of a myth of the future, but it is just as good a recommendation to say that gods will trace their descent from us, as that we trace our descent from gods.[2]

A myth of the future the vision still remains, though every trend in the last fifty years of unparalleled scientific advancement would seem to be bringing it somewhat nearer. But Lewis's concept of a ruling class almost akin to a priesthood would seem to have more to do with religion than with science. In Machiavellian terms, politics had been placed above morality: they were excluded from all the rules of conduct demanded in private life. But politics—or rule—conceived of in such terms as Lewis envisages would be liable to no such exclusion: they would be at one with morality once more. And where morality's influence upon government is strongest, he believes, government will be most just. So much so, that from the historical analogy of the Hebrew state, he is even prepared to affirm that 'theocratic and theurgic forms of government are the highest form of democracy—a kind of super-democracy, in fact'.[3]

Perhaps this idea of theocratic government and a ruling caste sounds more Asian than European: Pakistan and India currently provide rather questionable examples of each. But in any case, Lewis was plainly thinking of a very different kind of rule from any that was enjoyed by Europe during the twenties. The pattern of future government might have to be set by a complete revolution in political thinking, but it was still his belief that 'the permanent state of mind of the revolutionary *ruler* will now be that of the philosopher; a more cultivated, in addition to a more able, ruling class than Europe has ever possessed is promised'.[4]

If so, that promise also remains to be fulfilled.... But enough has been quoted to show clearly that the sort of ruling caste that Lewis had in mind was essentially an intellectual one. Government by such a dedicated caste, he felt, would be the most likely to promote and protect the status of the intellectual in society. And it was his firm conviction that only under such protection could the intellectual ever be enabled to give of his best to society as a whole. Left at the mercy of the admass—and the debased standards which the admass mind imposed—the intellectual tradition of the West was being constantly eroded and would ultimately be lost. Summed up in a phrase, he put his case quite clearly: 'Instead of the vast organization to exploit the weaknesses of the Many, should we not possess one for the exploitation of the intelligence of the Few?'[5]

One might have supposed that this idea was reasonable enough to have passed without argument—at least, among the Few. But there is something about the very concept of fewness which is unacceptable to certain critics. There was a suggestion about it, to the liberal theorists of the twenties and thirties, that caused them once again to accuse Lewis of trying to create a privileged intellectual élite at the expense of the rest of mankind. Any such aim was held to be a denial of the rights of average man to a full share in the benefits of culture: at best, it was a penalization of his lack of educational opportunities. (Whether average man wished to avail himself of such opportunities, they insisted, was really beside the point.) William Morris's vision of a Socialist world in which the workers could be freed from the tyranny of degrading labour was certainly no more dear to his critics than it was to Lewis himself. What he did not share with them, however, was any belief that with leisure upon their hands, most people would promptly devote themselves to cultural pursuits—and that every man would accordingly become his own intellectual. To Lewis, such an idea was utter nonsense. Cultural pursuits never had been—and never would be—most people's dream of self-indulgence. How many of the ruling and privileged classes of the time, he wondered, indulged themselves in such pursuits with all the opportunities in the world? Did the average statesman, politician or tycoon? Why then should anyone insist upon them as the frustrated aspiration of all and sundry? Where some prefer to study philosophy, others prefer to cultivate their gardens. Given the bread, a regular supply of circuses (as of now—football, racing and television) is all that the majority demand. The Russophile's wistful vision of 'ballet every evening' is hardly calculated to appeal to them—nor did Lewis see any particular reason why it should. Happiness for the average man, no less than for the intellectual, is where he finds and enjoys it. The pleasures of the intellect are there for all who seek them: those who do have only to start using their minds individually and creatively.

The frontier which Lewis believed to be drawn between what he called the changeless Many and the unchangeable Few, he defined as the frontier which divides the unfree from the free.[6] He agreed that the intellectual would always be critical of his rulers—no matter how 'intellectual' government itself might become, given the rulers for whom he hoped. And this he saw as in the best interests of everyone. But if the freedom of the intellect was not to be swallowed up forever, he insisted that the frontier must be kept: there was no other way by which freedom could be guaranteed for anyone at all.

He was willing to concede that the mere idea of the Many being on the wrong side of a frontier might be interpreted as a tacit desire to keep them there. But he denied any such desire on his own part: the Many had chosen that side for themselves, or been persuaded to choose it. On the other hand, he cheerfully admitted that the privileged position of the intellectual which he was advocating would benefit himself, among others, but he saw 'no dishonour in such a conclusion to the argument'. He merely pointed out that the tendency of the Many to herd together was itself forcing the Few to draw apart, since within the herd there was 'no play for the inventive and independent mind'. And while the intellectual was normally the last person likely to associate himself with anyone, the time was coming—in spite of himself and in spite of Lewis's critics —when he would be driven into forming some sort of cartel of his own. Such a time, Lewis foresaw, might well mark a turning point in history, for 'had the best intelligences at any time in the world been able to combine, the result would have been a prodigy of power, and the result for men at large the happiest'.[7] From Socrates to Shaw, most intellectuals might well have agreed with him.

But before that turning point was reached—if indeed it ever *were* to be reached—the lot of the intellectual in the modern world was singularly *un*privileged. As Lewis was to emphasize twenty years later in *Rude Assignment*, before the days of commercialism, a ruling aristocracy had always extended some degree of patronage to the arts and sciences. And while the practice had many shortcomings (not least of them, the arbitrary way in which patronage was dispensed) it had occasionally ensured the intellectual such independence as allowed him to concentrate on usefully creative or experimental work. No such patronage was being extended by modern society—unless, in the case of the scientist, it was extended by commercial or militaristic interests for the wrong reasons. (During World War

II, for example, nuclear physics benefited notably by such patronage: in peacetime, the research which went into production of the Atomic Bomb would have occupied unsubsidized science for the rest of the century.)

But apart from lack of patronage, the intellectual in the modern world had increasingly to contend with positive hostility and interference. And if the scientist found his discoveries menaced by prejudice, ignorance or commercially vested interests, Lewis believed that the lot of the writer and the artist was no better. As What the Public emphatically Did *Not* Want, the intellectual had been turned into a target for every kind of ridicule and envy. So far as his creativity went, the popular press had been only too quick to belittle what the majority were incapable of appreciating and to dismiss what they were incapable of understanding. All this, said Lewis darkly, was a conscious policy designed to curtail and eventually to overwhelm the independence of the intellectual position. This position, he asserted, must be safeguarded by 'a *separation*, limited in kind, between creative man and his backward fellow'.[8]

Naturally enough, one begins by wondering what is implied by 'limited separation', with its suggestion of some sort of cultural *apartheid*. It was already one of Lewis's complaints that 'the writer or painter is isolated from the general public to an unparalleled extent, at the present time'.[9] Further 'separation' would therefore hardly seem to be called for—unless it amounted to a privileged position in society which guaranteed the intellectual a measure of economic independence. It would seem, in fact, that no more was in Lewis's mind than patronage in the old sense. But patronage of what kind? If it was to be paid for by the State, who would administer the fund—and on what terms? Would the intellectuals themselves be responsible for the arrangement, presenting an annual budget for the Exchequer to meet, as did the Service Departments? Possibly so. But could the intellectuals have been expected to speak with one voice? Wouldn't intellectual factions immediately begin to struggle for ascendency and monopolize benefits to the detriment of all rival factions? That was certainly the way it was in the publishing world, and probably the way it always would be. In his coming role of The Enemy, Lewis would hardly have received very generous treatment from those who liked to re-

gard themselves as his peers! Nor would he probably have
done any better at the hands of the Arts Council as we know it
today....

One thing he was definitely *not* prepared to consider was any
direct patronage which was at the discretion of the British
government—either in 1925 or ten years later, when he was
invited by the B.B.C. to give his considered opinion on the
matter. Indeed, he roundly declared on that occasion that *'any*
patronage is better than one deriving from the politicians'.[10]
Stanley Baldwin could hardly have been regarded as even a
poor man's choice as a discriminating Maecenas.

Nor did the authoritarian government of Fascist Italy appear
to have been the answer either. The Italian intellectual had not
benefited notably from his privileged position under Mussolini,
and Lewis was careful never to make any such suggestion.
Indeed, if patronage of the arts had been introduced by the
Duce—who more likely to have enjoyed it than Marinetti and
his Futurist *squadra*—the intellectual begetters of Fascism, as
Lewis fully appreciated? As an avowed anti-Futurist, he could
hardly have expected to benefit by the *same* patronage—even
if it had existed, and he had been entitled to it. Nor was the
record of government patronage under the Soviets likely to have
pleased him any better. Even in those days, endorsement of the
Party Line would have been his only hope, and any attempt at
criticism would have earned him nothing more than a one-way
ticket to the labour camps or even the asylum.

All in all, Lewis's 'limited separation' seems to have bristled
with difficulties, which is probably why he refrained from giving
even the first hint as to what in fact he meant by it. He was
perfectly justified in feeling the lack of patronage and encouragement in the modern world as he found it. But it seems highly
questionable whether any existing form of government—autocratic or otherwise—would have been likely to have supported
him any better. He appears to have resigned himself to the fact
by leaving the matter at that, for as he frankly admits towards
the end of the book, 'no logical future has taken pictorial shape
in these pages. All that has been done is to lay down a certain
number of roads joining the present with something different
from itself; yet something necessitated, it would appear, by its
tendency. Both what is desirable and what is not in it contribute

contradictorily to this impression. It is this *double* movement (proceeding from combined disgust and satisfaction) that must make the planning of these roads so difficult.'[11]

'Contradictorily' would seem to be the operative word. As he admits elsewhere: 'Politics has nothing to do with the idea of perfection.'[12]

So much has been said about Lewis's advocacy in the cause of the intellectual, that some clarification of his own intellectual position would seem to be called for. His unique achievements in the creative field—either as a writer or as an artist—are too well known to need any mention here: it is only the nature of his critical and philosophical thinking which need concern us. This would be easy enough to decide, if he had not explained it so often and so consistently himself. Lewis was a classicist, and stands—as a critic no less than as a creative artist—for the classical conception of life and art. As a painter, he has defined classicism as 'a *progress* backwards ... to the great, central, and stable canons of artistic expression, *away from* the atmospheric, impressionistic, molecular-pointilliste, vibratory-plein-air nineteenth century aesthetic'.[13] He might well have agreed with Blake that 'the more distinct, sharp and wiry the bounding line, the more perfect the work of art'. As a writer, he explains: ' "Classical" is for me *anything* which is nobly defined and exact, as opposed to that which is fluid—of the Flux—without outline, romantically "dark", vague, "mysterious", stormy, uncertain.'[14] And he emphasizes that the Hellenic age had no monopoly in the classical: it is to be found in the art of every culture since. He explains his own art in this way: '*To solidify, to make concrete, to give definition to*—that is my profession ... to crystallize that which (otherwise) flows away, to concentrate the diffuse, to turn to ice that which is liquid and mercurial— that certainly describes my occupation, and the tendency of all that I think.'[15] And in general terms: 'The "classical" is the rational, aloof and aristocratical; the "romantic" is the popular, sensational and "cosmically" confused. That is the permanent political reference in these terms.'[16]

Lewis's concern is with the external world rather than the world within—with what he calls the hard carapace rather than the fluid core. He is fascinated and stimulated by the logic of pure form; he is uninterested in the changing patterns which merely reflect impermanence and imbalance. His art is an art of the eye—an art which dwells upon outward appearance, rather than the shifting states of mind which hide behind it. He is an accurate observer, and his world is a floodlit world from which the shadows have been eliminated. In his writing no less than in his painting he is obsessed with 'clarity of form' and his care is always to avoid 'romantic blur and blotch'. His world is the world of Signorelli and Cézanne, rather than that of Giorgione or the Impressionists.

There is a philosophical basis for this insistence upon the precise to the exclusion of the imprecise and approximate. It is derived from his antipathy for the world of Bergsonian philosophy, with its insistence upon Time as a necessary factor in all our ideas of being and form. Lewis's girding at Bergson would make up a book in itself—as indeed his destructive analysis of Bergsonism makes up the substance of *Time and Western Man*. But there is quite enough in *The Art of Being Ruled* to suit the present context. It is Bergson's emphasis upon the value of intuition to the detriment of the intellectual process which arouses Lewis's wrath; for as Bertrand Russell once put it, much of Bergson's philosophy is 'a kind of Sandford and Merton, with instinct as the good boy and intellect as the bad boy'. This fact, coupled with Bergson's obsession with the kinetics of the temporal and his denial of the permanence of the spatial was responsible, in Lewis's opinion, for the undermining of every value in contemporary life and thought:

Bergson ... has been the great organizer of disintegration in the modern world: it is he who has found all the *reasons* (eloquently dressed in a 'style that bribes one in advance,' as William James says of it) for the destruction of the things of the intellect, and the handing over to sensation of the privileges and heirlooms of the mind, and the enslaving of the intelligent to the affective nature. His philosophy of *movement* and *change* makes him the best spokesman of the life lived by the typical american business man. The vulgar frenzy of Nietzsche, and Bergson's gospel of fluidity and illiquation, form in about equal measure the philosophic basis of futurism and similar movements.... His is the doctrine of *sensation for sensation's sake*, a worthy fellow of *art for art's sake*.[17]

Luckily, we do not have to go into the rights and wrongs of Bergsonism: we are merely concerned with the aesthetic and political implications of Lewis's distrust of it. Enough emerges as to that in Part XII of *The Art of Being Ruled*: the later elaboration in *Time and Western Man* adds little to our understanding of his political point of view. So far as his intellectual standpoint was concerned, in opposition to Bergson's preoccupation with temporal fluidity, Lewis fell back upon spatial immobility. Art for him, as we have seen, was a freezing into permanence, the classical concept of stasis and the stability of repose. Art for the Bergsonian, on the other hand, implied an acceptance of the changing and the sensational, a belief in instinct and intuition as an essential part of 'vitalism' or 'dynamism', and a surrender of self to what he regarded as the *élan vital*. All this was the exact antithesis of everything that Lewis himself regarded as right and proper to art: rather than being objective, logical and classical, it was being subjective, emotional and romantic. So far as Lewis was concerned, romantic and wrong were 'commutative terms'.

In his classicist antipathy for the Bergsonian school, Lewis was hardly original: he had been anticipated in France by some thirteen years. He had himself attended Bergson's lectures at the Collège de France back in the 1900s, when Bergson's influence in Paris was at its height. Indeed, it was those lectures and his discussions with friends at the École Normale which developed Lewis's interest in philosophy. (He had first read it at Rugby, as he explained later, 'in spite of the demands made upon me by football and other athletics'.) Nor did Bergson's teaching seem to have aroused any hostility in him at the time: perhaps he paid little attention to it, for he claimed to have known very little about it until the twenties. But in 1912, Julien Benda had published *Le Bergsonisme ou une philosophie de la mobilité*, and two years later his *Réponse aux défenseurs du Bergsonisme*. In *Belphégor* (written about the same time, but only published in 1918) he returned to the attack once more; and it was largely Benda's point of view which Lewis himself took in the *The Art of being Ruled* and *Time and Western Man*. It was no doubt out of deference to Benda that Bergson had been blasted by *BLAST* in 1914.

Quite obviously, Benda had been a major influence upon

Lewis's thinking, and he is quoted with relish as having 'not left much in Bergson worth destroying'.[18] The very section-headings of *Belphégor* sound like a reeling off of Lewis's objections to Bergsonian romanticism—*That Art must be a Mystic Union with the Essence of Things, Proscription of Clarity in Art, Cult of the Indistinct &c, Musicization of All the Arts, The Quest of the Emotion of Surprise, Thirst for Novelty &c, That the Artist shall live the Emotion he is dealing with and not rise above it by means of his Understanding*—and so on. All these 'rules' for the aspiring Bergsonian, as attacked by Benda, are again demolished by Lewis in his own—more withering—indictment.

There is no need here to go into any discussion of the French neo-classicist movement with which Julien Benda was associated, or to consider Lewis's indebtedness to the movement in any more than general terms. (For those who are interested, the question has been ably covered by Geoffrey Wagner in his *Portrait of the Artist as the Enemy*.) The highly heterogeneous group included, among others, Henri Massis, Ernest Seillière, Pierre Lasserre, Paul Bourget, Edouard Berth, Jacques Maritain, and Charles Maurras. Some of their ideas were undoubtedly very similar to Lewis's own, though he dissociates himself from the Bergsonism of Maritain and the rabid *Action Française* outpourings of Maurras—as indeed did Benda himself.

Even so, Maurras, with his monarchistic ideas of *ordre* as the first necessity of government is underlining one of the factors that Lewis himself believed to be the foundation-stone of sound politics. And as Alastair Hamilton points out in his recent book *The Appeal of Fascism*, even Malraux had called attention to the fact that by the emphasis he placed on 'order', Maurras had been reminding us that only in order could we hope to find 'strength and beauty'. Lewis also insists that the rule is no less true of the State than it is of art, and agrees with Maurras at least to the point of asserting that 'any little organization that Europe has ever had has been centred in France, and symbolized by her classicist culture'.[19] While organization and order are not necessarily synonymous, there can be little of the one without the other. Indeed, it was the breakdown of European order before what he regarded as the disruptive nihilism of

Rousseau that, for Lewis, had brought political death into the world and all our woe.

Any careful reading of *The Art of Being Ruled* will clearly show that it was because of its classical overtones that authoritarianism first appealed to Lewis as the natural corrective for romantic *dis*order, revolution as a state of becoming, and democracy with its approximations of the many at the expense of the clear-cut precision of government by the few. As he remarks in another context, there is nothing wrong with democracy except the people who compose it. Democracy sprawls: it is an open acceptance of the intuitive and the fortuitous in government. It is not only 'romantically' unstable, but fluid and 'Bergsonian' in the worst sense of the word. If the State is itself to be regarded as a work of art, something far more structural and tightly integrated would seem to be called for by the classicist—whether monarchical or not. Lewis never endorsed the monarchism of Maurras, though he admits to having toyed with the idea of a Patriot King as predicated by Bolingbroke. But there is every reason to believe that it was the French neo-classicist demand for order and permanence which had interested him in rule as an art form in the first place. Authoritarianism is rigid and exact: democracy is not. Therefore, he seems to have argued, how can classicism in art hope to thrive under a form of government which, in its very nature, is opposed to a classical ordering of its political affairs?

This whole concept of the romantic at war with the classical, Faustian Man and Music displacing the Plastic ideal in art, Bergson's flux of time distorting the spatial appearances of Berkeley, and Einstein cutting the ground from under Newton's feet—what was it but a war in which the political theorist no less than the artist was committed to taking sides? There were, of course, difficulties: Berkeley himself could be dim and dark, though his was still 'the best of all possible philosophic worlds'.[20] And even Lewis was the first to admit that the arch-romantic Shakespeare had utterly out-written the classical Racine. But these were merely the anomalies of warfare. And while the argument of classicism versus romanticism seems to us nowadays little short of quaint (at least, as applied to politics) the argument is still with us in terms that are more immediately acceptable to the post-war intellectual. As we should choose to put it in our own phraseology, it is now the argument of the Hip versus the Square.

In his highly stimulating *Advertisements for Myself* (1959), Norman Mailer has pursued just that line of argument. Taking 'romantic' as an instance of the hip, he places 'classic' as its antithesis in squareness. Similarly, we find 'spontaneous' listed in opposition to 'orderly', 'instinct' in opposition to 'logic', and 'nihilistic' in opposition to 'authoritarian'. Further examples of the hip are Negro (for which now read Black), crooks, Heidegger, sex, the body, the differential calculus, Marx as a psychologist, Thelonius Monk, Trotsky, Dostoyevsky, D. H. Lawrence, Churchill, anarchists, Picasso, to seduce by touch, and the present. The square alternatives are listed as white (now read honkey), cops (now read The Fuzz), Sartre, religion, the mind, analytic geometry, Marx as a sociologist, Dave Brubeck, Lenin, Tolstoy, Aldous Huxley, Clement Attlee, socialists, Mondrian, to seduce by reasoned argument, and the past and/or the planned future. And much as Sir Winston Churchill may have demurred at being classed with the anarchists as hip, Lewis would certainly have been willing to add himself to the list of squares in opposition to a hipster like James Joyce.

The principle of squareness, in fact, was what Lewis was defending throughout *The Art of Being Ruled, Time and Western Man, The Diabolical Principle, Paleface* and nearly every political or critical 'essay' that he was to write for the rest of his life. He would, we may be sure, have *gloried* in the name of square: it is so much a matter of precise and analytical geometry. The universe may try to be passing itself off as curved (or shaped like an American doughnut, in the latest theory) but the State, the individual, art and philosophy, Lewis would have kept foursquare by any means at his disposal.

Much as one is amused by Mailer's listing, one can generally see clearly enough what has been the thought behind his sifting of the goats from the sheep. On the other hand, he lists 'Catholic' as hip and 'Protestant' as square—despite the fact that he regards free will as hip and credits Protestantism with giving it to 'the emotional history of the West'. But he explains that the listing reflects his 'sense of the present' rather than a square sense of the past. Perhaps because he would have denied any 'emotional history' to the West at all, Lewis, on the other hand, was never in any doubt that Catholicism was classical and Protestantism was romantic. (Maurras was certainly of the same opinion, and went so far as to charge Protestantism with being Jewish—than which nothing in his canon could be more abominable!) While their listings would have been the same for the most part, Lewis and Mailer would still have been at odds here and there. Nor is this really at all surprising, since any such assessments must always be subjectively hip and can never quite attain to the objective squareness which Lewis would have preferred. As Bergson would have explained it, objectivity may enable one to analyse reality—but never quite to achieve it.

This would be obvious enough in Lewis's changes of opinion, which he freely admits, but which have resulted in his being forced to attack on philosophical grounds what he has elsewhere been ready enough to praise aesthetically. Despite his initial appreciation of Joyce's *Ulysses*, for instance, he explains that he had not then come to have 'the clear picture of the contemporary scene' which forced him later—reluctantly—to attack it at considerable length for its 'disintegrating metaphysic'. Not merely that, he came to deplore the fact that it had 'no firm and logical linear structure', but was rather 'a chaotic mosaic'.[21] He even accuses Joyce of having been 'very romantic indeed' about its Homeric form—a 'framework of classical antiquity' which he finds it whimsical that Joyce should have adopted in the first place.[22] Pound and other romantics, on the other hand, were of a very different opinion. More recently, even the classical structure of *Finnegans Wake* has been coming up for discussion—among the hipsters, if not among the squares.

As we are not here concerned with Lewis's literary criticism, we need not go further into his objections to the work of Henry James (occasional), Gertrude Stein, Jolas and the *transition* school (invariable), Ezra Pound himself (a 'Revolutionary Simpleton' in *Time and Western Man*), and eventually his fellow-classicist T. S. Eliot (in *Men Without Art*). It is sufficient to say that by the time he had launched himself upon *The Art of Being Ruled*, his critical opinions could all be traced back to the use of a metaphysical yardstick—and that the same yardstick was being used for his political assessments also. That his assessments were no less personal and subjective for that, goes without saying. Indeed, his yardstick itself seems to have been subject to almost Bergsonian variations in length—or should we say to its own kind of Fitzgerald Contraction?

But leaving literature out of it, Lewis's political thinking was also liable to change whenever he moved over from theorizing in general terms to a consideration of particular instances. The 'sovietic' system which he had praised so highly in theory was already beginning to lose its initial charm. In 1926, Lenin had been 'a Lion, and consequently a portion of eternity too great for the life of man to measure'[23]—at least, in a world of rats and foxes. Two years later, Lewis had 'come to believe that Russian Communism not only should not, but cannot, become the creed of the Western peoples'.[24] To the hypothetical question 'Is there one God and is Lenin his prophet?' he now replied with an emphatically muttered negative—'Nee-ee-een-Oce', as he chose to put it in contradiction of *transition's* reputed 'EE-EE-EE-ee-ee-arse'!

Italian Fascism also began to lose its attractiveness, when Lewis ceased to regard it as a theoretical system and at last began to look at it rather more closely. In 1925, Mussolini's dragooning of his *squadre* into a latter-day facsimile of the Roman Legions had seemed like the start of a new Renaissance, despite the fact that the Romans had never been particularly strong 'in art or speculative thought'. By 1927, however, the *fasces* of the lictors, the *Roman* salute and all the other claptrap was being ridiculed as so much romantic *passéism*. As for the Fascist insistence upon 'action'—that was now dismissed as mere 'futurism in practice'. 'Action' was Fascism's magic word, 'recurring in all their speeches and incantations'.[25] It merely served to emphasize that violence was its god, and that Fascism itself represented 'the habit of mind and conditions of war applied to peace'.[26] In metaphysical terms, it was no more than Faustian Man's substitution of 'Action' for 'The Word', and as such was yet another Bergsonism. Indeed, if Lewis had come up against the shabby-romantic trappings of Fascism at first hand, he might have been quicker to recognize the comical uniforms and general gimcrackery for the fustian that it was. He might even have been reminded of Byron's weakness for dressing up as an Albanian chief, and the helmet that he designed for himself to wear at Missolonghi. How much further could the romantic idea in politics be pushed?

Indeed, the more one considers it, the more 'romantic' the concept of authoritarianism begins to seem in itself. The Nazi version, with its mammoth rallies, its torchlight processions, its wild hysteria and Wagnerian overlay, we shall be considering later on. But the whole tone of authoritarian pamphleteering—not least of it, the worst of Lewis's own—has an overstatement and a pushing of argument to extremes which is more than a trifle suspect. One is reminded of Julien Benda's gibe at the violence and vehemence of Maurras in *Belphégor*: what is so 'classical' about violence or over-emphasis of any kind? It is certainly at variance with the seventeenth century classical tradition in France, which Maurras pretended to value so highly—or with any other tradition that we recognize as classical in any sense at all. As Benda concludes ironically: 'Apostleship can never be classic.'

But whether one chooses to list authoritarianism among the hips or the squares, very little can be argued from one listing or the other. It might seem to many of us that the argument is completely academic, and that in neither the one category nor the other can any excuse for its excesses be found. The same is of course true of the excesses committed by democracy. Judicial murder may be carried out under the latter with all the 'classical' decorum and formality which went to the elimination of Socrates. Is it any the better for that, in its implications for humanity? As Benda points out in *La Trahison des Clercs*, it is one of the anomalies of the authoritarian position that it tends —as did Sorel—to range itself against Socrates along with his accusers. And as he sadly remarks, such an alliance of the intellectual has never before been known 'since Crito closed his master's eyes'.

By his change of mind over Sovietism and Italian Fascism, Lewis made it clear that he was perfectly aware of the ill uses to which authoritarianism can be put. On the other hand, he was equally aware of the shortcomings of government in the western democracies, and the lowering of all standards to which it appeared to be giving rise. As he saw it, western culture and western society were rapidly in process of disintegration. This he blamed upon the destructive tendencies inherent in much modern thinking, upon a fashionable acceptance of change as an end in itself, and upon a resulting collapse of all belief in authority as anyway necessary to good government. If he was right in his estimate, then he was right in the means he employed to redress the balance by a vigorous insistence upon the rehabilitation of classical order. It did not necessarily mean that he was throwing out all forms of romanticism with the Bergsonian bath-water: it merely served to counteract one over-emphasis by an unremitting insistence upon another in his polemic. When he identifies Bergsonism with all that is muzzy in contemporary thinking, he is at least focusing attention upon that muzziness. When he identifies it also with the restless urge for change which he finds at the back of most contemporary behaviour, he is reminding us that change is valuable only for the results which it may bring in its wake. The fact that—largely as a result of the Bergsonian metaphysic—we have become used to regarding revolution as a way of life does not mean that revolution is necessarily to be equated with progress. And the revolution which he sees as having been brought about by the democratic free-for-all, in Lewis's opinion, has definitely been a change very much for the worse.

To begin with, he questions whether our modern concept of democracy is a sound and realistic one in itself. In essence it derives from Rousseau and his romantic belief in the freedom of Abstract Man. But has Abstract Man ever existed as a factor in any social system? His freedom was certainly not the point at issue in the American Revolution, however much he may appear to figure in the Declaration of Independence. Nor was he able to claim any freedom as a result of the various revolutions in France, except insofar as he could identify himself with the rising power of the *bourgeoisie*. As for the so-called democracy of Athens, that had nothing in common with the Rousseauesque ideal either, being based upon a solid substratum of slave labour. Democracy may have been enjoyed by a proportion of the Athenian citizens, but hardly by the populace as a whole. And taking it at its best, says Lewis, 'our democracy is a flower—if a wilted and shrivelled one—of that distant Hellenic servitude'. Over the years, it has never failed to keep "a substantial section of our own people in a servile condition'.[27]

Wherever the State has paid lip-service to the romantic ideal of democracy, some form of privilege has resulted—the *bour-geoisie* being generally the class to enjoy the benefit of it. And for Lewis, the 'small man' is emphatically *not* synonymous with 'the people' in any democratic sense at all. The 'small man', on the contrary, is the very worst product of democracy, 'making an unreal, small *middle-world*, or no-man's-land, from which his vanity and uselessness can bite at and checkmate those above him and exploit those beneath him. He is not only the enemy of a unification of the intelligent forces of the world; he is the symbol of what has always held back our race.'[28] Need-less for the intellectual to add, his mediocrity has 'always brought to nothing the work of the creative mind'.

Yet it is the 'small man'—the middle-man—who has assumed the role and claimed the identity of 'Abstract Man' on behalf of everyone else. By virtue of that middle-world of the 'small men', and their innate conservatism, democracy had resulted in a large measure of subjection for the rest. Out of deference to the 'small men', democracy had also been at pains to devalue all that they distrusted and all they could not appreciate. As for the 'superior wills' in the background—what more effective cover could they ask for behind which to operate? Or carrying it a stage further, what more unwitting tools could they ask for in achieving their own ends?

This being the case, Lewis concludes, democracy can hardly be expected to hold out any great hope for the future. By encouraging belief in a romantic abstraction—the freedom of Abstract Man—Rousseau had merely made it possible for one segment of society to entrench itself to the detriment of the rest. By pretending to dispense that freedom—which most of society did not really want—'democratic government' had then been able to hold the rest in comparative subjection. And in line with the romantic nostalgia inherent in Rousseau's initial concept, this mock-revolution had been accepted as social pro-gress! As it had worked out in political terms, Rousseau's initial concept had merely resulted in the negation of all it had been intended to promote.

It was not the idea of freedom itself which Lewis was attack-ing in *The Art of Being Ruled*: that would always be the first need of the intellectual and the artist. What he was attacking was the fact that *un*freedom was being accepted by most people as though it were the same thing. And if *un*freedom was what they wanted—at least let it be organized. By way of paving the way, therefore, to a future which had better things to offer, he ended the book with a final plea:

> Our minds are still haunted by that Abstract Man, that enlightened abstraction of a common humanity, which had its greatest advertisement in the eighteenth century. That No Man in a No Man's Land, that phantom of democratic 'enlightenment', is what has to be disposed (of) for good in order to make way for higher human classifications, which, owing to scientific method, men could now attempt.[29]

It will be clear enough by now that the attempt, so far as Lewis was concerned, should be towards the attaining of a more classical order in government than so far democracy had shown a disposition to adopt.

In *Time and Western Man,* published some eighteen months after *The Art of Being Ruled,* Lewis admitted that his attitude to democracy had changed in the interim. He felt that he had dwelt too insistently on the shortcomings of democratic government as he saw it to be, and had been too obsessed with the implications of admass gullibility. But whatever redeeming features might be found in it, he still insists that 'its political realization is invariably at the mercy of the hypnotist'.[30] Unfortunately, he did not go on to admit that 'people are simply made that way', and infer that a far greater danger was to be feared from the hypnotism exerted by authoritarian leadership. He could have saved himself a great deal of embarrassment if that simple inference had been drawn.

Taking his new look at democracy, however, he is persuaded in *Time and Western Man* that people should be 'compelled to be freer and more "individualistic" than they normally desire to be'. And he ironically suggests that this end could best be achieved by making them individually 'remain absolutely alone for several hours every day', and placing them in solitary confinement once every two months 'under pleasant conditions (say in mountain scenery)'.[31] This happy suggestion at least has the advantage of being romantic. It would certainly have recommended itself to Rousseau....

But it is doubtful whether the class-ridden and impoverished democracy of the twenties could ever have appealed to Lewis much more than what he was then prepared to call 'its doctrinaire and more primitive relative, communism'.[32] Its standards were no less suspect to him than those of the 'small man' squatting in its midst. As for Communism itself, he is even clearer in his mind: 'The emotionally-excited, closely-packed, heavily-standardized mass-units, acting in a blind, ecstatic union, as though in response to the throbbing of some unseen music.'[33] That would hardly be the proper environment for one so insistent upon individual values and a return to the canons of classical art.

Borrowing a pragmatic attitude from William James's proto-Bergsonian philosophy, therefore, he was prepared to 'muddle through' with democracy until a better alternative presented itself. And his final attitude, as of 1927, is admirably summed up in a single sentence: 'Let us behave *as if* the West were free, and as if we were in the full enjoyment of an ideal democracy.'[34]

Some of his less exacting readers may well have added: 'Let us indeed!'

NOTES

1. *A of B R*, p.374.
2. Ibid., pp.155-6.
3. Ibid., p.419.
4. Ibid., p.99.
5. Ibid., p.89.
6. *R A*, p.187.
7. *A of B R*, p.420.
8. *R A*, p.184.
9. *D P and D S*, p.vii.
10. *B.B.C. Annual*, 1935, p.186. In the article which he contributes on *Art and Patronage*, Lewis concludes that 'the kind of patronage represented by the B.B.C. as it exists to-day is the best in the worst of all possible worlds for the artist'. It is pleasant to know that sixteen years later, after Lewis had gone blind, the B.B.C. were to afford him the patronage which enabled him to write *The Human Age*.
11. *A of B R*, p.413.
12. *The Calendar*, April 1926, p.44.
13. Ibid., p.29.
14. *Paleface*, p.255.
15. Ibid., p.254.
16. *T and W M*, p.26.
17. *A of B R*, p.386.
18. Ibid.
19. Ibid., p.359.

20. *T and W M*, p.480.
21. *R A*, pp.54-56.
22. *T and W M*, p.132.
23. *The Calendar*, April 1926, p.18.
24. *The Enemy*, No. 2, p.xxx.
25. *T and W M*, p.213.
26. Ibid., p.56.
27. *R A*, p.181.
28. *A of B R*, p.108.
29. *A of B R*, p.434.
30. *T and W M*, p.42.
31. Ibid., p.138.
32. Ibid., p.42.
33. Ibid.
34. Ibid.

CHAPTER 4

No Blues for Mr Charlie

In January 1927, Lewis had emerged on the literary stage in what was to prove his favourite role—that of *The Enemy*. The literary review which he published under that name ran to only three issues over the next two years, each of which was built around a long essay which was later to appear in book form.[1] But it was as The Enemy that Lewis was to function throughout his critical career; and it was in that capacity that he had appointed himself the literary and political Cato of his time.

It has generally been supposed that the leading writers and intellectuals of any age establish the trend of their time. But this, Lewis was at life-long pains to challenge by his own example. In *Time and Western Man*, he quotes Professor Samuel Alexander's contention that 'truth means the settling down of individual believings into a social whole and the condemnation of the heretical or unscientific believing.... The divergences of standard minds from the isolated minds of the victims of error are the mode by which we come to apprehend propositions as true.'[2] But Lewis is very much of the opposite opinion: 'In contradiction to this theory of a collective truth, our experience shows us that it is always an "heretical" minority that imposes its truth upon the majority.'[3] In *The Art of Being Ruled* he was even prepared (for once) to quote Sorel in defence of his argument, and add that Émile Faguet had also maintained that 'good writers, far from embodying, as was generally supposed, the prejudices of their time, did the exact contrary—namely, they opposed them'.[4] This idea of swimming against what appeared to be the *Zeitgeist* was very much after Lewis's temperament; and while not in his lifetime able to reverse the current of twentieth century political thinking, he at least succeeded in rocking many boats which were content to paddle along with it.

His ideas on the classical nature of authoritarianism had already made him a target for those critics who preferred the libertarian comforts of democracy: with his essay *Paleface*, he drew down a great deal of abuse for what was regarded (quite unfairly) as his 'racialist' attitude towards the Black American and the American Indian. When it was published in book form (1929), *Paleface* was the subject of some unfavourable reviews— one of them, in *Time and Tide*, by the otherwise highly appreciative Rebecca West.[5] Her objections to the work were mainly on political grounds, whereas Lewis's object in writing it had been purely aesthetic; but as he himself might have been the first to foresee, politics and aesthetics are hardly to be kept apart in contemporary criticism. Lewis excused his failure to realize as much some years later, when he came to consider the work retrospectively in *Rude Assignment*. For any liberal, the repression and ill-treatment of the Black American was a matter of sincere concern; and the question of the Black contribution to White culture was accordingly a matter of some importance— or, as Lewis chose to put it, a primary emotional asset of the revolutionary, a prime target for agitation'. As he explains: 'These revolutionary interests were not paramount for Rebecca West: but she was better acquainted than I was with the circumstances, since she had lived in the States, and knew the extent to which discrimination against coloured people constituted a monstrous social injustice.'[6] While he still defends the tenor of his criticism on aesthetic grounds, therefore, he regrets that it might seem to have unfortunate implications for the cause of Black emancipation, since he regarded this as 'an elementary necessity, outside and irrespective of the stratagems of politics'.[7] There is nothing in *Paleface* or any other of Lewis's works to suggest that he was not fully in sympathy with the cause of Black emancipation.

If anything, *Paleface* is a book about *White* emancipation. It is a protest against the sense of inferiority which the white race is being invited to feel when faced with the moral integrity,

75

innate understanding and artistic achievements of the coloured races—the invitation coming as much from certain white intellectuals as from the coloured races themselves. It is, in fact, one more broadside in Lewis's onslaught against a Bergsonian over-selling of the intuitive in art at the expense of the intellectual tradition. We are back once more with the hip and the square—the Black and the Hopi being the hipsters on this occasion, and Lewis once more the square determined at all costs to defend his classical values. It is the insistence of certain writers on the moral superiority of the primitive that he is disputing. Such an insistence, allied as it was to a modern obsession with the primitive in art, he sees—once again—as a deliberate undermining of the intellectual position. It is to substitute the instinct for the intelligence, the emotion for the thought, and the spontaneous for the calculated. It is to repeat Rousseau's apotheosis of the Noble Savage—a ceremony hardly likely to appeal to latter-day Black Panthers. It is, in short, a dangerous form of sentimentality; and when he finds writers of the calibre of D. H. Lawrence and Sherwood Anderson indulging in that sentimentality, Lewis once more moves up his artillery.

Sherwood Anderson's *Dark Laughter* had been parodied by Hemingway's *Torrents of Spring* before it was subjected to Lewis's criticism in *Paleface*. It was a novel in which the diffidence and indecisions of White America, its hypocrisy and intolerance, were thrown into relief against a dark background —the simpler, all-wise derision of America's black servants. Theirs was the dark laughter before which white supremacy was beginning to lose all faith in itself, and white assurance lose all sense of adequacy. While the idea is interesting in itself, it is hardly helped across by the sentimental terms in which it is worked out. Indeed, the laughter was no more called for by the story than by the story-teller—as Hemingway's parody made abundantly clear.

As for D. H. Lawrence, it was his *Mornings in Mexico* which supplied the occasion for Lewis's heavy sarcasm. Lawrence had spent half his life looking for the antidote to modern man's destructively analytical self-consciousness. He had sought it primarily in sexual relationships, where the urge and the orgasm at least brought temporary relief from the tensions of social self-restraint. He had toured the world looking for a way of life that was more instinctive, less artificial and less inhibiting than that compounded by western civilization. The later Sardinians and Sicilians had been found somehow wanting; even the gipsies and the Australian aborigines had not supplied him with every answer. Nowhere, in fact, had he found the answer so convincing as among the Indians of New Mexico. Watching their ritual dances and listening to their music, he found them spontaneous in a way that no westerner could hope to be. To the rhythm of their tom-toms, they answered with a rhythm in their blood: they were in direct touch with Nature in a way that urbanized man had lost the art of being. They were Natural Men where we were merely Civilized Men. This, Lawrence decided, was a truly excellent thing.

There is, however, one disconcerting fact about the North American Indian: as with all primitive peoples, his way of life may be ideal for him, but it is not necessarily the right way of life for visiting Englishmen. As Lawrence puts it: 'The Indian way of consciousness is different from and fatal to our way of consciousness. Our way of consciousness is different from and fatal to the Indian.'

Lawrence himself had a knack for instinctively 'understanding' the Indian way of consciousness—as he did that of the bat, the tortoise and Bibbles the little black bitch in *Birds, Beasts and Flowers*. He had a 'little ghost' inside him which enabled him to 'understand' very many ways of consciousness. But that did not mean to say that even he could *adopt* more than one way of consciousness at the same time. He could, if need be, forsake one way for another—as he was tempted to do in New Mexico. But as he freely admitted, a man 'cannot go both ways at once'. That, he asserted, simply 'can't be done'.

With all this, Lewis was in full agreement. But why, then, he wonders, does Lawrence insist so hard on trying to win us over to the Indian way? If he himself finds the Hopi way of consciousness fascinating, why not at least 'keep this as a private luxury', and not try to involve the rest of the world? As we might say today, why was Lawrence a pusher? The answer, quite obviously, was that Lawrence himself was hooked: he really did believe that the Indian way was somehow superior to his own. Not so Lewis, who found no great fascination in tom-toms, folk-song, ritual dancing or any other such forms of self-expression: 'If we followed Mr. Lawrence to the ultimate conclusion of his romantic teaching, we should allow our "consciousness" to be overpowered by the alien "consciousness" of the Indian. And we know what he thinks that would involve.'[8] On Lawrence's own admission, so far as the white way was concerned, it would be 'fatal'.

Lewis makes much good fun of Lawrence's grudging acknowledgment that among the fishermen of the Outer Hebrides he had found folk-singers whose singing style was a tentative approach to that of the Indian—but while they sang with 'vivid mindless eyes', they were still under the initial disadvantage of realizing that they were human, and so 'outside the great naturalistic influences'. Ah, says Lewis sadly, that is too bad! 'The poor White Hebridean still, alas, remains *human*, he is not totally *mindless*, though more nearly so than any other White Mr. Lawrence offhand can bring to mind.'[9] But perhaps the clinching argument in favour of Indian superiority, for Lawrence, is to be found in the way that when the Hopi gives himself up to song, 'face lifted and *sightless*, eyes half closed and *visionless*, mouth open and *speechless*, the *sounds* arise in his chest, from the *consciousness in the abdomen*.'[10] (Lewis's ironical italics.)

This is it, then: 'consciousness in the abdomen' or what Lewis prefers to call *visceral* consciousness, which 'takes the privilege of leadership away from the hated "mind" or "intellect", established up above in the head'.[11] We can now see clearly enough what Lewis is attacking in *Paleface*: it is the sentimental assumption that the primitive—in life and in art—is somehow superior to the sophisticated, that the primitive is 'romantic' and that the intellect is its natural bane.

It is significant that Lewis goes on to link Lawrence and his noble savagery with the pessimism of Spengler, whose *Der Untergang des Abendlandes* was in process of being translated when this section of *Paleface* first appeared in *The Enemy*. Spengler also had his weakness for mysterious overtones—words which were beyond mere definition, being 'symbols' rather than 'notions'—into whose warm euphoria of significance one was invited to sink as into a German feather-bed, the idea of Destiny demanding 'depth, not intellect'. Lewis likened Spengler to Lawrence in his Germanic conception of Woman as the

Great Mother, whom he equated with Destiny and Time. His 'musical' consciousness was even more suspiciously familiar; and indeed Spengler's whole philosophy had been swingeingly attacked in *Time and Western Man* as one more unfortunate example of the Bergsonian aftermath. 'Upon the *feminine* nature of "Time" or "Destiny",' says Lewis ominously, 'Spengler insists a great deal.'

From this point on, it is only a short step to accusing Lawrence also of 'a glorification of the Feminine principle' (which he would surely have admitted), and even charging him with being a 'natural communist' (which must have taken him by surprise). The Mexican Indian, as Lawrence understands him, is for Lewis, by virtue of the unreasoning nature of his responses 'the perfect Bolshevik'. He certainly is guilty of no individual, isolated experience of the sort which is 'such an offence to communism'. To adopt the Indian way of consciousness, to identify oneself with the whole, as the Indian does, is indeed, as Lawrence affirms, to feel 'the dark blood falling back from the mind, from sight and speech and knowing, back to the great central source where is rest and unspeakable renewal'. Or as Lewis sums the matter up: 'On the same principle as "Back to the Land", the cry of Mr. Lawrence (good little Freudian that he has always been) is "Back to the Womb". For although a natural communist and born feminist, it required the directive brain of Freud and others to reveal him to himself.'[12]

All this is good knockabout fun, but how is it anyway political? And *Paleface* becomes political only when it moves on to examining the reasons behind the fashionable acceptance of Lawrence's love for the primitive by an audience that could hardly have been expected to share his 'little ghost'. The fact is, says Lewis, that the popular acceptance of the 'superiority' of the coloured races by liberal intellectuals is based upon something far deeper than a romantic liking for the strange and the exotic. It is an outcome of the inferiority complex which the white race has been developing over the years, and which the writings of Sherwood Anderson, Lawrence, the *Green Mansions* of W. H. Hudson and other works were doing far too much to encourage.

In *Time and Western Man*, Lewis had pointed out that half the White Man's Burden in conquering, and then trying to govern, the coloured races consisted in the fact that his Bible was highly confusing to his sense of purpose. If he had been guided from the start solely by the Old Testament, his conduct 'could not have been less humane'. On the other hand, if he had been guided by the Gospels only, he would never have set out to enslave anyone in the first place. 'It was this unhappy blending of disparate things that was his curse.'

As it was, Lewis admitted, either end of his Bible notwithstanding, the White Man had certainly proved to be the curse of the coloured races. In Asia and in Central and South America, he had put down civilizations which were in many ways superior to his own. The fact that Lewis could not bring himself to say the same for the civilization of Africa was due, no doubt, to the fact that African art (apart from Benin bronzes, perhaps?) could not be defined as classical.... Neither could the art of the American Indian; though he was prepared to admit that totem-poles (like the canoes of the Solomon Islanders) were built up 'according to a rigid geometric plan', a characteristic which they shared in common with 'all the most splendid plastic and pictorial art....'

But one thing Lewis made no bones about at all: in his opinion, the art of the Far East represented the finest plastic and pictorial art that the world had seen. He was ready to assert that 'Europeans have never understood the fundamental problems of art in the way the Indian, Persian or Chinese have done'.[13] That being the case, he could hardly be accused of racial intolerance on his favourite stomping ground of aesthetics. Nor could he be accused of racial intolerance on any political grounds—or for that matter, on any grounds at all.

He was more than ready to admit that the white race had been guilty of militant imperialism and much injustice, that they had little to feel 'superior' about except the temporary technical advantages given them by science, and that these advantages were rapidly being overtaken by races which science had enabled us to enslave. 'Further, the charge has to be met of having imposed a rotten, materialist civilization upon all sorts of people with great cruelty often, of having wiped out races of very high quality, such as the Indians of North America, in the name of a God who was all compassion: so he (the Paleface) is convicted of hypocrisy of the ugliest, of the "civilized" kind, on top of everything else.'[14]

Such being his considered opinions, Lewis declares, he is hardly qualified for the role of White Deliverer or Champion, for which various critics were apparently trying to cast him— or with which, alternatively, various other critics were trying to saddle him. Indeed, he is rather surprised to find himself even considering pigmentation at all, having no racialist theories to peddle. It is merely what he calls 'the excesses of the anti-Whites' which have pushed him into appearing as a kind of Devil's Advocate in defence of white parity. (Most of the 'anti-Whites' he quotes, of course, are no less white than he is.) But as for the idea of preaching any sort of racial superiority—on either side of the colour line—that he is not prepared to do.

It is hard enough for anyone in the modern world to retain any sense of adequacy, Lewis points out. Particularly is this the case in Europe or America, where science has gone such a long way to drive us all down into 'our primitive private mental caves, of the unconscious and the primitive'.[15] For this we have to thank 'the successive waves of "Newtonian" innovation' which have driven us back upon our particular kind of 'sub-jectivity'. For where Lawrence and others would claim that cultures are at the mercy of alien races, Lewis would prefer to regard them as at the mercy of alien ideas. And for him, 'scientific' was coming to be a dirty and pejorative word. The scientific 'progress' which the modern world has been taught to accept automatically, he insists, has been anything but an un-mixed blessing. It has tended in itself to make us a kind of cave-man in the wilderness of unnecessary achievement. It is hardly a sufficient compensation for the lost values of self-sufficiency that 'a million sheep's-heads, in London, can sit and listen to the distant bellowing of Mussolini; or in situations so widely separ-ated as Wigan and Brighton, listen simultaneously to the bellowing of Dame Clara Butt'.[16] Nor, we are to imply, would it be very much better if they were listening to the gravelly voice of Satchmo himself: such pleasures are not an adequate substitute for 'the art of Sung or the philosophy of Greece'— (though science can hardly be blamed for their loss).

But it is the world which modern man has built for himself, with the aid of science, which is responsible in great part for the 'sense of inferiority' which he feels—leaving the question of

colour out of it altogether. He has become overawed by his own
achievements, and by his own equally monumental stupidity.
For most of all, perhaps, can his 'sense of inferiority' be regarded as an aftermath of the First World War, 'when all the
Whites, in one glorious *auto-da-fé*, for four years did their
best to kill and ruin each other'.[17]

In America particularly, white civilization had built itself up
into 'a towering babylonian monument to Science', and it was
there most noticeably of all that the old sense of power enjoyed
by the White Man during the years of conquest and settlement
had become crushed by 'the great technical achievements of
the same instruments that had secured him his new empire'.[18]
When that had been added to his growing sense of guilt in the
way that massacre and slavery had gone to the process of conquest and settlement—and the fact that racial injustice was still
a condition of social life—it was hardly surprising that the
White Man in America was beginning to feel unsure of himself in every way. It was in America, therefore, that Lewis had
looked most carefully for symptoms of the complex which he
was trying to diagnose. More to the point, it was there that he
looked for contributory causes of the complex in the literature
fashionable at the time.

Those who know America today will probably agree that such
a sense of guilt and inadequacy is to be found there on almost
a national scale. The breakdown of much social order, the
revolt of the students, the spread of drug addiction and mental
illness, the rioting and the violence—these are hardly the
symptoms of a society that has any great faith in itself. Nor
can the blame be laid upon America's long involvement in
Vietnam *entirely*: it goes a great deal further back than that.
One thing is clear enough: Lewis would have found much
more to adduce in support of his case today than the quotes
from Mencken's *Americana* and the rest which went to the
making of *Paleface*.

If one accepts Lewis's belief in the White Man's increasing
'sense of inferiority', of course, his reasons for indicting Lawrence, Sherwood Anderson and the rest of the visceral school
become quite clear. So far as he was concerned, their books
were merely calculated to exacerbate a condition which already
he found critical enough. While he would lay the original blame

for that condition upon an unquestioning acceptance of scientific 'progress'; while this had itself given rise to the modern demand for novelty at all costs; and while by reason of that demand Bergson's philosophy of impermanence had gained such a dangerous ascendency—nostalgic yearning for a neo-primitivism, either in art or in life, was hardly likely to bring about anything better than increased confusion. To close one's mind and wrap oneself in instinct would not be to find the lost answers for which Lawrence had been searching; it would be merely burying one's head in the sand. It would be leaving the way clear for still more irresponsible ventures by utterly un-primitive science. And from that one could expect nothing better than a rapid acceleration towards a scientific holocaust in which civilization and *all* values might well be lost forever.

On that particular tack, Lewis even went so far as to suggest that by letting ourselves accept the Noble Savage as a blood-brother, we were being subtly persuaded to accept savagery as an end in itself. If that was the case, then the visceral school were certainly playing into the hands of those who were *planning* the scientific holocaust, for 'all those forms of organized violence must be gone into absolutely against human reason; they are henceforth motiveless, and hence mad'.[19] This idea he promptly develops into the doctrine of 'political primitivism' and goes on to draw the sinister conclusion : 'It is not difficult to see how beautifully it agrees with the artistic primitivism of Mr. D. H. Lawrence—with Aztec blood-sacrifices, mystical and savage abandonments of the self, abstract sex-rage, etc., or Mr. Sherwood Anderson's more muddled and less up-to-date primitivist bag of tricks.'[20] In terms of political primitivism, after all, the Borneo head-hunter would represent a model recruit; and he could surely be relied upon to make sounds in his chest as he added each further trophy to the tribal collection.

Lawrence and Anderson may well have been startled to find themselves in such an unholy alliance with the armament manufacturers and their 'superior will'. But as Lewis cheerfully admits, many a good book may be 'saturated with some political philosophy or other—even unknown to its author'.[21] As he also admits that there may be 'some exaggeration' in his analysis, however, one can only suppose that he is having a little quiet fun on the side; and we should be well advised not to take him always too seriously. He probably never made that mistake himself—as witness the jolly high jinks of *One-Way Song*. In *Paleface* he acknowledges that he is writing as 'a sort of extremist', but suggests in another context that 'it is always from exaggeration, however, on one side or the other, that the actual comes into existence'. Fortunately for us, 'political primitivism' does not seem to have taken any firm root in Britain; but we have seen many sickening examples of it elsewhere....

Paleface is not so much concerned with Lawrence's Poor Indian, however, as with the Blacks whose laughter had inspired Sherwood Anderson. In every way, this is unfortunate, though the fault derives from Anderson far more than it does from Lewis. It is Anderson's sentimental ideas about the Black, indeed, which brought him into *Paleface* in the first place. Until he has become de-tribalized, the American Indian can fairly be regarded as a primitive, without using the word in any derogatory sense. But the case of the Black American is completely different—as different, indeed, as that of the Hindu or the Chinese, whom Lewis is always careful to differentiate from either. The Black American is as much a part of modern America as the White American, and that not merely in language but in every other way. It was this obvious fact, of course, which was rankling at the back of most of the adverse criticism to which *Paleface* gave rise at the time, misguided though most of it was. The fact that the Black American has retained much of his race-consciousness as a displaced African, and the fact that this is clearly reflected in his music, is quite beside the point. There is infinitely more in his culture, by now, that is wholly western—as witness the fine achievement of his creative writing. To equate the Red with the Black, therefore, would be no more sensible than to equate the Japanese with the Ainu or the Maori with the Australian Bushman. To be fair, Lewis never tries to do so; but the fact remains that some of his thinking about the one spills over into his writing about the other.

In the America of the twenties (to say nothing about the America of the seventies) discrimination against the Black was all that Lewis called it—'a monstrous social injustice'. But since he was not writing a book about racial politics, he took little notice of the fact in *Paleface*. He was simply concerned with the way that liberal white writers were persuading the White American to think of himself in relation to the Coloured (Black and Red) and how he was being written about, at the same time, by the Black American. (Since the Red Man expressed himself mainly in grunts, the Black was the only articulate Coloured American in the field.)

Lewis's analysis of *Mornings in Mexico* had gone half way to dispose of the first question. Contributory evidence in general terms was gathered from H. L. Mencken's *Americana*, Aldous Huxley's *Jesting Pilate* and elsewhere. But it was mainly from Anderson's *Dark Laughter, Poor White* and *The Triumph of the Egg* that Lewis gathered the quotations to show how the Black American was being romanticized—or to use his own term, sentimentalized. His analysis of all these works is admirably astringent—so much so, in fact, that he tends to destroy his own case. For a truly depressing array of obsequious peons Anderson makes of his favourite race! Indeed, the Black American as we meet him in such characters as Bildad ('the kind Dusky Uncle Tom with the Dickens tear in the corner of his pathetic rolling benevolent black eye') is *precisely* that—the archetypal Uncle Tom. And Lewis is to be credited with recognizing Uncle Tommery long before it was officially denounced by the Black militants. Anderson's Blacks are 'superior' in nothing but Christian resignation and their willingness to accept their shoddy lot; and they are calculated to make the modern advocate of Black Power turn pale with righteous indignation. They are full of laughter and loyalty, kindness to children and dumb animals, much given to bandying about (and accepting) the sobriquet of 'nigger' (in the way that some of them still bandy the disgusting word among themselves)—but they are otherwise as unlike the Black American of today as Uncle Tom himself was unlike Malcolm X. Anderson's Blacks, in short, belong to a way of life that had ended even in Lewis's time, as he was the first to suggest: 'What blissful ignorance of really *dark* realities is displayed by these old-fashioned habits (of theirs)—old-fashioned because they came into existence amongst and were proper to conditions that have passed! There are many duskier things than the big black honest open face of the poor Negro.'[22] This being the case, the fact that they are 'made to take the White down a peg or two' every so often is hardly evidence of

Anderson's complicity in a plot to undermine white civilization.

Nor was the preaching of 'black superiority' much better served by some of the black novelists of the time—at least, not by those that Lewis quotes in defence of his own argument. It will be realized, of course, that back in the twenties the new school of Black American poets, dramatists and novelists was still only just emerging. And it is a pity that there was no James Baldwin or LeRoi Jones or Eldridge Cleaver or George Jackson around at the time to have helped Lewis's case along! Even so, there were many fine writers in the field, most of whom had been published by Alfred Knopf, whose New York imprint was known to Lewis (by reason of the house emblem) as that of the Borzoi Books. Knopf is credited with 'a compassionate sense of the Negro's sufferings, coupled with an intelligent dislike of that certain shallow cocksureness shown by many Palefaces, both of which feelings,' Lewis remarks, 'if they are his, I share with him.'[23] But while he quotes aptly from Nella Larson's novel *Quicksand* (Knopf, 1928), it is from W. E. B. DuBois's *Dark Princess*, a rather embarrassingly naïve novel published elsewhere, that Lewis quotes most fully —that being, he says, a story that 'combines the characteristics of one of the cheaper films with a violent political tract'.[24] In modern terms, the tract appears remarkably *un*violent, and it is certainly not at all well written. But it is not as literature that Lewis considers it; and at least he does it the justice to believe that as a tract it is quite sincere.

Yet there is little enough in *Dark Princess* to convince the modern reader that it was particularly tendentious. Its hero, Matthew Towns, is a Black American medical student who revolts against discrimination, and like many another Black since, takes himself off to Europe. There he falls in with a set of coloured intellectuals, whose leader is an Indian princess. They are in process of planning a world-wide rising against the dominance of the white race. At first, Towns is rather abashed to find that the Black American and the Black African are both dismissed airily as 'the lower classes', and lumped in with the proletariat generally. But at least he finds it amusing to hear the white proletariat described as 'rabble' and the white rulers written off as members of 'an inferior race'.

It is some time, in fact, before he can get his people accepted by the club as full members, and so as legitimate allies in the Great Plan of casting off white domination throughout the world—a plan in which the Chinese and the Japanese were apparently happy to contemplate joining forces. But by the time the book ends, and Towns has married his princess, he is hailed as 'the Messenger and Messiah of all the Darker Worlds', and Black America has been given its part to play in the coming struggle.

The idea that the Indians, the Africans, the Arabs and the rest—even back in the twenties—were beginning to organize resistance to imperialism can hardly surprise us in this day and age. (Nor did it disturb Lewis at the time: he had already hailed Gandhi as 'one of the only saintly figures in the world'.[25]) We cannot be unduly alarmed to find DuBois suggesting that Black Americans had a part to play in the overall strategy, or startled by his wistful hope that they would be accepted as co-combatants by the other coloured races. One is reassured, rather, to be told that Indian princesses are apparently so un-race-conscious....

All in all, *Dark Princess* would be far more likely to raise a giggle than one white eyebrow if it were read today. As we have said—and as Lewis said more ironically, though not at all unkindly—it is all very Phillips Oppenheim and all rather sadly ingenuous. It romanticizes in the way that all works written from a sense of social injustice are apt to romanticize: wishful thinking is not peculiar to the black or any other race. It presumes that racial conflict is coming, because it cannot quite believe that the White Man will ever give up an ascendency until it has been wrested from him. It suggests that 'five years of intensive struggle' will probably be necessary before that ascendency can be overthrown; and it sets the date for what it calls the liberation of 'the Dark World' as 1952. In that it was a little over-hopeful; but at least by 1972 most of the Dark World has its own seats in the General Assembly of the United Nations. Matthew Towns might well have been depressed to find that Black America has no independent seat of its own among them, but after all, President Lincoln himself had put paid to all such separatist aspirations!

It is worth stressing, of course, that in picking his way

through the fantasy-building of *Dark Princess*, Lewis takes no exception to its voicing of a legitimate will to *emancipation* on the part of the coloured races. As to that, he makes no comment at all. He merely regrets that the book appears to be advocating the replacement of one ascendency by another: 'the Coloured Peoples are urged to develop a consciousness of *superiority*, and the same book seeks to force upon the Paleface a corresponding sense of *inferiority*. It is this that is unfortunate: the mere reversal of a superiority—a change in its *colour*, nothing more—rather than its total abolition.'[26]

This being his only real objection to the book, it must be admitted that Lewis's choice of excerpts does not really prove his case. The only quotation where white 'inferiority' is mentioned attributes the charge to the Indian, Egyptian and Japanese conspirators—who happily lump the Blacks and Whites together as both being sub-yellow and sub-brown. Even Towns himself can find this no more than wryly 'amusing'. Either way, however, as the book was obviously written in reaction against 'a monstrous social injustice', one should not have been surprised if now and again it was guilty of over-compensation. Nor should Lewis, of all people, have blamed a fellow tract-writer for overstating his case....

Even so, his criticism of *Dark Princess* is perfectly fair and reasonable in tone. As a novelist, DuBois was certainly no worse than Harriet Beecher Stowe. It was simply the cumulative effect of the sudden plethora of pro-Black, anti-White books and plays and films that Lewis was dubious about. From where we are sitting now, many of us can only feel relieved that the cumulative effect of liberal writing—black and white —has, over the years, brought the evils of racial intolerance and the facts of Black victimization out into the open, and gone some way to redress them. Nor is there anything in *Paleface* to suggest that Lewis himself would have been in any way unhappy at such an outcome, provided that it did not lead on inexorably to racial strife. But as he saw it, the Paleface himself had plenty of injustice and poverty and suffering to complain about on his own account. The vast majority of both black and white races were virtually in the same boat: they were both on the receiving end of social exploitation. Therefore the Black should not be encouraged to believe that he had any sort of monopoly in suffered injustice—or in revolutionary fervour.

But so far as the fervour went, Lewis could find small evidence of it among most of the Black Americans of his time. They were much too happy-go-lucky and easy-going to make good revolutionary material for the propagandist to work upon. Like his white brother, Lewis feels, the average Black American 'wants to be left alone: above all, he wishes to identify himself with his Paleface neighbour as far as possible, not to be put in opposition, and so in *contrast*. He has more in common with Babbitt than with the Coloured Intellectual.'[27]

Despite the embittered advocacy of Black Power, this is still probably true of the majority of Black Americans outside intellectual circles: it was certainly true at the time when Lewis was writing. That being so, like the black intellectual himself, Lewis could only feel rather depressed by the prospect for the future, 'for the middleclass ideal of the Paleface is not a very high one in the first instance'. Even so, it is rather more comfortable to be a Black Babbitt than to be a Bigger Thomas —as many a native son must have realized before now....

But it is not with the would-be Black Babbitts that Lewis is concerned so much as with claims by the black intellectuals as to the contribution which had been made by their culture to the intellectual heritage of the West. So far as he was concerned, that cultural contribution could be summed up in a single word. And whatever Shylock may have felt personally about bagpipe music, there can be no doubt at all what Lewis felt about jazz —or what he thought of as jazz.

Perhaps his aversion would not have been so comical if he had been an enthusiast for music of another kind. He could oblige with a spirited rendition of *Pretty Little Polly Perkins* to amuse his friends on occasion, but that was merely by way of clowning. The fact was that music was an art about which he found it hard to wax enthusiastic. He could enjoy the classical formality of Bach as a kind of aural geometry, but the unbridled extravagances of Beethoven were obviously so much more 'romanticism'. As for Brahms and Wagner—definitely, the less said the better! So far as Lewis was concerned, in fact, music was what the German imagination had brought in along with Faustian Man: it had probably been thought up simply to pave the way for Bergson, Einstein and Spengler. Insofar as it was dependent upon 'time' for its very existence, music represented a dangerous drug which could wean the judgment away from a true appreciation of the plastic. But at least classical music (if one could pardon the contradiction in terms) was architectonic after a fashion: it had a formal structure and a logical progression of its own limited sort. But what on earth was one to think about music which was essentially *improvised*, which was intuitive and instinctive? More particularly, what was one to think about music which was so emotional in its appeal, and which aroused such an intolerable itch for capering, finger-snapping and general excitation in the listener? Jazz, Lewis decided, was a Very Bad Thing Indeed!

Why then was jazz being universally accepted by the western world as a cultural activity? Why was it not decried on all sides as a raucous, frenetic reversion to the jungle-rhythms which had pounded their way across from the upper reaches of the Congo? How could anyone with any cultural pretensions at all be led to accept the cacophonies of Louis Armstrong or the ecstatic blatherings of Cab Calloway as anything but the stridulation of the savage? That they should appeal to the Rousseauist —such as D. H. Lawrence, if he happened to like them—was understandable. After all, the singing and drumming and dancing of the Hopi was only one remove away from them. But so far as Lewis was concerned, any suggestion that jazz represented culture of any kind at all was ridiculous, if not downright provocative!

The fact that even a black intellectual such as Alain Locke— for whom he expressed a certain respect—could refer to jazz as one of 'the Negro's cultural gifts' to White America which had not received 'the reward that all genius merits and even requires' was enough to rouse Lewis to unusual vehemence. The singing of Roland Hayes and the acting of Paul Robeson—yes! *They* are 'handsome presents to our civilization'. But jazz—or the dance music which Lewis confuses with jazz—that was a different matter entirely:

> What Mr. Locke might say with great reason is somewhat as follows: 'Although the Blacks have produced nothing but a barbarous, melancholy, epileptic folk-music, worthy only of a patagonian cannibal; and although this sort of art has been fast-

ened upon the White World, as a result of a given set of circumstances, that is no reason why the White Man should look down
upon *all* Negroes, or should too lightly assume that, given equal
opportunities, the Negro would not produce something that
would put the foolish jazzing White in the shade.' That would
be unanswerable, I think.[28]

There is more in the same vein in *Paleface*, not invariably
expressed in quite such courteous terms. The 'cultural gift' of
Black America, as Lewis understands it, is closely akin to the
black art of Faust and Bergson—something which he would
rather be without. And it is quite in line with his private opinion
of the admass Paleface that 'jazz' should have been taken to
the western heart in the way that it had. As he points out, the
Chinese and the Hindu 'would never have been captivated' by
it at all! And he can even look forward, ironically, to the days
of full emancipation when the Black will be dancing waltzes
and minuets, while his dimmer-witted white brothers are dancing the Black Bottom round the corner. It seems unlikely, however, that Lewis would have been dancing with any of them:
he might well have preferred to spend the evening with his
favourite Polly Perkins....

So what is the overall message of *Paleface*? Put at its simplest,
it is Lewis's reply to those who would suggest that Western
Man is entering upon his decline, for which he refuses to accept
Spengler's assurance. It expresses his belief that too much is
being done to *persuade* the West to enter upon a decline. This,
he feels, can hardly be accidental, for the campaign 'has all the
appearance of attacks upon a disintegrating organism, by some
other intact and triumphant organism: it has very much too
human and personal a flavour.'[29] The true nature of that
'triumphant organism' is never identified explicitly, though
one presumes that it is probably Communism. Other contribu-
tary factors would seem to be Big Business (still in search of
cheaper labour), Coloured Imperialism (*à la* DuBois), Rousseauism (*à la* D. H. Lawrence), Borzoi Books (*à la* Knopf), and
'jazz' (*à la* Tin Pan Alley—which had commercialized but
hardly improved it).

Lewis is concerned, first of all, for the future of western
culture; he is also indignant that *all* Palefaces should be mis-

represented as arrogant 'overlords', whereas most of them are just as put upon and exploited as anyone else. When it comes to the final push, he admits that he finds 'the average White European (such as Chekov depicted) [!!] often exceedingly ridiculous, no doubt, but much more interesting than the average Hopi, or the average Negro.'[30] (He does not give us his opinion of the average Southern American demagogue or the average Alabama Klansman.)

He is, however, firmly opposed to the putting down of any race by another, and freely admits that the White Man's treatment of the coloured races in the past had been barbarous and deplorable. But that does not mean that he will accept a different racial ascendency as any way preferable. He sees no merit in the Black aping the White: he sees even less in the White aping the Black—in view of his longer and more remarkable cultural tradition. He is prepared to believe—with Lawrence—that the culture and ideas of one race can indeed be fatal to another if politically imposed upon it; and while he can see no such danger for the West as yet, he has no desire to see western culture eroded meanwhile by an insistence upon some alien 'superiority'. The fact that he denies 'superiority' to some of the coloured races, however, does not imply that he is assuming it on behalf of the Paleface. It implies no more than a refusal to sell the Paleface short: so far as he is concerned, there will be no Blues for Mr Charlie. Still less will there be a wake.

Lest there should be any suggestion that he is again advocating some sort of cultural purism or exclusiveness, however, he goes on to make it clear that no such thought is in his mind. Races should *not* be manoeuvred into mutual opposition. There should not be *two* Americas: there can and should be only the one. Cultures, like races, can mingle to advantage; and as an example of the racial melting-pot, he regards America as an excellent prototype for the World State of the future. Indeed, he underlines the fact that 'it is not the Melting-pot I object to, but the depreciation and damage done to one of the ingredients'.[31]

America, in fact, provides an example which he feels that Europe would do well to study. Europe also should be breaking down her barriers, and strengthening her local cultures by intermingling them. Like Goethe, he would even prefer to write in Volapuk—a world-speech of the Esperanto order—rather than in a purely national language. But even Volapuk should be careful to preserve its individual accents and idioms. He is in favour of an internationalism with local differences, rather than a series of nationalistic enclaves, each of which promptly becomes as like the others as possible. The object of *Paleface* 'is much more to propose that we set up a Melting-pot in Europe—which would be as it were a Model Melting-pot, not at the boiling-point but cooking at a steady rate day in day out —than to venture any criticism of the principle underlying the american or african Melting-pot or, alternatively, Colour Line. Indeed a quite irrational attitude is often adopted by the American to miscegenation....'[32]

Just how far Lewis would have been prepared to follow up this last argument in general terms—as opposed to individual instances—it is interesting to speculate. Not very far, one rather supposes. But it is not the current tendency of Black militancy to pursue it very far either. Miscegenation is not a live issue—or at least, not until emancipation and integration have been fully achieved. Meanwhile, to the advocate of Black Power—Black is Beautiful. To Lewis, White was Beautiful—but he could see no earthly reason why White or Black should be mutually exclusive or mutually destructive. Black Militancy or backlash were equally distasteful to him, and he could only hope that his point of view might 'offer some resistance to the colour-blind fanatic who can see only one colour at a time'.[33]

In Lewis's view, Lawrence and his disciples were the ones at fault in their insistence upon the 'unassimilable seed in the matrix' of race, which would leave East exclusively East and West inviolably West. He himself would prefer something far more universal, even though he may privately hope that in the final amalgam, the culture of the Paleface 'may blanch or bleach the entire Melting-pot'. But whatever the end-product, by all means let East and West meet meanwhile no less than Black and White, so long as we can be sure that they are all meeting on free and equal terms. In that at least, most Black Americans, Africans and West Indians might well agree with him.

As for the dwindling Hopi—he, of course, might still prefer

to keep his private sounds locked up in his chest.... And has anyone the right to blame him?

NOTES

1. *The Revolutionary Simpleton* (subsequently Part I of *Time and Western Man*); *Paleface* (subsequently Part II of that work); and *The Diabolical Principle* (subsequently published along with *The Dithyrambic Spectator*, an essay first published in *The Calendar of Modern Letters* for 1925).
2. Op. cit., p.466.
3. Ibid.
4. *A of BR*, p.387.
5. *Time and Tide*, 24.5.29.
6. *R A*, p.203.
7. Ibid.
8. *Paleface*, p.175.
9. Ibid., p.176.
10. Ibid., p.177.
11. Ibid.
12. Ibid., pp.183-4.
13. *Paleface*, p.69.
14. Ibid.
15. Ibid., p.103.
16. Ibid., p.106.
17. Ibid., p.126.
18. Ibid.
19. Ibid., p.246: (earlier draft, *The Enemy* No. 2, p.93).
20. Ibid., p.247.
21. Ibid., p.229.
22. Ibid., p.223.
23. Ibid., p.29.
24. Ibid., p.30.
25. Ibid., p.296.
26. Ibid., p.41.
27. Ibid., p.42.
28. Ibid., p.66.
29. Ibid., p.84.
30. Ibid., p.196.
31. Ibid., p.257.
32. Ibid., p.278.
33. Ibid., p.21.

CHAPTER 5

Hitler or The Art of Being Fooled

The year 1930 was to be a highly important one in Lewis's life as a writer. In its ultimate effects, it was also to prove unfortunate. It was in June 1930 that he published *The Apes of God*, which ranks not only as his finest and most trenchant satire, but also as one of the comic prose masterpieces of the century. A re-written collection of his early stories, *The Wild Body*, had appeared in 1927, along with *The Lion and the Fox* and *Time and Western Man*. A heavily revised version of *Tarr*, and *The Childermass* (advertised as the first section of a trilogy) had followed in 1928. *The Art of Being Ruled* and *Paleface* were still fresh in the reading public's mind. Along with three issues of *The Enemy*, sundry articles and Lewis's many paintings and drawings, the whole muster constituted an almost incredible achievement for some four years of one man's creative and critical output.

The fact that he was now being assailed on many sides for his political ideas (to say nothing of his withering satire) was meat and drink to The Enemy: he asked for nothing better of his outraged contemporaries. He hastened to the defence of *The Apes of God* with another polemical pamphlet, *Satire and Fiction*, in which he quoted some of the highly appreciative notices which the work had elicited from those not included in its gallery of charlatans. He promised completion of *The Childermass*, which had been equally praised in friendly quarters, and prepared for further battle with *transition* and various other hostile groups. Meanwhile, he found that history appeared to be catching up with certain of his political predictions.

The Wall Street Crash of October 1929 had only confirmed him in his distrust of a world made over to the financiers, in which none could hope to survive for long except the most ruthless of financial interests, and in which 20,000 American local banks could add to the confusion by closing their doors on a disaster they had done more than somewhat to promote. As yet, the economic blizzard had not begun to blow full force in Britain; but it had already wrought havoc in Germany, where American loans were being withdrawn and where the political situation was rapidly getting out of hand.

As we have seen, Lewis's momentary appreciation of Italian Fascism had begun to wane. While it had not gone completely into reverse, as had his early respect for Soviet Communism, it had nonetheless become rather more sardonic than enthusiastic. He was already referring to Mussolini as 'a noisy ice-cream agitator', and his whole claptrappery of black shirts and a blue chin had begun to seem slightly ridiculous. In *The Apes of God*, one of the characters, Starr-Smith, himself appears in a black shirt; and while Lewis uses him as a critical stick to belabour the apes, and while he is identified as a true disciple of the mysterious Pierpoint (who speaks for Lewis himself), like his co-disciple Zagreus he is turned into yet another comical butt before the book is through. The fact that he emerges as a sort of latter-day Fluellen, and is reduced to punching an ape in the eye, does not suggest that he was a disciple of the kind that Lewis valued:

> 'I will show you what *violence* is, that I will quickly show you too—you will tell me when you know—I wonder! Take that for your *violent* now—take that too look you—when next—and that now! Ah!'[1]

And Julius Ratner is knocked off stage into the pit....

Indeed, there is something almost symbolic about Blackshirt's last appearance in the book: he is made to leap from the stage himself to avoid being bowled over by the descending curtain! And it might well be supposed that the explanation he offers for attending Lord Osmund's Lenten Party in the costume he does is somehow applicable to Lewis himself:

> 'Why do you suppose I am here with two more, who are volunteers, as 'fascists' of all things, tonight? Nothing to do with *Fascismo*—the last thing—can you guess? It's because I picked

up three khaki shirts for a few pence and dyed them black—the whole outfit for the three of us did not cost fifteen bob! That is the reason.'[2]

Lewis also, perhaps, might feel that his temporary appearance in the black shirt disguise required some sort of explanation. For he was hardly the man to allow himself to be seen in any uniform for long—black or otherwise.

He had recently defined his political views in *The Enemy, No. 3*, as 'partly communist and partly fascist, with a distinct streak of monarchism in my marxism, but at bottom anarchist with a healthy passion for order'. And provided he was not immediately required to join the Anarchist Party, no doubt it amused him to pass as some such deviant. So far as he was concerned, it provided a handy cloak for his independence.

Even so, his initial endorsement of Italian Fascism lingered on in many memories; and insofar as this aroused an automatic antagonism in all critics of the Left, Lewis was still prepared to play devil's advocate for Fascism whenever he felt the urge. Events in Germany during 1930 were to provide him with an unluckily convenient opportunity.

On 14 September 1930 a General Election in Germany had brought a new figure into world prominence: an Austrian ex-corporal by the name of Adolf Hitler had led his so-called National Socialist or Nazi Party to a remarkable success at the polls. Not very many people outside Germany had previously heard of him—unless as a rabble-rousing demagogue who in 1923 had failed miserably in an attempt to lead a March on Berlin from Munich, after the pattern of Mussolini's earlier March on Rome. For that abortive *Putsch* he had been imprisoned, and on his release in December 1924, had appeared to be something of a forgotten man. By skilfully reorganizing his party, he had slowly fought his way back to prominence by rather more orthodox means. And after three years of violent haranguing, street-fighting and Jew-baiting, the Nazis had emerged at the elections of May 1928 with 12 seats in the Reichstag out of a total of 491.

Unemployment in Germany at that time, thanks to large American loans and a consequent trade revival, had been reduced to some 650,000, a vast improvement on the black days of the fall of the mark in 1922. But the Wall Street Crash, the withdrawal of American credit and the world trade recession which followed had put an end to Germany's economic recovery; and by the time of the 1930 elections, unemployment had again risen to something over three million. The German electorate had been plunged into a mood of reminiscent anxiety from which only revolutionary policies could be expected to arouse them. Such were on offer by both the German Communist Party and the Nazis—but only the Nazis had made their appeal to the dispossessed bourgeoisie no less than to the workers. And their noisy, violent campaigning was to pay off only too well; for the September 1930 elections brought about a truly remarkable change in their political standing. Their 1928 total of 810,000 votes rocketed overnight to close on six and a half million, which gave them 107 seats in the Reichstag in place of their previous 12. From being a minority party —placed ninth in the final count—they had suddenly emerged as the second largest political party in Germany. And it was clear to everyone that the days of Brüning's moderate government were numbered.

What was equally clear was the fact that *democratic* government in Germany appeared to be in danger of coming to an end. Though the Nazis had risen to prominence by democratic methods (more or less), and though they had been loud in their assurances that only by democratic methods would they come to power, the fact remained that they were in no sense a democratic party. Once power had been won, they openly boasted that they would use it dictatorially—and would never relinquish it. 'Democracy,' Hitler had announced before the elections, 'must be defeated with its own weapons.' And he left nobody in any doubt that once he was in full control, democratic government would be abolished. It was to be superseded by something of a very different order—the government of the Third Reich.

It would be fair to say that the German election results of 1930 had caused alarm throughout Europe. Headlines from *Pravda* to *Le Figaro* reflected the general uneasiness, and there were persistent rumours of a coming Nazi *coup d'état*. Though these were loudly denied by Hitler himself, anxiety continued. There was a panic rush to withdraw gold from Berlin and the

Paris Bourse slumped heavily. The Nazis proclaimed their intention to repudiate all war reparations and indemnities once they were in power, and were obviously bent upon a threateningly militaristic programme if they could attain to it. Under the terms of the Young Plan, endorsed the previous year, First World War reparations had been agreed at a reduced rate, and the occupation forces of Britain and France had been withdrawn from the Rhineland five years ahead of time. It now seemed possible that the French would repeat their action of 1923 and re-occupy the Ruhr in defence of their treaty rights. The threat of another conflict in Europe was suddenly being discussed again only two years after the signing of the Kellogg Pact, which had seen the nations of the world united in agreement to outlaw war forever as an instrument of national policy.

Though it shared the apprehensions of the French, the Czech and the other continental papers, the British press preferred to wait upon events before resigning themselves to the worst. 'It would be a mistake to put too sinister an interpretation,' said *The Times*, 'upon what after all may only prove to be a very transitory phase of German politics.'[3] The *Manchester Guardian* followed much the same line in its leader, and thought that 'fortunately there are few things less likely' than Hitler moving on to enjoy sole power. But the *Daily Express* was not quite so sanguine: 'The evidence is there for everyone to see that at present Germany is politically out of hand, and that she must go through yet another shattering experience before unclouded counsel directs her troubled destiny once more.'[4]

The *Daily Mail*, in which Lord Rothermere was carrying on a flirtation with the Duce, viewed the sudden eruption of the Nazis with such disfavour that they feared it might give Fascism a bad name: 'The German National Socialists ... have been freely called Fascists. They are nothing of the kind. Italian Fascismo is a constructive creed; where it destroyed it lopped off dead wood and remedied deep-seated abuses. The German National Socialist programme is purely subversive.'[5] And two days later their Berlin Correspondent reported that: 'The German people are beginning to understand that the folly of the electors in packing the Reichstag with revolutionaries has placed Germany in a perilous position.'[6]

But this misreading of history was suddenly corrected by Lord Rothermere himself. In a dispatch from Munich, which appeared in the *Daily Mail* on 24 September, he set the record straight for all his readers: 'The sweeping success of the German National Socialist Party—in other words the Fascist Party —at the general election of September 14 will it is my strong conviction, prove to be an enduring landmark of this time.' And he went on to declare (in heavy type) that the success of the Nazis represented 'the re-birth of Germany as a nation'. The Nazis had been returned to the Reichstag, he explained, by the votes of those 'between the ages of twenty and the early thirties' —a fact which he found peculiarly significant. 'They have discovered,' he said, 'as, I am glad to know, the young men and women of England are discovering, that it is no good trusting to the old politicians.' (All which, as Lewis would have been quick to point out, was typical campaigning in the age-war.) As Lord Rothermere saw it, in fact, it would be 'of the best possible augury' that the Nazis should come to power in Germany, as they were 'inspired with the same sound principles' as those with which Mussolini had ruled Italy for the last eight years. So far as he was concerned, the rise of National Socialism 'sets up an additional rampart against Bolshevism,' and so would eliminate 'the Soviet campaign against civilization'. Indeed, this blow struck by Germany against the corruption of Communism reminded him that it was 'with some such purpose' that he himself had founded the United Empire Party in England, since 'no strong Anti-Socialist policy can be expected from a Conservative Party whose leaders are themselves tainted with semi-Socialist doctrines.' And despite the 'Socialism' of their own title, nobody could accuse the Nazi Party of any such taint as that. As the *Mail* had explained the week before, Nazi 'Socialism' was 'only the lime to catch the bird'.

Lord Rothermere's warm support for Hitler was unique in the British newspaper coverage of the time: it was certainly not shared by his quondam ally Lord Beaverbrook. Indeed, the *Daily Express* viewed the emergence of the Nazis with obvious distaste, and proceeded to stress the anti-Semitic aims of the party as particularly odious. 'When a nation starts persecuting Jews as a whole,' a leader declared two days after the election results were announced, 'it is a confession of decadence and defeat.'⁷ And Germany was accused of following Russia's lead by turning anti-Semitism into a national policy.

It so happened that in November 1930, two months after the German elections, private business took Lewis over to Berlin. He had no intention of writing anything on the political scene in Germany when he set out, but found himself 'at first casually, and then more carefully' observing the political in-fighting and general unrest when he got there. Chance had taken him in a similar way to Italy on the eve of the March on Rome (the only time he was there); and it had even caught him up in an unsuccessful military rising against the dictatorship of Primo de Rivera in Spain. But he had never before been tempted to write about the political situation anywhere as a journalist: his books had confined themselves to political theorizing rather than political reporting.

On his return to London, however, he offered a series of five articles on the German scene to *Time and Tide*, which was then under the editorship of Lady Rhondda. These were accepted, and appeared weekly in the issues of 17 January to 14 February 1931, under the general heading *Hitlerism—Man and Doctrine*. They comprised an introductory study of *The Weimar Republic and the Dritte Reich*, a colour piece on *Berlin im Licht*, an affirmation of *The Oneness of 'Hitlerism' and of Hitler*, some thoughts on *The Doctrine of Blutsgefühl*, and a final satirical flourish which Lewis called *Creditcrankery Rampant*. These articles were to be subsequently expanded and provided the groundwork for his book *Hitler* which was published in April.

The articles were not intended as an apology for Hitlerism so much as a plausible explanation for its sudden emergence. Lewis explained at the outset that he was writing 'as an exponent—not as critic nor yet as advocate—of German Nationalsocialism'. And insofar as no British reporter (apart from Lord Rothermere) had so far looked at the subject with anything less than mistrust or hostility, this declared intent was clearly all to the good. After all, there must have been *some* explanation for Hitler's meteoric rise: six and a half million votes could hardly have been indicative of nothing at all. What, then, was the secret of Hitler's appeal to the German people?

Leaving politics out of the matter altogether, of course, a great deal of his appeal could be simply the result of German nationalism itself. Not even the Jews could ever have longed more ardently for the coming of a militant Messiah than nineteenth and twentieth century Germany had longed for its militant Führer. This was due in large part to the nationalistic cast of German academic thought: Herder, Fichte, Hegel, von Haller and the rest had been preaching the supremacy of the State, power-politics and pan-Germanism for over a century. There was also the Prussian militaristic tradition.

This, no doubt, was something which Lewis remembered from his student days in Munich. But what he was most concerned about in his articles was the putative Messiah himself. What *did* Hitler mean to the German people? What was he promising to achieve for Germany, as distinct from what he was trying to secure for himself? Had the anomalies of the Treaty of Versailles given him a case to argue? Was he potentially dangerous to the peace of Europe, as was generally supposed? Or did he represent an insurance policy for Europe against the spread of Bolshevism, as Lord Rothermere had suggested and the French reporter Frédéric Hirth had hopefully echoed?[8] Finally, what could be said in clarification of his doctrines, if not necessarily in favour of them?

Lewis's declared object in writing the articles on *Hitlerism* had been to answer these questions as impartially as he could. And so, for the most part and on balance, he can be said to have done. Unfortunately, he did not let it rest at that. He had admitted in *Paleface* to being 'not more informed than the next' on the subject of Russian Communism, and to have written about it 'merely judging from report'. And despite the fact that he had spent some weeks in Berlin, where he had watched the nightly brawling of the Communists and the Storm Troopers, the same could have been said about his knowledge of National Socialism. His articles were hastily written, and very sketchily researched. On the strength of what he had seen, what he had read (largely in the Nazi papers) and what he had heard (partly from Nazi sympathizers) they appeared to be offering some defence for the open violence of Hitlerism and making a rather uncritical evaluation of the doctrines which Hitler himself had advanced in support of it. Finally, by accepting at its face value Hitler's assurances that his Storm Troopers were fighting the guns and bottles of the Communists with nothing better than their bare fists (the S. A. had been 'disarmed' by Presidential decree during the summer before the elections), and by accusing the Berlin police of aiding the Communists against them, he laid himself open to a charge of partisanship from the start.

A letter of protest to *Time and Tide* from Frederick A. Voight, Berlin Correspondent of the *Manchester Guardian*, took Lewis to task after his second article had appeared. It amounted, he claimed, to 'just a collection of the sillier tales and legends which the Nazis spread in their papers, their speeches, and in their talks with simple-minded visitors from abroad'. The accusation that the police were siding with the Communists against the Nazis he dismissed as 'one of the Nazi legends' that was 'completely absurd'. And protesting that the jackboot was in point of fact on the other leg, he challenged Lewis to come up with evidence of a single instance in proof of of his assertion. 'It is quite clear,' he asserted in turn, 'that Mr. Wyndham Lewis has simply been stuffed with Nazi propaganda,' and that he was writing 'without the slightest knowledge of the German situation in general and the Nazi movement in particular'.[9]

No doubt as a result of similar charges, the editor of *Time and Tide* saw fit to preface the last three articles of the series with a caveat:

> Whilst we do not find ourselves in agreement with Mr. Wyndham Lewis's attitude towards the German National-Socialist Party and the political situation generally, the vivid picture of present-day Germany which he gives in these articles seems to us of such unusual interest that we do not hesitate to publish them.[10]

As for the vividness of the article *Berlin im Licht* (a description of decadent Berlin night-life) there was a great deal there to think about; and a letter from Cecil F. Melville warmly applauded Lewis for the significant sidelights he had thrown on the German hysteria. Nor did Lewis have much difficulty in dealing with Cecily Hamilton's wry complaint that he seemed to have found more 'naughtiness' in Berlin than she had: as he remarked, she was perhaps less likely a target for transvestite propositioning. But the serious charge he could rebut with nothing better than a counter-claim that Voight had proved himself to be hotly pro-Communist—an idea which none of Voight's regular readers were ready to accept.

Even so, and allowing for their unfortunate bias, there was much in the articles which was worthy of careful consideration. They represented the first impressions of a lively mind on a subject of great significance; and the wrong assessments of which they were occasionally guilty were to be repeated by many others when there was far more evidence to go upon and far less reason to make the same mistakes. The final outcome of Hitlerism was still an open question; and many of the wrong judgments that Lewis made can be put down to an understandable exercise in wishful thinking. As Lady Rhondda had herself suggested in a far from cordial editorial at the time of the elections: 'It would be unwise to minimize the meaning of the Hitler phenomenon. He represents, above all, profound discontent with parliamentarianism, and the willingness of large sections of the community to take big risks in order to try to cut through to something better than the parliamentary régime has been able to give Germany.'[11] And it was this inescapable fact that Lewis was doing his best to make plain.

After all, no less important than what Hitler was trying to do was the reason why so many Germans should think that he was right in trying to do it. And when the articles had been expanded into book form, they went some way to explaining why this was the case. The final text of *Hitler* emphasized that a major factor in the success of the Nazi Party at the polls had been their declared intention to repudiate all war reparations, and their complete rejection of what they denounced as the 'war-guilt lie'. It was emphasized that a new post-war generation could hardly be expected to saddle themselves with a guilt of which they felt themselves to be innocent, and that many Germans—young and old—sincerely believed that the greed of the Allies in continuing to penalize them for what had been done by others was responsible for all they were suffering through industrial stagnation and rising unemployment. The collapse of the mark and the overnight wiping out of all personal savings still rankled with the deprived middle classes, and was a very real cause of bitterness and anxiety. What they regarded as the grasping demands of Wall Street—'the American Shylock'—

they resented almost more than the watchful hostility of the French, whom they still mistrusted as an implacable enemy determined to keep them in a state of national subjection. The German people as a whole were suffering from a sense of imposed inferiority, to which the rabid nationalism of Hitler offered an acceptable corrective. They were no longer content to have their economy and standard of living controlled for them by non-Germans (with whom, of course, they were invited to identify Jewish financiers both at home and abroad), and where the democracies appeared ready to accept a policy of drift, the younger Germans were not. They were far more in a mood to listen to a leader who offered them desperate remedies for all their ills, and who played upon their longing for a new and nationalistic sense of self-respect.

Lewis could hardly be accused of harbouring pro-German sympathies: his deadly characterization of Kreisler in *Tarr* (and his preface to the first wartime edition of that masterpiece) had made that abundantly clear. But there was plainly an intention in *Hitler* 'to break the European ostracism of Germany, call in question the wisdom of the Versailles Treaty and get it revised, end the bad behaviour of the French chauvinists, attempt to establish healthy relations in Western Europe' and generally to state the German case as fairly as he could.[12] And as he went on to point out: 'This was undertaken in the interest of Western civilization (the private interests of Germany had no weight with me at all: my "spiritual home" always has been, if anything, France).'[13]

Such an intention was soon to become the declared policy of the British government, before it had been pushed to the farthest limits of 'appeasement'. Lewis was right also—and proved to be so—in his contention that 'if Hitler continues to gain ground, as there seems every chance of his doing, Germany will then act *as one man*,'[14] for he saw clearly enough that the quality of leadership which Hitler represented was ardently wished for by a large section of the German people. His old contention that most people do not value abstract 'freedom' so much as release from the responsibility of thinking and acting for themselves, could certainly have found no better illustration than was offered by the sudden German acceptance of Hitlerism as a way of life. And while Lewis had never suggested that people *should* think and behave like hypnotized zombies, he refused to blind himself to the fact that very many people do. He realized clearly enough that Hitler's own 'eloquent workman's evangile' was a very different thing from the older nationalism of the Junkers and the Hohenzollerns—effective though that had been in itself with the bulk of the German people. Hitler's appeal was that of a pseudo-Everyman, a self-styled *Mann aus dem Volke*, who passed off his heady brand of nationalistic revivalism as a *Volksbewegung* in which everyone could relax and be carried along by a sort of self-generating impetus. As for Hitler himself, and the role which he had assumed:

> As even his very appearance suggests, there is nothing whatever eccentric about him. He is not only satisfied with, but enthusiastically embraces, his *typicalness*. So you get in him, cut out in the massive and simple lines of a peasant art, the core of the teutonic character. And his 'doctrine' is essentially just a set of rather primitive laws, promulgated in the interest of that particular stock or type, in order to satisfy its especial requirements and ambitions, and to ensure its vigorous survival, intact and true to its racial traditions.[15]

There was nothing about 'typicalness', peasant art, the teutonic character or primitive anything which was likely to appeal to Lewis very strongly, but he could accept them as so many German facts and deduce from them a likely pattern of events. He was correct in his belief that Hitler would not attempt a second *Putsch*, like the one that had failed at Munich, but was only too likely to get his hands on power by legal and 'democratic' means. As he said, 'When the majority of the electors are in favour of a policy (or when such a majority may be confidently expected in the near future) why attempt to carry that policy through by violent and uncertain means? That would indeed be a senseless proceeding!'[16] And while the Nazis never did achieve an absolute majority in a free vote at the polls, Lewis was right in his belief that once power had been made over to Hitler, the majority would certainly be content to leave him in possession of it. The only question was—to what use would that power be put?

Oddly enough, although Lewis had attended a mass meeting

at the Berlin Sportpalast which was addressed by Göring and Goebbels ('whose voice rose constantly to a scream') he had never heard Hitler speak in person. (He admitted later to having heard him speak on the radio, but apparently not in one of his 'screaming' moods.) It may well be, therefore, that the dementia which came over in all the major speeches that Hitler made would have warned him far sooner than newspaper reports of the dangerous paranoia which Hitler represented—one might almost say, the national paranoia. As it was, and judging solely from what he read, Lewis was gulled into making a monumental misjudgment in his estimate of the man.

According to Lewis, in fact, Hitler was at bottom a 'Man of Peace'. His brand of nationalism was not of the predatory kind —in which Lewis felt that it differed from the *Action Française* nationalism of Maurras. He believed that the consolidation of a Third Reich, the mastering of Germany's economic problems, reorganization of industry to cure her unemployment, and the building-up of a limited and permitted armament for defensive purposes—this would be more than enough to keep Hitler and Germany herself occupied for the foreseeable future. As for Hitler's irredentist aims—the *Anschluss* with Austria, the return of the Sudeten Germans, the problems of Danzig, the Polish Corridor and the rest—these, he felt, were matters which could be settled peaceably in due time. The fact that Germany had been 'so scrupulously disarmed' was itself a guarantee of peace: and the idea of Germany representing any sort of military threat could be 'entirely dismissed from the most apprehensive mind'. The French might continue to insist upon the fact, but the explanation of that, no doubt, was easy enough to find: it was 'good for the armament firms'.[17]

Given the benefit of hindsight, all this sounds remarkably naïve. But one has to remember that precisely those arguments provided a basis for British foreign policy over the next eight years, by which time even the French were advancing them with increasing optimism. The fact that a casual reading of *Mein Kampf* would have caused even the least apprehensive mind to view them with misgiving can hardly be urged against Lewis exclusively. The fact remains that the few who could be bothered to wade through that dreary book at all were unwilling to take its vapourings at all seriously. They doubtless agreed with Churchill about its being 'turgid, verbose, shapeless', but failed to allow, as he did, for the fact that it still remained 'pregnant with its message'. As for Hitler's declared aim of carving out a new empire in the East—in the sacred name of *Lebensraum*—nothing was apparently felt to be wrong with that in any way: his declared intention of leaving overseas colonialism to the British and the French had a pleasantly analgesic ring to it. Jack, it seemed, was the only one who wasn't going to be all right.... Lewis may have made his monumental misjudgment, but it was shared by the majority of the British people, if not by the majority of his readers.

It is well to remember that Lewis had always insisted that the politics of the future must be a form of Socialism. It must be remembered also that he had a strangely unorthodox idea as to what Socialism implied—indeed, he had even tried to identify it with Italian Fascism. For him, Socialism was primarily a matter of setting one's national house in order: it did not consist in burgling the house next door. When he insisted, therefore, that Hitler's nationalism was actually 'national-*socialism*',[18] he seems to have convinced himself that it was purely a matter of domestic aims and issues. After all, Socialism was fundamentally a political philosophy for have-not nations —rather than an evangile for haves or let's-have-mores. Hitler's brand of Socialism might appear to be militant domestically, but that was merely a matter of expediency: control of the State could only be won after control of the streets, as the Nazis had always insisted. But Hitler's militancy extended only as far as the frontier: like Mussolini's Fascism, Lewis believed it was strictly not for export. It represented the militancy of 'an armed peasant', rather than that of 'a dispossessed aristocratic class'. The nationalist phobias of Maurras and Coty in France, always itching to get at 'the traditional enemy across the Rhine', could not be equated with the peasant's determination to fight for undisputed possession of his acre of land. Peasants, after all, were not in the habit of attacking their more powerful neighbours—neither, for that matter, were Socialists. Nationalism of an *un*socialistic order might very well lead to the 'Balkanization' of Europe—which, Lewis protested, he would be the first to deplore. But he still could see no reason to believe that Hitler was a 'nationalist' of that 'Balkanizing' order—as indeed he was not! Yet when he went on to assure his readers that 'Adolf Hitler is not a sabre-rattler at all', he was forgetting one rather obvious fact: on Lewis's own showing, Hitler had so far no sabre to rattle. Once he had one to hand—in the shape of a revived Reichwehr—the case was likely to be altered....

As to the nature of Nazi 'Socialism', even the *Daily Mail* could have disabused him: Lord Rothermere, who looked for Socialists under his bed each night, would never have wasted time looking for one in the ranks of the Storm Troopers! Amusingly enough, even Lewis seems to have been slightly puzzled by *one* anomaly of the Hitlerite brand of 'Socialism'. He had insisted upon the fact that Hitler 'was a sort of inspired *german peasant*', and later went on to explain why he found the economic programme of the Nazi Party entirely consonant with the aims of the peasant proprietor and the small trader. 'But there is a paradox,' he added with some surprise. 'It is one of the first difficulties in understanding who-is-who in this particular mêlée. The interest of the industrialist, so it seems, is in many ways identical with that of the peasant: or at least it can be made to accommodate itself to the latter. That is certainly contrary to what one would expect.'[19] It is certainly contrary to what one would expect under orthodox *Socialism*....

At the same time, Lewis was at least right in finding the economic programme of the Nazi Party at variance with the outworn and stagnating policies of the democracies. The New Deal in America had yet to be called into being, and the American Depression under Hoover was even more hopeless than the British Depression under MacDonald. No government currently in power seemed willing to take a new look at the problems created by a trade recession; and probably the nearest approach to Nazi thinking had been the economic proposals put before the Labour Party by Sir Oswald Mosley while he still belonged to it. Needless to add, the proposals had been far too unorthodox for Philip Snowden or any other British Socialist, though they have been described since (if Mosley's own) as 'evidence of a superlative talent which was later to be wasted'.[20]

The truth was that Hitler's vague ideas about the evils of loan capital—*Leihkapital*—as opposed to the usefulness of 'productive' capital had all the appeal of a new approach to the problem of restrictive credit. They appeared to be a threat to the stranglehold of international finance—*Zinsknechtschaft*, or credit-slavery, as Hitler chose to call it. The Banks, the 'Profiteers', the financial moguls and market-manipulators—these were the subject of much Nazi abuse. Needless to add, they were to be abused no less in Britain during the 1931 Financial Crisis. And knowing no more about economics than Hitler himself, Lewis was at least encouraged to find that his natural antipathy to international finance was shared by a Party which appeared likely to do battle with it on a national scale. As he admitted: 'I do not feel inclined to condemn a party like that of Hitler because I find that they would make it hot for the Stock-jobber.... It depends what comes after that, and why it is done.'[21] And by convincing himself that Hitler was some sort of a 'Credit Crank' (at which he expressed ironical dismay), who was bent on introducing a local variant of Social Credit (which Pound and Eliot had also blessed), Lewis was somehow hopeful that great things might be done indeed. If he had only realized just how much had been contributed to the building up of the Nazi Party by German barons of Big Business, he might have felt rather less hopeful of the event....

But perhaps the most serious charge that could be levelled at Lewis's *Hitler* is the fact that the book failed to take any real notice of the virulent nature of Nazi anti-Semitism. In the third of his *Time and Tide* articles—*The Oneness of 'Hitlerism' and of Hitler*—he had briefly referred to the subject, had made no attempt to excuse it, but had dismissed it in these terms:

> To reassure the Anglo-Saxon too much upon this head would give a false idea of the Hitler Movement, and that I do not wish to do. All one can say is that Hitler *himself*—and I have shown how much depends upon him—is, though not a man of compromise, yet not an unreasonable, a violent or fanatical man. I believe that, if he should come into power, he would discourage his followers from any reckless pursuit of any policy calculated to antagonize the rest of the European world. The Anglo-Saxon would not, I think, turn his back entirely upon Hitler because of his precious *Judenfrage*.[22]

In expanding the article for book publication, Lewis replaced this passage by a chapter on *Hitlerism and the Judenfrage* in which he freely admits that in the forefront of the Hitlerist

Programme stand drastic proposals directed against the Jews'.[23]
He agrees that this is likely to prejudice opinion in the Anglo-
Saxon countries, and proceeds to offer what he can in explanation of the Nazi attitude. He is afraid that this can not be
much, but hopes that it will be able 'to soften somewhat the
contours of this preliminary snag'.

His reason for trying to do this was perfectly fair and above
board: however mistakenly, he believed that the Nazi brand
of anti-Semitism represented no new phenomenon in Germany.
Anti-Semitism, after all, had been rampant in Germany and
Austria for as long as anyone could recollect: it was a sort of
Germanic psychosis which anyone visiting either country had
to shrug his shoulders and learn to accept. Lewis himself had
learnt to accept it while studying art at Munich in 1905. As he
remembered it (and he had had his Jewish friends), the anti-
Semitic sentiments of the Germans had not been unlike the anti-
Welsh sentiments of many Englishmen—or as Hugh Kenner
aptly puts it, 'no more sanguinary than Dr. Johnson's sparring
with the Scots'.

Admittedly, the Jews in Germany had been a rather easier
target for persecution than they were in Britain. Where honest
Bavarians wore nothing more ridiculous than socks without
feet, leather shorts and embroidered braces, Jews were still to
be seen in Munich with prayer-curls and rabbi-hats! In Britain
and America the Jews had been rather more assimilated into
the national life: they wore their tweeds and fedoras like so
many natives. And as Lewis remarked, a Jew in the patriarchal
sense and in his Jewish gabardine had not been seen in Britain
'since the days of Dickens', and had almost become 'a Shakes-
pearian myth out of *The Merchant of Venice*'. In the Anglo-
Saxon countries the Jew has long since ceased to be regarded
as an alien: his contribution to government and culture is
appreciated or taken for granted. As for his business acumen,
that is merely an improvement upon the trading habits of his
gentile neighbours. And though, like Eliot, Lewis could be
mildly witty about the Burbanks and the Bleisteins, that was
as far as he was ever prepared to go. More to the point, that
was as far as he advised the Nazis to go themselves: 'a pinch
of malice certainly, but no "antisemitism" for the love of
Mike!'[24]

Harking back to Lewis's student days in Munich, it is worth remembering that sniping at the Jews had been a pastime in Linz and Vienna at roughly the same time. There it had offended the delicate sensibilities of Hitler himself, as he explains with disengaging honesty in *Mein Kampf*: 'As I thought they were persecuted on account of their Faith my aversion to hearing remarks against them grew almost into a feeling of abhorrence.' Indeed, he goes on to protest, 'I considered the tone adopted by the anti-Semitic Press in Vienna was unworthy of the cultural traditions of a great people.'[25]

This early squeamishness on Hitler's part, of course, was quickly overcome. He observed how the anti-Semitic outbursts of his favourite Burgomaster, Dr Karl Lueger, proved highly successful as a means of catching the popular vote. At the same time he realized that by insisting upon its *religious* basis, Lueger's anti-Semitism was not really getting him very far: 'a few drops of baptismal water' was enough to take the curse off the scapegoat. In fact, the Viennese Christian Democrats, with their 'shilly-shally way of dealing with the problem' were satisfying nobody at all, least of all the electoral xenophobes. This deplorable state of affairs would obviously have to be remedied, Hitler decided. And with his 'amazing intuition', he realized that if it was to get him anywhere at all, his own form of anti-Semitism would have to be given a *racial* basis. No amount of baptismal water could douse the fires of hatred then! Racial anti-Semitism could be worked up into a truly murderous instrument of policy....

Lewis himself quite clearly failed to draw a distinction between anti-Semitism of the old-fashioned kind and anti-Semitism as perfected and practised by Hitler. He pointed out (while never attempting to condone it) that anti-Semitism was hardly peculiar to the Germans: it was also to be found among the Poles, the Czechs and Slovaks, the Hungarians, Romanians and Balts—to which he might well have added the Russians. But as practised by all these 'inferior' peoples (in Nazi terminology) no doubt it was still rather primitive and inefficient. Only Hitler had refined the blood-sport till it now seemed worthy in every way of the 'cultural traditions of a great people', provided, of course, that the Hitlerites could be accepted as such.

The fact that Lewis had failed to notice the peculiar virulence of Nazi anti-Semitism would have seemed odder, perhaps, if he had not equally failed to notice so many other things on his trip to Berlin. But because he did not believe that Hitler had in any sense *invented* anti-Semitism, he could not bring himself to believe that Hitler took it at all seriously. He regarded it as so much *Agitationsmittel*—so much playing to the gallery and dressing of the political shop-window. It was an unpleasantness which would be forgotten, once power had been attained and the Nazis were playing to a world audience in place of a purely Germanic one.

But Lewis, after all, was not alone in his refusal to take Hitler at his own word. It did not occur to many people that when he was uttering blood-curdling threats against the Jews, the 'Traitors of 1918' or anyone else, Hitler was in deadly earnest. It had not yet occurred to most of the British Press that when he promised in a Leipzig courtroom that once he had come to power 'heads would roll in the sand', he meant precisely that. 'This was clearly a rhetorical flourish,' said one leader writer: 'Those who expect wild measures from him will be disappointed.' And for once in his life, Lewis appeared to be echoing the popular press: 'I believe Hitler himself—once he had obtained power—would show increasing moderation and tolerance. In the *Dritte Reich*, as conceived by Hitler, that great jewish man of science, Einstein, would, I think, be honoured as he deserves.'[26] Luckily, Einstein did not stay to put the matter to the test. Like every other German Jew who knew his Nazis at first hand and believed *Mein Kampf* when he read it, he realized that on one subject at least Hitler was a man of his word.

In his consideration of the 'Aryan' side of Nazi racial policy, Lewis begins by noting that race is in theory a less divisive element in society than class or nationality. In *The Art of Being Ruled* he had pointed out how the 'class-war' was capable of infinite proliferation once 'class' was taken to include age, sex, occupation or any other basic difference. As for nationality—or its militant offspring, nationalism—the Treaty of Versailles had notably increased the dangers inherent in that by the creation of new and unstable nations. With Europe as frontier-conscious as it was, race could well be regarded as a unifying factor, since one great race-group accounted for most of the continent.

But moving on from race to militant racialism of the Nazi kind, the matter became rather more complicated. To begin with, Lewis had dismissed the latter contemptuously as 'the dogmatic "Germanism" that the Hitlerist takes over lock, stock and barrel from Gobineau and Houston Chamberlain, and then develops in new directions for his own present purposes'.[27] Nor could he possibly have defined it better.

When expanding his consideration of *Blutsgefühl*, however, he began to find one or two redeeming features in what he believed that Hitler's private brand of 'Aryanism' represented. He found the word 'Aryan' useful at least insofar as it 'conveys something that is well defined enough, for me at all events', while admitting that it was no doubt 'ethnologically indefensible', which it certainly was, as used by Hitler. (One is reminded of Max Müller's drily Germanic observation that: 'To me an ethnologist who speaks of Aryan race, Aryan blood, Aryan eyes and hair, is as great a sinner as a linguist who speaks of a dolichocephalic dictionary or a brachycephalic grammar.')

At the same time, fresh from his writing of *Paleface*, perhaps it was not surprising that Lewis should find something to say in defence of a 'philosophy' which called for '*a closer and closer* drawing together of the people of one race and culture,' when the people also happened to be white. He admitted that such a doctrine was easy enough to ridicule; but he was persuaded that 'the *opposite*—the diffusionist, racial-olla-podrida camp—is equally if not more easy to ridicule'. And he could think of no easier way of doing so than by identifying it once more with D. H. Lawrence's 'fetish of promiscuity and hysterical paeans to all that is "dark and strange"'.[28]

This was hardly in line, of course, with what he himself had written in favour of the Melting-pot. And he failed to realize that when Hitler used the word 'Aryan' he really meant 'Teutonic', whereas when Lewis used it he invariably meant 'Western'. Being no racialist himself, Heine and Jacob Epstein were just as much a part of western culture for him as Goethe or Schopenhauer. But in that, Hitler would hardly have agreed with him.

Where Hitler and Lewis were on the same side of the fence— the 'square' side—was in their denunciation of 'jazz' and *Negertänzen* (Hitler regarding them as Afro-Jewish), 'decadent' art (Hitler would have included vorticism under this head, of course), primitivism, and the sort of exoticism that Lewis himself traced back by way of Lawrence, Gauguin, Baudelaire (with his mulatto mistress), Walt Whitman, Byron and Shelley, to Rousseau's Noble Savage himself. And when Hitler's attitude towards democracy and his dark threats against international finance had been thrown into the balance, no doubt Lewis could convince himself, almost wistfully, that 'the Hitlerist dream is full of an eminent classical serenity'—the operative word, of course, being 'classical'.

But it is mainly on what he calls the 'Exotic Sense' that Lewis concentrates when considering the subject of race. Once more he returns to the attack upon what he feels to be the modern predilection for the strange and the unfamiliar: 'The Exotic Sense, in the nature of things, is a direction taken by the mind that implies a decadence. For it is a flight from the Self, is it not —a yearning for violent change?'[29] By many of his readers, Nazism itself might have been described in exactly those terms, for nothing was more likely to do violence to the Self than submersion in the mystic 'Instinct of the Blood' upon which the Nazi was always insisting. If he had been examining any programme other than one which he regarded as 'classical' in its creation of monolithic order in the State, Lewis would surely have been the first to deride this talk of 'instinct', this lauding of the blood above the intellect (which might, after all, happen to be Jewish), this blind stampeding of a herd-mass which ran gallumphing wherever the 'intuition' of its Führer decided that it must go. But because he had supposed that Hitler was inspired by his own concern for western culture, Lewis allowed a great deal of arrant nonsense to pass under review without comment. Once convinced that western society was in process of disintegration, he was prepared to tolerate *Blutsgefühl* as merely 'a violent affirmation' of his own aesthetic beliefs! From there on, it was only one step further to admitting that the sort of 'Hands-off-Aryanism' which Hitler appeared to represent was 'not entirely to be despised, though not necessarily to be swallowed whole'.[30]

If Lewis had put himself to the boredom of analysing the Nazi racial doctrine through all its illogicality—by Rosenberg out of Houston Stewart Chamberlain crossed with by Nietzsche out of Gobineau, he would have been forced to deride and denounce it for what it undoubtedly was—a romantic farrago of childish absurdity. As it was, he was willing to swallow only those bits of the doctrine which happened to square with his own independent thinking. (He might even have done as much for Stalinism.) But when Hitler would try to persuade him that 'all the "Science and Art, technique and invention" in the world is the work of the White European, or "Aryan",' Lewis begins to demur. It is certainly not true of Art, he protests, and the Chinese, Aryan Persians and Hindus, Hamitic Egyptians and the rest are back in the argument. He is certainly not prepared to accept 'Aryanism' as a sort of Germanic monopoly. If race is at issue, the Shetlander, the Bavarian and the Breton are blood-brothers in the club together, but unlikely to ally themselves as such. Nor will he allow anti-Semitic nonsense to obtrude in serious debate: 'in matters of the technique of art, as opposed to the technique of science, and at this in fields where a great deal of taste and intelligence is required, the Hitlerist's arch-enemy, the Jew, can make rings round him in all that universe that is not war, or mechanical technique.'[31] And he adds, with a certain irony, 'no "aryan" mathematician has succeeded in putting Einstein in his place'. The fact that 'aryan' mathematicians were following Einstein's theory 'like obedient mooing cattle' might, perhaps, be unfortunate for philosophy, but that had nothing to do with the question of race. Neither had the deplorable influence of Bergsonism!

There is no conscious humour, one feels, in Lewis's apology: 'I feel that this part of my account of Hitlerism may fall short of what I should wish, and may sound too much like criticism, instead of just the work of a detached exponent.'[32] Perhaps it was the severity of Lewis's criticism on the subject of art and culture which induced the Führer to have the German translation of *Hitler* pulped and burned when he came to power, and 'classical serenity' reigned in the Reich at last....

What, then, is one to say of the book in the light of subsequent events? It proved, for Lewis personally, little short of a publishing disaster, and did his reputation probably more harm in Britain than any other book he wrote. This was certainly unfair, though perhaps hardly surprising in the circumstances. His estimate of Hitler as a 'Man of Peace' who could never conceivably afford to attack either France or Poland was almost laughable in its wrongness. His failure to realize the full horror of Nazi brutality—and the evil nature of its murderous anti-Semitism—was unfortunate, to say the least: it led many people to assume that Lewis secretly approved of what he merely failed to recognize and denounce. The fact that he took a great deal of Nazi propaganda on trust may have been surprising but not so surprising as all that: many millions of Germans did the same, with far more reason to be suspicious. And in his desire to 'expound' Hitlerism impartially, it must be admitted that now and again he came perilously close to appearing as an advocate for what he was expounding. Perilously close, but that was as far as he actually went. It was by those who had not read the book at all that *Hitler* was often decried the loudest during the later thirties.

If Lewis had really set out to write a serious book in the first place, he would certainly have written a better one. He would have researched his subject far more thoroughly, related the Nationalism of the Nazis to the academic nationalistic tradition in German history, and might even have read *Mein Kampf* through for himself. (Though he quotes from it occasionally, he later admitted that he had never read the book right through until the time of the Munich crisis.) And if he had not thought that Hitler's racialist vapourings occasionally appeared to chime with his own aesthetic and cultural thinking, he might have taken a far harder look at the 'classical' tendency which he somehow seemed to believe that Hitlerism represented.

The fact remains that Lewis's object in writing the book at all was perfectly reasonable. No book on the subject had appeared in English before. Like many others, he saw in Germany a nation that had been made to play the scapegoat for 1914 militarism throughout Europe. He felt that the terms of the Treaty of Versailles were harsh and unwise, and that they had bred in the Germans a feeling of resentment and a will to regain—at all costs—their sense of national self-respect. He saw that Hitler's new evangelism was taking the German mind by storm, and he felt that the nature of the doctrine deserved to be understood. Believing that Hitler had been misrepresented by the majority of the British press (which he had not), it seemed to Lewis in the best interests of everybody that Hitler should be given a fair hearing. In his self-appointed role of exponent, therefore, he tried to set the record straight and to lessen prejudice by reasoned explanation. This, it must be admitted, he sadly failed to do.

As already suggested, if Lewis had met up with Hitler in person, had watched him in vicious action or heard him in one of his hysterical and screaming tirades, he might have assessed him rightly from the start. Or might he? There were many who failed to do so, however mistrustful of Hitler's secret aims. 'Those who have met Herr Hitler face to face in public business or on social terms have found a highly competent, cool, well-informed functionary with an agreeable manner, a disarming smile, and few have been unaffected by a subtle personal magnetism.'[33] Those words were written by Winston Churchill four years later than Lewis's own estimate. Churchill also was to revise his early opinion.

NOTES

1. *As of G*, p.596.
2. Ibid., p.509.
3. *Times* leader, 16.9.30.
4. *Express* leader, 16.9.30.
5. *Mail* leader, 17.9.30.
6. *Mail*, 19.9.30.
7. *Express* leader, 17.9.30.
8. *Hitler ou Le Guerrier Déchâiné*, par Frédéric Hirth, published October 1930.
9. *Time and Tide*, 31.1.31.
10. Ibid.
11. *Time and Tide*, 20.9.30.
12. *R A*, p.209.
13. Ibid.
14. *Hitler*, p.33.
15. Ibid., pp.31-32.
16. Ibid., p.55.
17. Ibid., p.56.
18. Ibid., p.45.
19. Ibid., pp.176-7.
20. *English History 1914-1945* by A. J. P. Taylor, p.285.
21. *Hitler*, p.180.
22. *Time and Tide*, 31.1.31.
23. *Hitler*, p.35.
24. Ibid., p.42.
25. *Mein Kampf*, trans. James Murphy, 1939.
26. *Hitler*, p.48.

27. *Time and Tide*, 31.1.31.
28. *Hitler*, p.109.
29. Ibid., p.115.
30. Ibid., p.124.
31. Ibid., p.137.
32. Ibid., pp.142-3.
33. *The Truth about Hitler*, by the Rt. Hon. Winston Churchill, P.C. *The Strand Magazine*, November 1935.

CHAPTER 6

Thou Hast Robbed Me of My Youth

If 1930 had proved an unfortunate year for Lewis, in its own way 1932 was to prove another. Of the four new books that he published, along with a portfolio of portrait-drawings, two were to be withdrawn by the publishers, and another banned by the lending libraries which could normally be relied upon to guarantee an adequate sale and circulation. The seeds of this unlucky half-crop had been sown the previous year.

In *The Art of Being Ruled*, Lewis had dwelt at some length on what he described as the 'age-war', which he regarded as a significant concomitant to the 'sex-war' and the 'war of the brows'. In the interim, he had collected a number of press-clipped stories and articles which he felt would provide all the evidence he needed in support of his theory that crabbed age and youth were being freely incited to attack each other in the interest of sinister forces pursuing their sinister ends. In 1931, *Time and Tide* published a series of seven articles on *Youth-Politics* which Lewis was later to expand into his book *Doom of Youth*—the title, of course, being a play on that of Alec Waugh's wartime best-seller, *The Loom of Youth*. These articles appeared weekly from 13 June to 25 July and considered, in sequence, *The Everymans, The Age-Complex, Youth-Politics upon the Super-Tax Plane,* how *There is* Nothing *Big Business Can't Ration, The* Class-War *of Parents and Children, Government by Inferiority-Complex,* and *How Youth-Politics Will Abolish Youth.* While they were recommended to readers as 'a series of stimulating and controversial articles', each of them again bore an editorial caveat: 'We do not wish to be taken as being necessarily in agreement with all the opinions expressed by Mr. Wyndham Lewis.' The series was rounded off by two further articles on *The Doom of Doom* by G. K. Chesterton, in which he gave his own views on the controversial questions raised by the series; and a final editorial (presumably by Lady Rhondda herself) summed up the whole under the heading *Big Business, Youth and Age: Mr. Wyndham Lewis and Mr. G. K. Chesterton.*

In his opening article, Lewis had affirmed that 'in England it might almost be said that it was the Popular Press that voted, rather than the populace', and that 'it is the newspapers that tell the populace which is the party most likely to bring them immediate and unexampled prosperity and redress for ever for all their wrongs'.[1] Perhaps it occurred to him subsequently that the electorate still preserved the right to ignore the advice with which they were fed so sedulously—as witness the fact that two Labour Governments had been returned to power in the twenties in defiance of a popular press which was overwhelmingly conservative. Whether or no, since politics as such were not his immediate concern, this assertion was silently suppressed when the text of the articles was worked up for book publication. In its place appeared the statement that 'the spell-bound public, at the hands of the Popular Press or by way of the film, has notions and beliefs pumped into it that are the *reverse* of any recognized Tradition—either in Religion, Law, Government, or Ethics. In this sense it is "revolutionary" propaganda—the propaganda of a power always *In Opposition*.'[2] And having what he defined as 'a revolutionary sort of mind' himself, Lewis was not averse to such indoctrination in principle. If he had any objection to it at all, it is simply because of what he regarded as the 'purely destructive' nature of such journalism—destructive, that is, of the standards which he personally favoured. Not least destructive of all, he believed, was the conscious promotion by the Popular Press of what he called 'Youth-Politics'.

In a scientific age, as he had already insisted, the will to progress had become a motivating force in society. Progress meant change, and change implied a revolution in which a demand for the 'new' became obligatory and incessant. In the philosophical world of the relativists, the New God was 'an embryo-god'—a *'God-in-the-making'*. In the same way, Man was now Man-in-the-making, and every new machine was merely a step towards the evolution of a machine that was never still. 'It is very easy to see,' says Lewis, 'how Youth-Politics must find, in such a soil, the necessary material for a full-blooded success. Men begin regarding themselves—instinctively, of course—as machines; as machines that rapidly wear out, and that, *of necessity*, every two or three years, are succeeded by slightly better machines. And *that* is a state of mind that is ideal for a Youth-Politician.'[3]

As Lewis defines it, the business of the Youth-Politician is a constant promotion of the age-war by an insistence that the young must demand their rightful place in the world. From that, it is an easy step to demanding that the old move over and make way for them. 'Youth at the Helm' was the sort of catchphrase on which the Youth-Politician thrived, and the great spate of human-interest stories, pseudo-news items, gossipcolumnry and leading articles which featured 'Youth' and all its goings-on were so much shot and shell in the warfare. In short, 'the Youth-Politician is the witch-doctor who juggles with this popular magic—to his own and his master's great profit'.[4]

These quotations from the original *Time and Tide* articles set the theme of the coming book clearly enough, particularly when related to the economic factors involved. Production costs were obviously cheaper when juvenile labour could be substituted for experienced labour—or even female labour. And in the modern world, much of the work done was of a kind in which experience was quite unnecessary. It was mechanical work which the young could often do more spryly and energetically than their fathers. Therefore the old had indeed to be induced to move over—preferably, in fact, to move out of the picture altogether. The sooner the old could be persuaded to die off, the sooner they could be replaced, and the sooner the production costs of the Modern World, Inc., could be reduced to a satisfactory level. Put at its simplest: 'Youth-Politics is, upon the purely economic side, a technique for mobilizing and manipulating the herds in office, workshop and factory. It is there that the effects of the Youth propaganda are principally to be looked for—the wage question is the critical one.'[5]

Essentially, that became the main theme of the book *Doom of Youth*, which can now be examined most usefully in its own text. It was published in New York in April 1932, and the London edition followed in July. Unfortunately, it was not to be available in Britain for very long.

The book contained a chapter on *Winn and Waugh*, in which Lewis examined what he called *Youngergenerationconsciousness* (no doubt the Germans have a word for it) as exemplified in the journalism of Evelyn Waugh and Godfrey Winn. The chapter was maliciously amusing, and made some play with Waugh's articles on *The Attitude of Mind of the Younger Generation* and *Matter-of-fact Mothers of the New Age*—the latter, a squib which he had fired off in the *Evening Standard* three years before. Lewis cited Waugh's dictum that 'Loyalty to one's own age is the only really significant loyalty remaining to us', post-war disillusion being what it was. In response to Waugh's defence of the Younger Generation, Lewis explains, 'it seems whole Brigades of red-faced Old Colonels wrote threatening letters—with minatory gestures of great horsewhips in the direction of his naughty *Youngergenerationconscious* b.t.m.'[6] Time, in fact, was declaredly Evelyn Waugh's god—in Lewisian terms, at least. In the contemporary field of youth-politics journalism, unbeknownst to himself, he was dutifully playing the game in accordance with the rules laid down for him by the witch-doctors and their unseen masters.

It seems that Evelyn Waugh took the charge in good part—being flattered, perhaps, to find himself described as a new 'Max'. Not so his fellow-journalist Godfrey Winn, who was subjected to rather more quizzical attention. Two of Winn's articles are given the full Lewisian treatment—*Give us our Latchkeys!* which had appeared in the *Sunday Graphic*, and *A Modern Young Man Moans: I Wish I Had a Sister*, which had recently graced the pages of a weekly called *Modern*. Lewis points out, with some irony, that the 'Latchkey' article opens with the words 'When I was young (*really* young!)...' whereas what he calls 'I *wish* I had a *siss*!' or 'Mr. Winn's "Sissie" article' merely starts off with 'When I was six years old...' Whether a longish quotation from the latter article was seen as a breach of copyright, or whether he objected to being called the author of a 'Sissie' article, Godfrey Winn was clearly not amused.[7]

An application was made for an interim injunction against

any further sale of *Doom of Youth*. The appeal was heard before a judge in Chambers on 16 August 1932, and dismissed— possibly on the legal grounds that 'you do not obtain injunctions for actionable wrongs for which damages are the proper remedy'. But rather than risk incurring any such damages, *Doom of Youth* was withdrawn from circulation by the London publishers. Whatever the rights or wrongs of the affair, the suppression was regrettable: removal of a few offending sentences would have left the book in the clear—and there is much of far greater interest which vanished along with them. In retrospect, one is irresistibly reminded of the scene in *The Childermass* when an outraged Barney objects to being called a 'Cissy', but on this occasion it was rather the Bailiff's head that was sliced off by the heiduk Mannaei....

By way of epigraph, *Doom of Youth* quotes Trotsky to the effect that 'the education of the young is for us a question of life and death'—in which context, 'us' means, of course, the Soviet Union back in the early twenties. Comparing this to the Jesuit dictum 'Give us a child up to the age of six, and do what you like with him after that,' Lewis goes on to quote the *Manchester Guardian* on the subject of *Marxism for Babes*. In the fifteen years since the October Revolution, he reminds us, a new generation had been growing up in the Soviet Union which had been indoctrinated with Communist teaching since birth, and a new seriousness had been given to them by *Pioneer Pravda* and other juvenile reading matter. The result had been an 'extraordinary precocity' which was totally at variance with the 'prolonged, lazy, animal period of "Growing-Up", sheltered from the realities of life to a greater or less extent which had previously characterized the life of Western Man' in the democracies. Rather surprisingly, Lewis wonders whether this is not due in large part to 'the jewish Intelligence' which he felt had played a preponderating part in establishing Soviet rule. (Respectful as it was, it is easy enough to see where *this* idea came from!) Whether or not the result was a good thing for the Russian people, Lewis is not prepared to say, though he admits that 'to *read about* they were nicer before'. The fact remains, he declares, that a new preoccupation with Youth had begun to spread throughout the West of recent years, and he believes that 'in all lands to-day the acuter, more intellectual, jewish nature has set the pace'. And he goes on to speculate: 'May not the jewish consciousness (that, of course, of a very ancient race) have set a quite unusual store by just that thing which formerly the European paid no heed to—mere freshness and Youth—in the way that an old person is attracted by the very young (or as King David procured virgins to warm up his old bones in bed)?'[8]

This is an interesting (if unlikely) speculation, but as Lewis admits it has nothing to do with Youth-Politics as such. The fact remains, however, that the appreciation of *'youth-for-youth's-sake'* has undoubtedly made Youth-Politics possible. And much as he deplores them, he is prepared to admit that they are 'a specifically Western, even teutonic, or anglo-saxon thing'. He protests that no intelligent civilization—such as those of the East—would ever have allowed itself to become party to such an activity, which can merely result in the poisoning and destruction of its own true nature. 'It remained,' he says, 'to the half-baked—the ill-cooked—Western Man to indulge, in the first instance, in this last suicidal sentimentality and egoism.'

For whether or not 'the jewish Intelligence' had helped to foster Youth-Politics in the Soviet Union, it could certainly not be blamed for their later development under Italian Fascism or in Nazi Germany! Youth-Politics in Germany, of course, had merely been built upon an already existing Youth Movement which dated back at least to the time of the Napoleonic Wars. The romantic idea of wandering and gipsying freely through the woods and forests of the Fatherland had long appealed to the German student. But the Hitler Youth had quickly absorbed all the non-political *Wandervögel* groups that had flourished during the twenties, and had supplanted them by a highly regimented political movement which could be used to indoctrinate all future generations with Nazi ideology.

Lewis is not prepared to find the Youth-Politics of the Nazis anyway more culpable than Youth-Politics of any other sort. He still retains a sneaking respect for the way that German Youth had rallied to Hitler 'with all its characteristic passion and "idealism"', and joins issue with an article in which Gilbert Seldes had bitterly denounced the way that Youth in Nazi Germany was being corrupted and militarized. Why, says Lewis, attack one brand of Youth-Politics more than another simply because it has accepted a political creed to which you happen to be ideologically opposed? And he gravely warns his readers that—'like most active-minded american correspondents'—he suspects Seldes of being 'dogmatically communist in sympathy', which hardly accords with what he quotes Seldes as having written.

But it was not Lewis's purpose to discuss Youth-Politics under Nazism, Fascism or Communism, nor indeed had he acquired the data to do so. He is prepared to dismiss all three varieties as 'ugly' and leave it at that. His first concern is with the way that he believes Youth-Politics are to be found at work in the democracies, and the secret aims that lie behind their obsessive insistence on 'Youth' as a virtue in itself. Avoiding the temptation to get embroiled with the Boy Scout movement (oldest youth-regimentation of them all), therefore, he confines himself to analysing Youth-Politics as he finds them at work in the British press.

We have already quoted Lewis's argument that the basis of the age-war was primarily economic. And he rightly describes *Doom of Youth* as 'a very extensive appendix' to the case that he had first presented in *The Art of Being Ruled*. This time, however, the argument is pushed considerably further, illustrated with a wealth of documentation, and followed through to what he regards as necessary conclusions. Once more he emphasizes the fact that the constant stressing of the importance of 'Youth' by the media is all in accordance with a carefully worked-out plan. As for those responsible for the plan, he is once more guardedly unspecific. They are either 'hardened old criminals', or an 'old political ruffian', or a 'bald-headed Press Magnate'—or even (in theory), 'Super-Economic Intelligence'. In any of these or similar guises, the 'superior will' still stands with Lewis for Big Business in all its old and evil ways. And for Big Business, as he assures us, the newspapers are no more than a propaganda department. They are there to ensure that the public is fed upon the fare which will predispose it to serve the unseen master's interests—and serve them as cheaply as possible.

It may have seemed to some of the book's readers that Lewis had tried to make Big Business an over-convenient scapegoat, and that he had again endowed it with Machiavellian cunning and a power of co-ordination in excess of all likelihood. But in his reply to the *Youth-Politics* articles in *Time and Tide*, G. K. Chesterton was ready to accept this part of Lewis's argument whole-heartedly. It was only Lady Rhondda, winding up the whole series in an editorial, who remained unconvinced. She agreed that exploitation was made easier when people were divided among themselves—as the age-war tended to leave them —since 'the isolated, the divided, the insecure find themselves at the mercy of those with organization, co-operation and security behind them'. But she went on to remark that 'the contemporary world makes an odd comment upon any theory which flatters Big Business by attributing to it such co-operation, foresight and security'.[9] After all, Big Business had proved singularly unable to foresee the economic blizzard from which it was currently suffering, and still less able to find a cure for it. As the Depression showed plainly enough, Big Business was itself at the mercy of circumstances, frequently mistaken in its forecasts and frequently the victim of its own mistakes. Perhaps her most cogent observation was that Lewis may have tended to over-simplify the issues, and that 'one curious phenomenon about the human race is that it almost always moves in two directions simultaneously'.[9]

While he shared Lewis's distrust of Big Business, however, even Chesterton was unprepared to accept all Lewis's conclusions as to the final outcome of its Youth-Politics programme. If pushed to its logical conclusion, Lewis had implied, this would involve not merely the doom of Youth itself, but also the doom of sex and the doom of the family. Chesterton, in fact, was of the opinion that only doom was doomed, since the very *notion* of doom had disappeared with the nineteenth century in the same way that inevitable damnation had disappeared with the seventeenth century. He found Lewis's dogmatic predictions touchingly innocent, and on a par with such assertions as that 'the nose is obviously destined to disappear from the human face within the next few years'. And because Lewis's dogma did not accord with that of the Roman Church nor his philosophy with that of St Thomas Aquinas, he found it hard to gather what he was trying to save, and what he was trying to save it from. He was, said Chesterton in his best dogmatic manner, 'the surgeon who does not know whether he is cutting the leg off the man or the man off the leg'. And he summed up Lewis and all other non-Chestertonians as 'often remarkable for the breadth of their generalization and the narrowness of their experience'.[10]

Despite this jolly rebuttal, Lewis's conclusions in *Doom of Youth* are well worth considering, if only for the benefit of non-dogmatists. Whatever may be felt by the open-minded reader, for instance, Lewis maintains that his treatise 'is not a work of literature' but rather 'a work of science, pure and simple'. He himself, in fact, is to be judged in this instance as 'a man of science'.[11] And it is intriguing to discover just where he felt that science was leading him.

As we have seen, he regards the age-war as merely one among the many 'class-wars' that he had been discussing in *The Art of Being Ruled*. He finds it the natural successor to the sex-war which had promoted feminism—and which, presumably, has found recent renewal in the birth of Women's Lib. (It is to be hoped that the Liberators are at least aware of the Father whose business they are about.)

First of all, then, it is worth recording that Lewis is no less opposed to class-warfare than he is to warfare in the purely military sense. ('I am not one of those who believe in the ultimate "triumph" of *any* class in these class-wars. All equally will be defeated, I think.'[12]) And although the sex-war was still to be slugged out in his time, he already notices many ways in which he feels it has proved inimical to the interests of Modern Woman:

> That crafty ant, Man, thought that it was high time that most women ceased to regard themselves as luxury-objects only. Even upon quite simple luxuries Big Business began to frown. Woman, the old sort of woman, was an absurd luxury. Woman must be made to *do work*. So their big crop of cumbersome romantic hair —'woman's crown of beauty' (away also with all crowns, of whatever sort, and what the hell *is* 'beauty', anyway!)—that ridiculous handicap where *work* is concerned, must be cut off. Skirts (another hindrance where *work* is concerned) must be shortened: women must immediately be turned into little, cheap workmen. Men formerly wasted endless time and money upon these absurd dressed-up dolls.[13]

Chesterton was at least with Lewis thus far: he also believed that the promotion of feminism was merely a means to exploitation, and was on record as having said so. For him, the 'economic independence of women' was worth about as much as the independence of 'Chinese Cheap Labour'. He did not follow Lewis in his summing-up of the short skirt—short for work, not play or sex—nor did he commit himself openly to Lewis's contention that by allowing herself to be persuaded out of the 'luxury' of her long hair and her long dresses, Modern Woman had lowered her own market value, being 'never so cheap—for those who like "a bit of skirt"'. Least of all (understandably) did he dally with the subject of slimming: even as Lewis saw it, this was a sad attempt to acquire the profile of Youth, and so no part of feminism proper....

On the subject of love, Lewis had perhaps a better case to make. Regimentation of women could be expected to proceed, ultimately, upon the lines laid down by the Soviet Union, where the regimentation had surely been perfected. He quotes Professor C. E. M. Joad to the effect that there—in the Land of Love Locked Out—no evidence of the existence of romantic love between man and woman could then be seen, and that 'people might be born in parsley beds' for all Joad had been able to observe to the contrary. Bernard Shaw is then invoked in an admission that 'if Bolshevism succeeded in evolving a more civilized attitude to sex', he would not be at all surprised. (In which case, sex would indeed be doomed, for all that Chesterton might have done to save it.) After all, feminism implies an outright denial of the old sentimental idea that Woman Lives for Love: it gives her far more things to get on with, and far less time to spare for the beck and call of her organs or her proclivities. And, says Lewis: 'Feminism having in large measure destroyed "sex" (in the old, romantic, overheated sense), the *age-bogey* with woman (which was a sex-bogey, of course) has disappeared.' The only advantage in this that he can see is that the old idea of 'chocolate-box' beauty has passed completely out of vogue: in the Feminist Era, it seems, anything goes. Apart from that, feminine values—'the most featureless, boneless, softest, the most emotional'—may well prevail in the coming matriarchy. Ah yes, warns Lewis, but they will still be 'feminine values promoted by men, and a pseudo-matriarchy (of a puppet-matriarch—a pantomime figure in the "modernist" carnival) which conceals a figure (or a congeries of figures) in trousers.'[14] As he sees it, by uniting in the cause of feminism, the women workers of all countries have lost nothing by way of chains....

What, then, can Youth be expected to gain from its involvement in the age-war? And so far as Lewis is concerned, once again the answer is—nothing at all! If one is to use the word at all, 'Youth' has indeed everything to *lose* by the age-war. For the war will result in the total *suppression* of Youth at the hands of the Youth-Politician—who, be it noted, is certainly old enough to be its father, and probably is.

It is easy to see how the young, post-war generation had been induced to engage in the age-war, since the Great War itself (World War I) had left them with an urge to blot out all that stood for them as a symbol of the *pre*-war. Those whom they thought of as 'pre-war', after all, were those who had brought that war about. And where to be old was to be guilty, to be young was obviously to be innocent.

For the middle and upper classes at least, in the years before the war, youth had been a leisurely period of growth in which the child had prepared itself for the business of becoming a man. For the affluent classes, youth might last until the age of twenty-five before adult life began: in Lewis's own case it might be said to have lasted until he was thirty. Needless to say, the same had never held for the working class, for whom education had been compulsory (and therefore accepted) only up to the age of thirteen. But even among the working class, youth had been regarded as a period of apprenticeship: wage-earning of a self-sufficing order had begun far later. In any such scheme of things, youth had been regarded merely as the raw material, where the finished product had been manhood. But in the post-war world, Lewis notes, this segregation had rapidly broken down: the young were being encouraged to regard themselves as little adults at the age of ten.

On the other hand, where once the young had been impatient to achieve adulthood, this was no longer true. Modern youth had been taught to think of *itself* as the finished product. It had certainly lost all confidence in its future, for since the war futures had become highly problematical. Post-war youth, says Lewis, had begun to say to itself: ' "all I shall ever have is what

I have got, I shall only get older—everything I shall have *after* this will be less than this. I will spend all my energy in simply *being* what I am, I will put all my eggs in *that* basket, and spend the capital I have at once. After Me the Deluge!" '[15] And that, Lewis thinks, is probably true enough.

This attitude was understandable where growth was being equated increasingly by the media with obsolescence, and where to be old was simply to be in less demand. And certainly, during the years of the Depression, the business of growing old was becoming something of a tragedy. Lewis quotes a typical article from *The Sphere* for 28 February 1931, which paints a grim picture of hopelessness among the unemployed miners of South Wales for whom, once unemployment insurance had ended, the only palliative to existence was 'relief' and the distant hope of an old age pension. He might have quoted hundreds more, describing similar hopelessness in any of the so-called Distressed Areas. He had already written in bitter terms about the general indifference to the sufferings of the unemployed, which was one of the charges he had rightly levelled against democratic government as he knew it. 'If you make life too awful,' he points out, 'people will not *want* to live beyond a certain age. (As it is, the *average* life of the workman is not much over forty.) So what is there surprising if people should tend to curtail it at the other end: or, *making it start sooner*, bring it more quickly to a conclusion?'[16] And it is here, of course, that Youth-Politics begin to operate.

If Youth is already showing a tendency to cling to its youth, he finds it likely that business interests will promptly decide that it must be harnessed as such. For them, youth 'is not a human thing at all, but something like water or wind—to drive a mill, or make electricity'. It must be taught to regard itself as a motive force which had previously been found only in full maturity and experience. It must cease to think of itself merely as a state of becoming: it must be extolled and publicized for itself alone. It must be persuaded that the future is in its hands, and that the only obstacle to its assuming its rightful and proper place in the world is the envious, guilt-ridden, moribund generation which refuses pigheadedly to make way for it. Youth must be mobilized for an age-war in which the older (and higher paid) generation can be utterly demoralized and finally squeezed out of life altogether. As for the leaders of that older generation—pilloried in the popular press as the Old Gang—had they not done far too much harm already? Surely it was high time that they were swept away for good and all—or so the New Gang of Youth-Politicians and their masters would have the young believe. And if the New Gang were no less hoary and decrepit than the Old Gang (for which Press Baron was less than *sixty*?) who could be expected to notice that? After all, they were not asking power for themselves: the New Gang were merely disinterested spectators on the political sideline. No, it was rather for *Youth* that they were campaigning—Youth which should be at the Helm, wherever that left Pleasure....

Things being as they are, Lewis is not convinced that this perpetual indoctrination can ever really be countered. He certainly regards it as vicious, and likely to have the worst possible effects upon society. He distrusts the idea of youth-for-youth's-sake as he distrusts any other form of inexperience: in terms of art, it is likely to result in the primitive rather than the accomplished. In social terms, by destroying the authority of the father, we are destroying authority itself—which is merely to move towards anarchy. It certainly does not make for classical stability, unless, of course, youth were being regimented for classically authoritarian ends, which was hardly the case in Britain. There, the old was merely being discredited, and nothing comparable was being formed to take its place.

But the most significant outcome of the age-war, as Lewis believes, will be to shorten life itself. It is certainly designed to make effective life start sooner, and it has little use for life once effectiveness goes into decline. Youth can hardly be expected to last beyond the age of thirty—it was in his thirtieth year, after all, that 'Villon began his *Testament*'. But the idea of thirty marking the end of effective life was distinctly a new one. Under the old pre-war dispensation, according to Count Keyserling, effective life had been retarded—in Britain at least—to the point of merely *beginning* at thirty, since in those days maturity had been regarded as the first requirement of effectiveness. That in itself had been bad enough, since a man was generally felt to have passed his prime by forty, and the ten full years vouchsafed for him, said Keyserling, was 'about as long as the life of a dog'. But by starting life earlier, the effective life-span was certainly not being lengthened—for now decline was beginning earlier also. By starting life prematurely, therefore, modern youth was merely being induced to die off prematurely as well. It was allowing itself to be harnessed for business ends at far more economic rates than had previously prevailed, and would hardly be allowed to outstay its welcome. After all, so far as the Youth-Politician was concerned, 'To abolish the prolonged period of ignorance and primitiveness artificially maintained at great expense, for twenty years or more, at the beginning of life, is surely an excellent policy—something like "daylight saving", and the adjusting of the clock to suit the seasons.'[17]

But the result of this ingenious idea, Lewis thinks, is even more unfortunate than the shortening of life. By setting his unique emphasis upon Youth as such, the Youth-Politician was in process of abolishing it altogether. He was abolishing the prologue by turning it into the play itself. And that, in Lewis's view, is why Youth in the modern world is doomed indeed.

For what is left of life when youth in the old sense is no longer a preparation for life, but becomes one and the same thing with it? Youth, in any sense at all, can hardly last for long; and when youth and life become synonymous, they must end, to all intents and purposes, together. If youth is followed only by something describable as *not*-youth, that in itself will surely mark the beginning of the end. For the first essential of the age-war has been the creation of the age-complex, by which maturity can be cowed and demoralized into an admission of its own inferiority.

That such a feeling of inferiority was prevalent among the older generation in the industrial areas of Britain at the time there can be no gainsaying. Men in their prime were finding it increasingly hard to earn a living wage. Older men were being turned off from work as a matter of course, and if replaced at all, were being replaced by younger men at lower rates of pay. Once one was old and out of work, demoralization was inevitable: even while one was supposed to live on it, the dole was a miserable pittance that could hardly keep hunger at bay, let alone a feeling of being unwanted. And when the working son —by virtue of the iniquitous Means Test—was saddled with the responsibility of supporting unemployed parents, demoralization was often matched by resentment. But though this was admittedly a reflection of the age-war, its root cause was economic rather than anything else. The antagonisms of poverty stemmed from the Depression which was already beginning to affect both young and old alike. Youth-Politics and the Depression may have grown side by side, but essentially they were different things.

What, then, of Lewis's larger conclusion? Whether, like Hotspur, the western world had been robbed of its youth or not, *Doom of Youth* certainly makes out an impressive case for the reality of youth-consciousness. As we have seen, it avoids the issue of Youth Politics under the dictatorships, for there no exposure was called for: the ugly facts were glaring the world in the face. But the selection of clippings which Lewis culls from the popular press as evidence of an age-war in Britain is impressive, to say the least. *Open the Door to Youth, Strangling the Young Idea, Open Letter to Today's Young Men, Old Forms or New, Why Youth is Restless, The Spineless Young People, The 'Come-Back' of Youth, I Like This New Generation, Youth at the Wheel, Do You Fear Forty?, The Revolt of Youth, Battle of the Generations, Youths who Really Matter, Youth Must Make Its Own Chances, How Old Are You—A Little Address to the Middle-Aged, Don't Fear Old Age*—the headlines follow each other in a truly remarkable *Gallery of Exhibits*, and might have been multiplied almost indefinitely. Lewis is happy to make the most of them; and certainly no such mass of blathering evidence could have been gathered from the press of any earlier time: until the twenties and early thirties, Youth had been virtually no news at all.

But is Lewis right in believing that the sudden eruption of the age-war had been contrived by a sinister conspiracy of interested elders? That one might be forgiven for questioning. Admittedly, the concept of Youth versus Age had suddenly become saleable copy. And that the Press Barons and Big Business generally stood to benefit by playing the concept up for all it was worth is undeniable. If it had not been demonstrably a circulation builder, the newspapers no less deniably would have called an immediate halt to the campaign. But as we know to the point of infinite boredom, nothing is more calculated to whet the popular interest than the news of a 'row' in which every reader can take sides. As for Big Business, a New Generation is merely a New Market: new fashions, new cars and motor-cycles, new sports goods, new toiletries, new hair-styles, new magazines, films, tunes, cameras and whatever not can be unloaded upon it as soon as it can be persuaded to act as a new consumer-group. And the emergence in the twenties of Youth as a group of would-be Big Spenders was something that Big Business had not been slow to notice. Not so much among the working class, where lowered standards of living had begun to affect all age-groups equally: but the middle classes in particular were beginning to start life earlier, not perhaps because they had been conned into doing so, but because they *wanted* to do so. It was surely a case of demand creating supply; though once the possibility of such a new demand had been recognized, Big Business was only too ready to encourage the trend.

The simple fact was, that during the twenties effective purchasing power had moved far lower down the age-scale. And in view of the enormous losses among the older generation in World War I—to say nothing of the Spanish Influenza epidemic which followed it—what more obvious than that their place in commerce and industry should be taken by younger people? With money earned earlier, these new recruits had money to spend earlier, even if that money was less than an adult wage. The young, after all, lived mostly at home: until they got married, they had less to meet by way of living expenses.

But quite apart from that, tastes were changing and vast new areas were opening up to commerce as a result of new and improved techniques. A new generation requires new products for new interests and new outlooks: it even requires its own kind of music. The sudden arrival of jazz—or that part of modern dance-music which could be dignified with the name—was clearly sponsored by a generation that could afford to pay for it. We have seen an even more obvious example of this in the rise of folk, skiffle, rock and pop music which followed each other after World War II. Without the increasing Wages of Youth, L.P. records, hi-fi, tape-recorders, transistor sets and the rest would have been far slower in finding their way onto the market.

If Lewis had been trained in market research rather than in art, this would surely have been clear to him. He might still have despised the way that such demands lower the standards of taste; he might still have believed that this was acceptable to governments, in the way that circuses had been acceptable to the Caesars; but at least he would have realized that consumer trends can often be set by the consumer.

As for his insistence that the lowering of wages was a prime preoccupation of Big Business—there he was on firmer footing. Brought up as we have been on Keynesian economics, we realize that this simple method of lowering production costs can soon put an end to production itself. But neither Big Business nor government in the thirties had yet got around to reading Keynes. The Depression itself was largely attributable to that fact.

But while we may not always agree with his guess as to the cause of the disease, we are bound to admire the way that Lewis calls attention to its presence and analyses its hidden symptoms. His whole theory of the age-war is of particular importance to our time; and we can only regret that he did not live to consider such recent features as permissive sex, drug addiction and student unrest. As it was, his linking of the age-war with the Youth-Politics of the twenties and thirties was quite significant enough. Even in Britain, Youth-Politics were obviously at work —as witness the *Daily Mail* article by Lord Rothermere from which quotations were drawn in the last chapter. Yet for the most part, Youth-Politics in Britain were probably far more innocuous than Lewis chose to believe. It was only in the dictatorships that they were both avowed and highly dangerous, for there Youth was being doomed in deadly earnest.

The withdrawal of *Doom of Youth* was shortly followed by the withdrawal of *Filibusters in Barbary*, the account of his travels which Lewis had written after a holiday with his wife in French Morocco and the Spanish Sahara. The book had been expanded from another series of articles which had appeared in *Everyman*, and emerged as one of the liveliest travel-books of the time. Like all of Lewis's writing, it was quirky and opinionated, but nowhere was his gift of observation put to happier or more vivid use. It emphasized the fact, said the *Manchester Guardian*, that its author was 'perhaps supreme among contemporary filibusters of letters'; and its suppression after the threat of another libel action was certainly a sad *loss* to letters.

The virtual suppression by the libraries of his novel *Snooty Baronet*—this time, apparently, on the grounds of impropriety! —must have been the final straw of exasperation for Lewis that autumn. Another publisher brought out a portfolio of his drawings in a limited edition—*Thirty Personalities and a Self-Portrait*—as also a revised version of his play *The Enemy of the Stars*, which had appeared originally in the first number of *BLAST*. In the New Year, he also published a hastily written booklet of sixty-two pages on *The Old Gang and the New Gang*.

As a 'development' of certain arguments from *Doom of Youth*, this two-part essay adds little that is of much note. It has all the appearance of having been written not merely in haste, but also in acute irritation—perhaps not surprisingly in the circumstances. It re-states Lewis's theory of the age-war in a sort of told-to-the-morons jargon which is almost reminiscent of Cissy Caffrey—this, says Lewis, because he had been accused of 'writing above his readers' heads'. On the other hand, he coyly admits, this nursery-style is almost certain to enrage his critics by 'making everything so awfully clear', which always seems to 'get their goat'. If any readers at all were as gormless as the 'Mr. and Mrs. Everyman' to whom he was addressing himself, no doubt he got their goats as well, for the first part of the essay appears to be cocking a snoop at anyone fool enough to read it at all!

Once again we hear from Trotsky, 'a funny old Bolshie with a funny old name (it makes us English laugh fit to split ourselves to hear it spoken)', and are told that as regards Youth-Politics the Russians are the 'real past-masters'—all the more so, no doubt since they had exiled Trotsky as one of their Old Gang three years previously! We are also told about old Hitler (ha, ha, ha! It's as though he was going to hit you, isn't it?') who is in the Youth-Politics racket as well. Refreshingly (and accurately, for once) Lewis describes him as 'a military archimandrite' who 'inclines to the warlike, exclusively masculine, end of the business'.[18] He even goes on to tell us that 'Force and Action are the two demons that Hitler and Mussolini familiarly handle',[19] which is a theme that we can only be sorry he did not bother to develop. (For Lewis's ideas on 'Force' see

The Art of Being Ruled, and for his denunciation of 'Action'—
that most Bergsonian of all heresies—see *Time and Western
Man*.)

Instead, we are merely given a few footnotes to Youth-Politics
in Britain. Once again there is a girding at the professional
politician who 'retains his position until an advanced age by
selling and betraying every interest that he affects to represent'.[20]
The Old Gang at home may be an honester gang than similar
gangs abroad, 'but to compensate for that' they are 'a stupider'.
Even so, says Lewis, let us not make the mistake of supposing
that the New Gang who are trying to throw them out of office
will be any better—or any younger. (He might have pointed
out that Lord Rothermere, whom we have heard denouncing
'the old politicians' was sixty-three at the time—which happened to be the average age of Ramsay MacDonald's cabinet....)

Quoting typical age-war articles on *The Missing Generation*,
Lewis goes on to examine why there should be such an unlikely
age-gap between the Old Gang in office and the Youth to which
the New Gang were appealing. *Was* there, in fact, a missing
generation? Yes, Lewis decides, there were even *two* missing
generations. But in political terms, they were not missing because
they had been killed in Flanders: they were missing, as Quintin
Hogg had suggested, because they found it more profitable to
be in the City than to be in Westminster! They might well
have been disillusioned and 'destroyed' by the war, but that was
only a part of the trouble. Politics, like art, were no longer a
viable profession: they had become a hobby for the well-to-do.
And not everyone was willing to 'persevere through three or
four decades in which he may hope to demonstrate his fundamental ineffectiveness and safemannishness'.[21] Understandably,
both missing and younger generations were content to leave
politics to what Quintin Hogg had called their 'less intelligent
contemporaries'. As for the general public, its apathy was due
less to being 'bled white' on the battlefields of 1914-1918 than
to being 'bled white economically ever since'.

Dismissing the shallow irrelevance of the war-poets' wartime
attack on the Old Generals and the flashy journalism of
Remarque's recent best-selling *All Quiet on the Western Front*,
Lewis ends with a warning. Such attacks and sentimentality
only tended to occult and to mask more and more the prime

movers in the *background*'. War, after all, is not made by Old Generals any more than by Young Recruits. And as for the war of the Old Gang and the New Gang, that also provided a dangerous smoke-screen behind which anti-social interests could operate, since Youth-Politics were not waged by Youth. In its emotional roots, all too often the age-war belonged to 'the same mental climate as the Flanders Poppy'.

And that, as we all now know, was a flower that had to be plucked twice over.

NOTES

1. *Time and Tide*, 13.6.31.
2. *D of Y*, p.viii.
3. *Time and Tide*, 27.6.31.
4. Ibid.
5. *Time and Tide*, 11.7.31.
6. *D of Y*, p.107.
7. No more was Evelyn Waugh's brother Alec, who also seems to have felt that he had been over-roughly handled. In a brief consideration of his novel *Three Score and Ten*, Lewis suggests—among other things—that as a 'Youth' agitator he had even eclipsed his younger brother, for whose work Lewis also expressed far greater appreciation.
8. *D of Y*, p.47.
9. *Time and Tide*, 8.8.31.
10. *Time and Tide*, 1.8.31 and 8.8.31.
11. *D of Y*, pp.96-7.
12. Ibid., p.217.
13. Ibid., p.11. There seems to be some confusion here. Big Business could hardly object to money being *spent* on women, since its first principle is to persuade men (and women also) to buy as many luxuries as possible—the less useful and more unnecessary the better.
14. Ibid., p.211.
15. Ibid., pp.26-7.
16. Ibid., p.52.
17. Ibid., p.264.
18. *O G and N G*, p.22.
19. Ibid., p.23.
20. Ibid., p.39.
21. Ibid., p.42.

CHAPTER 7

Right Wings can be Wrong Wings

Fascism had provided no more than the occasional reference for Lewis's treatment of Youth-Politics. And after the disobliging references to Hitler and Mussolini in *The Old Gang and the New Gang*, one might have supposed that it would follow Communism into the limbo of his forgotten enthusiasms. In point of fact, Fascism was still an acceptable stalking-horse for his forays against the economic stagnation and general mismanagement for which he blamed the democratic governments of Britain, France and (latterly) the United States.

No doubt in view of the bad reception accorded to *Hitler*, for the time being Lewis appeared content to leave political journalism alone. The *Notes on the Way* which he contributed to *Time and Tide* in October 1932, for instance, had been mainly *un*political in content. Even so, he could not resist the occasional sally—as witness his reference to the Lytton Report on the Japanese invasion of Manchuria. The recriminations to which it had given support, he felt, seemed 'likely to result in a world-war to prevent the Bad Boy of the Earth at the moment, Japan, from encroaching upon the far-flung territories of that model state, Soviet Russia', and might be seized upon by 'the sympathetic masters of the United States to put off the evil day of final reckoning, bankruptcy and chaos, by a jingo oceanic "Armageddon"—with all the unemployed in khaki, or making munitions.'[1]

But apart from such asides, Lewis during the early thirties appeared to be keeping away from day-to-day politics and confining himself to matters upon which he could write with greater authority. This was particularly the case with the critical essays on literature and art which followed on his coverage of the age-war. In November 1933, he published his satirical verse diatribe *One-Way Song*, in which he returned to his attack upon the Bergsonian heresy, and also took cheerful swings at Ezra Pound (*The Song of the Militant Romance*) and, apparently, the *New Signatures* brigade of Auden, Spender, Day-Lewis and the rest in *Engine Fight Talk*.[2] The book was rounded off with an engagingly autobiographical excursus *If So the Man You Are*, which explains Lewis's position in a jauntily apologetic cake-walk worthy of Archie Rice himself:

> All that I know is that my agents write
> 'Your Hitler Book has harmed you'—in a night,
> Somewhat like Byron—only I waken thus
> To find myself not famous but infamous.
> But what have I done in this most mild brochure,
> Depicting german manners, to be sure,
> Which are so political, what man can write
> Unpartisan, without much of 'Left' and 'Right'?
> If so the man you are to provoke this hate
> I ask myself to what my crimes relate.
> High politics I shun—I gave but an impression
> Of the Berlin scene, in every impartial fashion.
> Are we forbidden (and if so by whom)
> To mention a man in Kun's or Lenin's room,
> Except in belittlement, column after column,
> A 'Germany puts the Clock back' sort of volume?
> I am puzzled by this ubiquitous virulence.
> I ask myself the Whither and the Whence.
> Is it not fitter that the Brit should know
> The sort of sunlessness makes Hitler grow?[3]

There seemed, after all, no reason why the Brit should not.

A year later, *Men Without Art* gathered together and expanded some of the critical essays which Lewis had recently contributed to *Life and Letters* and *Time and Tide*, together with extracts from his *Enemy* pamphlet *Satire and Fiction*, and much that had not previously appeared. As it is a book primarily of literary criticism (albeit with its political flavour) it need not be considered here at any length. It is a stimulating survey, in which brilliant critical analyses (particularly the studies of

Hemingway, Faulkner, Eliot as Critic, Henry James and Virginia Woolf) are built into an overall statement upon satire as art, and a critical system which may or may not hold water. But it had always been Lewis's way to insist upon *some* sort of systemization—this, no doubt, as a result of his philosophical training. And indeed, the fortuitous was always so repugnant to him, that only when it was offered as a necessary factor in some orderly progression, could he accept so much as a cup of tea!

In *Men Without Art*, however, he returns to the subject of *The Terms 'Classical' and 'Romantic'*, and it is interesting to note that his defence of the classical position, while still as forthright as ever, appears to be making some compromise with the times. He realizes—and apparently is now ready to accept—that 'in such enormous, sprawling, proletarianized societies as ours', it is virtually impossible to preserve any true classical values at all. Where Dryden or Pope, Racine or Molière could rely upon it, the proper audience for the modern classicist is lacking; and 'just as it takes two to make a quarrel, so it takes two to make a "classic" work of art'.[4] In an essentially romantic-minded age, therefore, 'the most classically-minded artist would also be the most personal'—a fact which he partly proved by his own example. And after discussing—and discarding—the various concepts of classicism put forward by T. E. Hulme (tainted by Bergson's *élan vital*), Professor Irving Babbitt (who was 'extremely ill-advised to advance his enlightened scholarship as a substitute for religion'), and Ferdinand Brunetière (confusingly contradictory and ascetically arrogant), he goes on to admit that in the modern world the terms 'romantic' and 'classical' are almost without meaning. We continue to bandy them about: 'But it is all extremely artificial—as artificial, for instance, as the Erse names in which the Irish at present masquerade.' Even so, we are expected (and even compelled, to some extent) 'to enter into the spirit of the comedy—that is the humble message of this book'.[5]

In accordance with that message, he follows Hulme in his belief that 'If you asked a man of a certain set whether he preferred the classics to the romantics, you could deduce from that what his politics were.'[6] We have already suggested that Lewis's own identification of authoritarianism with classicism had been responsible for his sudden interest in Fascism during the middle-twenties. In the middle-thirties the course of international affairs was seemingly to revive that interest. For having accepted authoritarianism in general terms as 'classical' and legitimate, he was to find himself hurried by events into a defence of Nazi and Fascist foreign policy. Such a defence, as he continued to point out, in no way meant that he was either a Nazi or Fascist sympathizer himself—at least, not in terms of *internal* politics. Indeed, what he found himself advocating was substantially the line taken later by the British government, whose policy of appeasement lasted longer than his own endorsement of it. Nevertheless, it was unfortunate that he failed to take proper note of Hulme's final conclusion in the political argument: 'it is in taking a concrete example of the working out of a principle in action that you can get its best definition.'[7] For in action, as Lewis and the world was to see shortly, the militarism of Hitler and Mussolini was to define itself as no more 'classical' than the excesses of Genghiz Khan or the Conquistadores.

And although for the most part Lewis had avoided comment upon them, international affairs had been engrossing more and more attention since the days of Hitler's first electoral triumph in 1930. The invasion of Manchuria by Japan the following year had been a faraway event which had made little immediate impact on public opinion in Britain. Even Churchill had regarded it as 'in the interests of the whole world that law and order should be established in Northern China', and seemed perfectly happy to leave the task to Japanese aggression. General agreement seemed to be that such aggression was understandable, irrespective of what America and the League of Nations might think about the matter. In that opinion, as we have seen, Lewis concurred.

His insistence upon the popular support in Germany for Nazi policy (and for Hitler personally) had been justified by the recent course of events in the Reich. In 1932, Hitler had pulled in no less than thirteen million votes in his token bid for the Presidency, and though inevitably defeated by the ageing Hindenburg, no less inevitably seemed destined to win office as Chancellor—which he did a year later. In the last free election that pre-war Germany was to hold, the Nazis polled 44.5% of the national vote.

On the death of Hindenburg in 1934, Hitler had succeeded to undisputed control of Germany as Führer, having already put the domestic affairs of the Nazi Party in order with his Night of the Long Knives. The Nazis of Austria—always obedient to his wishes—had obligingly murdered Chancellor Dollfuss, though they had failed in their bid to win control of the Republic. But the first move towards the future aggrandizement of the Third Reich came six months later, with the result of the plebiscite in the Saar—in which 90% of the electorate voted in favour of reunion with Germany and cheerfully accepted Hitler as Führer in their turn. This particular move—which had been expected—was followed by others that were rather more disconcerting.

By a curious quirk of fate, it was precisely at this point that Lewis was invited to contribute a further series of *Notes on the Way* to *Time and Tide*. Even while he was writing them, rumours were beginning to circulate that France and the Soviet Union were contemplating a pact of mutual assistance in the event of invasion by Germany of either's territory. And although the Soviet Union had been admitted to the League of Nations the previous year, the idea of a Franco–Soviet Pact was to cause more dismay in Westminster than might have been expected. It certainly caused dismay to Lewis himself, as he made abundantly clear. In view of Britain's obligations to France under the Locarno Treaty, any such pact would have the effect of bringing the Soviet Union to all intents and purposes into alliance with Britain—an eventuality which had so far been carefully avoided by British statesmanship. In point of fact, a Franco–Soviet pact was formally announced a few weeks later and ratified the following year. We have Austen Chamberlain's word for it that by many members of the Conservative Party, France's negotiation of such a pact was regarded as 'almost a betrayal of Western Civilization'.[8]

'Western Civilization', of course, was a concept which Lewis had done as much as anyone to promote: indeed, he might almost claim that 'Western Man' was his own invention. He clearly regarded himself as deeply involved in any events which might be held to threaten either. And his current series of articles in *Time and Tide* gave him just the chance that he needed to declare the fact. All that he had been quietly resenting over the years in what he regarded as the Left-wing trend of current political journalism rose to the surface and found expression. All that he felt he had been blamed for unfairly, four years back, in his 'expounding' of Hitlerism now impelled him to prove how right he had been. And in view of the fact that Britain was obviously at the critical point where she must soon decide, for better or worse, where her right course lay for the future—what could be more natural than that Lewis should make the decision for her, and point her the way in which her vital interests were to be served? During the next four years, his views upon foreign affairs were to take up much of his writing time. And as he was to admit, ruefully enough, after the Second World War was over—the time might well have been better spent.

The first of Lewis's *Notes* appeared in *Time and Tide* on 2 March 1935, and at once entered the plea which he was to reiterate regularly throughout the thirties:

> The world of Letters and of journalism is a 'Left-Wing' world. No student of politics can afford only imperfectly to grasp, much less to neglect, that momentous fact. The newspapermen of Fleet Street, as much as the 'intellectuals' of Bloomsbury and Hampstead, are ninety per cent 'Left-Wing' in sympathy. All the best advertized 'authors' are 'Left-Wing' in sympathy. Indeed, it is impossible to be a really well-advertized author unless you are 'Left-Wing' in sympathy. You *must* be a spiritual child of Macaulay—with a mind open on the side of Trotsky, but a mind shuttered on the side of Burke. To write, apparently, in England at this time, is to be 'Left-Wing.'[9]

It is interesting to remember that Lewis himself had begun as 'a spiritual child of Macaulay'—at least to the extent of quoting him on the subject of Frederick the Great in *The Lion and the Fox*. But even allowing for a change of opinion, there seems to be something highly exaggerated in his estimate of Left-wing sympathy in Fleet Street! The *Daily Mail* was very much of his own opinion on the subject of Hitler, and allowing for the fact that they might beg to differ with him, Lewis was hardly justified in lumping *The Times*, the *Morning Post*, the *Daily Telegraph*, the *Daily Sketch*, the *Daily Express*, the *Sunday Times* and the *Observer* along with the *Daily Worker*, the *Daily*

Herald, the *News Chronicle*, the *Manchester Guardian* and
Reynold's News! On the other hand, one has to realize that so
far as Lewis was concerned at that time, the Left-wing stretched
'from Baldwin to Pollitt'. That being so, perhaps it was hardly
surprising to find him complaining that journalistic opinion
was in fact not so much Left-wing as *One*-wing—'because there
is no Right there worth the name, to establish the duality'.

Needless to say, not many members of the Left-wing would
have been ready to agree with him—nor, for that matter, would
many members even of the Right-wing. The Labour Party at
least were less prepared than Lewis to accept Sir John Simon's
assertion that 'We are all Socialists today'. No more would
Lewis have been prepared to accept Stalin's assurance that the
British Government represented the forces of Fascist reaction.

The simple fact emerged that for Lewis—at this critical
juncture—everybody was Left-wing who did not happen to see
eye to eye with himself. That which was not avowedly classical
was necessarily romantic: all who were not wholeheartedly
with him were against him. Middle-of-the-road opinion—which
most opinion in Britain undoubtedly was—represented something which he declined to recognize as such. At the same time,
oddly enough, he insisted upon the fact that he himself was in
no way committed to either Right *or* Left: he declared his
neutrality and flew 'the flag of no party'. He admitted that the
term 'Left-wing' was no more than 'a convenient, though rather
ridiculous, term, which covers everything from the gentle
dreams of brotherhood of the Quaker sect to the "ruthless"
fanaticism of the Marxist'.[10] But in that case, the term 'Right-
wing' might equally have been held to cover everything from
the conservatism of the country vicar to the rabid truculence
of Mosley's Blackshirts. And as any Left-winger of the time
might have forecast British foreign policy over the next few
years was to be so Rightist—in its mildly British way—as to
endanger the future of Western Civilization indeed.

For although he could never bring himself to realize as much,
for all practical purposes, the British Government was often
almost embarrassingly of Lewis's own opinion. And as regards
its distrust of any involvement by treaty with the Soviet Union
—at that stage, at least, the same could well have been said of
the Opposition. Indeed, it was not so much with foreign policy

that Lewis was really at odds: it was with social trends as a whole. He had taken upon himself to swim against the *Zeitgeist*, and after ten years he was beginning to find the exercise not only tiring but also increasingly thankless and unrewarding.

For the last couple of years, as it happened, Lewis had been seriously ill. He had been in and out of hospital, had been operated upon to no purpose, and consequently been able to work only fitfully. As a result, he had found himself 'unusually hard up', and clearly his illness had left him with a sense of being unfairly discriminated against in certain quarters— quarters which were, he believed, some ninety per cent of the whole. If so, the discrimination was not merely due to his political opinions, but also to his expressed opinions on the nature of government and the future of society itself. The world was at variance with him, in fact, on the subject which had first engaged his attention—the art of being ruled. About this, his first *Notes on the Way* were quite specific:

> Not to be aligned, more or less, upon the side of society ... that accepts the regulation ideologies of Progress (the non-acceptance of which it stigmatizes as 'negative')—the side who as one man thrill (more or less) to the clamours of the salvationist politician's ballyhoo, is to be under a cloud perpetually. For my own part, I have been conscious for a long time of being under a cloud, and I have perfectly understood the nature of that cloud.
>
> To be penalized for one's unpopular opinions, because they are not conventionally 'Left-Wing' ones, has become commonplace with me.[11]

As the next few years were to show, Lewis did not allow the fact to stand in the way of his expressing unpopular opinions as he held them.

In order to understand just what Lewis felt he was being 'penalized' for advocating in March 1935, we must remind ourselves of the general reaction—in Britain and France—to the rising militancy of Nazi Germany. The coming to power of Hitler in 1933 had left France with a growing fear of attack by a revived German Army: her own arrogance in the twenties, when Germany had been helpless to resist her occupation of the Ruhr, no doubt contributed to her alarm now that Germany appeared to be growing strong once more. At the 1933 Disarmament Conference, Germany had firmly demanded military parity with France—which France in turn regarded as utterly unacceptable without adequate insurance. Her counter-proposal that parity would not be conceded unless her own security was fully guaranteed by Britain, in full and effective military alliance, was equally unacceptable to the British Government, which felt that the vague generalities of the Locarno Treaty were all that should be expected of them. By way of breaking the stalemate, Germany had withdrawn from the Conference, preparatory to her withdrawal from the League of Nations five days later. The inference was that she now intended to rearm at her own discretion, and in defiance of the terms of the Treaty of Versailles. This, in point of fact, she had been doing ever since.

In view of this threat, two policies were in course of being debated in Britain: reciprocal rearmament on a similar scale, or a wholehearted committal to the principle of Collective Security, in which all members of the League of Nations should bind themselves to resist aggression within the terms laid down in the Covenant. Few were in favour of the first course, very many in favour of the second—though without a measure of re-armament 'Collective Security' had little meaning. It was not for another year that Churchill was to accept the corollary, and adopt his policy of 'Arms and the Covenant' in contradistinction to his previous policy of rearmament alone.

It will be remembered that the principle of Collective Security had not before been accepted in Britain as a policy which could be taken altogether seriously. Nobody had really supposed, in 1931, that the Japanese invasion of Manchuria should be countered by either military intervention or even sanctions under the terms of the League Covenant. The Lytton Report into the affair had found Japan guilty of aggression, for which she had been duly 'condemned' by the League, from which she had promptly withdrawn. Apart from a few more speeches, that was the end of the matter. But the rearming of Nazi Germany was very much nearer home than Manchuria, and posed more immediate problems. If it were to result in an attack upon France, what—if anything—would Britain do to assist her? More to the point, without rearmament, what *could* Britain do to assist her? Obviously, this was a matter of some consequence —to the French, at least.

As some sort of gesture—to our own security no less than to that of France—on 4 March 1935, the British Government had published a White Paper on the urgent need for limited rearmament. (This White Paper bore the initials of the Prime Minister—James Ramsay MacDonald—though these had apparently been printed by mistake!) Two weeks later, loudly protesting that Germany was being 'encircled' by predatory enemies, Hitler replied by introducing conscription.

Coming as this did, halfway through his series of weekly articles, Lewis had two more *Notes on the Way* in which to discuss the implications of the move. Since the White Paper itself had singled Germany out as a potential aggressor, he found it natural enough that Hitler should have reacted as he did. Now, said Lewis, *all* countries are in breach of the terms of the Treaty of Versailles.[12] So having precipitated the crisis, what policy is Britain proposing to follow? And he proceeded to give his own analysis of the course which international affairs were taking. The standpoint from which he argued he described as that of an 'isolationist'—a standpoint, of course, which had already been created for him by Lord Beaverbrook in the *Daily Express*. Apart from isolationism, Lewis maintained, only two other policies could be considered. The first would associate Britain with the Franco-Soviet bloc which was already forming, and this he denounced as being a pro-Communist alignment which was wholly unacceptable. The other would be to establish understanding with Nazi Germany (which he felt need not imply any threat to French interests), and this policy he warmly supported.

While he was insisting upon his own 'isolationism', in fact, it was really the policy of 'understanding with Nazi Germany' that he was advocating. Isolationism, after all, would have involved support of neither France *nor* Germany. But unless it was to emerge as out-and-out pacifism (which Lewis disavowed) it would surely have implied a heavily armed neutrality. That in its turn would have implied rearmament, since general *dis*-armament had been rejected by everyone else. But even the limited rearmament which the White Paper was suggesting he had blamed as being provocative and only calculated to antagonize Hitler further. After all, Hitler would be easy enough to mollify, 'if we would only let him alone and not alarm him with every imaginable warlike threat of relentless encirclement'.[13]

Lewis can hardly be blamed for *not* advocating isolationism: one merely wonders how he came to believe that he was doing so. The isolationist position, after all, was not really tenable in a world where it was generally supposed—as Stanley Baldwin had assured the nation—that 'the bomber will always get through'. Common sense dictated a policy either of 'understanding with Germany' (always providing that this was practicable) or of 'understanding with France' (backed up either by a Soviet guarantee, or by full Collective Security within the League, or best of all—by both).

It was not merely that Lewis was convinced that this latter policy would inevitably lead to war (as it did): he was equally convinced that a new understanding with Germany was the surest way of safeguarding peace. He was convinced that understanding with Germany was being resisted by government and press alike on purely ideological grounds, out of a mistrust of Hitler and his authoritarian policies which Lewis did not share. In any case, as he saw it, authoritarianism as such was not the point at issue: it was rather a case of which *kind* of authoritarianism—Nazi or Communist. It was not merely the choice between Germany and France which Britain had to make, but the choice between Germany and the Soviet Union. And Lewis was not even sure that the choice remained open: 'it looks, from all the signs, as if the die has been cast upon the side of Russian Communism by our "conservative" rulers.'[14] And two weeks later, he sums up his attitude in these terms:

> All that I have said implies no particular partiality for Germany, nor yet any animosity for the French people, need I say, for whom I have the greatest affection. It is not the *beaux yeux* of Adolf that I am thinking about. I am solely concerned with the interests of England, which I, in common with a great many other people, regard as threatened by this incomprehensible policy, which sends Mr. Anthony Eden to Moscow this week.[15]

In the event, of course, Lewis need not have worried so much. The only result of Mr Eden's visit to Moscow was a nice fur hat and his name on an underground railway station.... But supposing that Nazi Germany were to be finally put down—with

British connivance—by France and the Soviet Union (both of which were 'feverishly arming'), Lewis wondered what could be expected of the future. 'If "the Allies" were successful,' he warned, 'and Germany for ever abolished, England would find itself comparatively unarmed, facing an all-powerful Continental coalition, with which it had nothing further in common, once the German bogey was out of the way.'[16]

The simple fact was, of course, that Lewis could *see* no German bogey. He could only see Hitler as the chosen leader of the German people—chosen because he promised to right the wrongs which they believed they had suffered at Versailles and ever since. He felt that after some sixteen years of territorial spoliation and occupation, crippling reparations and general ostracism, it was perfectly understandable that Germany should wish to rearm. It was certainly no more 'illegal' under the terms of the Versailles Treaty than was the continued increase of armaments in France, to which nobody appeared to take exception. Germany's declared aims did not seem to him aggressive or dangerous in any way: she was demanding no more than the right of every nation to security in its dealings with questionable neighbours. As for her internal politics, that was a matter for Germans alone to decide: it was up to them to manage their own affairs in any manner they chose. Only an obstinate determination by other powers to keep her in a state of vassalage could render Germany potentially dangerous, for such interference she was no longer prepared to tolerate. Britain had nothing to gain by alienating German friendship: she had everything to gain by deserving it. One hardly needs to add that a large number of people in Britain felt exactly the same about Germany at that time.

Nevertheless, there were many who felt very differently—some of whom took issue with Lewis in *Time and Tide*. A letter from John Brophy enquired whether it was not a fact that 'the only reason Germany has for resenting "encirclement" is her desire and intention sooner or later to burst her present frontiers by force of arms?'[17] Louis Golding, whose *Notes on the Way* followed Lewis's own, remarked indignantly that Lewis's apparent indifference to Germany's treatment of the Jews was worthy of *Der Stuermer*, let alone *Der Voelkischer Beobachter* or *The Blackshirt*—a charge which Lewis denied with equal indignation. And in the same issue (April 4) a long article by Sir Norman Angell, printed as a *Foreign Affairs Supplement*, came down firmly in favour of an agreement with the Soviet Union in a policy of Collective Security as the only possible means of safeguarding peace in Europe.

To Sir Norman Angell's article, Lewis replied in strangely prophetic terms:

> An alliance or entente today can only be a highly complicated matter, in which a country would find itself, before it knew where it was, risking its independent destiny in the defence of some obscure frontier or remote littoral, of which it had never so much as heard, at the other end of the world. And England (in contradistinction to Russia and France) has nothing to gain by engaging in any arrangement of that kind, but rather everything to lose.[18]

One is inevitably reminded of Neville Chamberlain's reference, at the time of the Munich betrayal, to 'a quarrel in a far-away country between people of whom we know nothing'! Perhaps the similarity of thought was not entirely fortuitous. For the policy of 'understanding with Germany' which Lewis was advocating—under its new title of 'Appeasement'—was subtantially the policy which the British Government was later to adopt.

Having once become embroiled with foreign affairs, it seems, Lewis was unable to let them alone. The pugnacity of The Enemy remained as great as ever, and he began to expand his ideas into book form once again. Even as he did so, however, events in Europe were running on ahead of him. In April 1935, the creation of the 'Stresa Front' (in which MacDonald, Laval and Mussolini agreed to resist any German moves against France or Italy) may well have exasperated him: it was one more example of the 'encirclement' of which he had been so critical. On the other hand, he must surely have been mollified by the Anglo–German Naval Treaty, which was signed on 18 June, and which completely undid any good which Stresa might have hoped to achieve. Not only did this new agreement disregard the Treaty of Versailles to the extent of 'allowing' Germany to build a new navy up to 35% of the strength of Britain's own (including a fleet of hitherto forbidden U-boats), but it also withheld from France all details of the naval plans which Germany had disclosed to us in confidence! As it had not even been consulted, the French Government understandably regarded this little matter as a virtual betrayal of faith. Mussolini, on the other hand, regarded it as an indication of the way in which Britain would probably react to a little buccaneering on his own account. Four months later, his troops invaded Abyssinia. Five months later again, Hitler's troops marched into the Rhineland. A plebiscite promptly declared that 99% of the German people were in favour of his action.

The book in which Lewis attempted to keep up with—and to explain away—these rather alarming events was originally to have been called *Bourgeois-Bolshevism and World War*—hardly a title calculated to win friends and influence people. In the event it emerged, in June 1936, as *Left Wings over Europe: or, How to Make a War About Nothing*. In this guise, it was much better received than many of Lewis's polemical books and was reprinted within a couple of months.

It is easy enough, with the benefit of hindsight, to disagree with most of the arguments that *Left Wings over Europe* advanced. A large body of opinion—not all of it Left-wing opinion, by any means—disagreed with them at the time. On the other hand, Lewis's sincere belief in the rightness of his arguments is undoubted, as also the fact that the book was motivated by nothing so much as a passionate desire for peace, and utter horror at the idea of Britain's becoming involved in another European war. Put at its simplest, the book was intended as an appeal to common sense: it was a plea that Britain should cease endangering her own interests by opposing either German aspirations in Europe or Italian aspirations in Africa. Such aspirations, Lewis insisted, were legitimate, and in no way put Britain's own security at risk. Playing watchdog for the League of Nations, going bail for a policy of Collective Security with the Soviet Union, endorsing Litvinov's contention that 'Peace is indivisible', and imposing sanctions against Italy over Abyssinia—these were the very last things that Britain should be doing. They were courses which were being forced upon her merely by Left-wing pressure: far from being in her own interest, they were the shortest way of making the world safe for Communism. The ready sale of the book showed that many people were prepared to agree with him.

Left Wings over Europe, in fact, has two main themes: what is so wrong with what Hitler and Mussolini are doing, and why is Britain reacting to it so violently? Remilitarization of the Rhineland was the more topical issue when the book was published, but Mussolini's invasion of Abyssinia while Lewis was actually writing it supplied an equally controversial talking-point. At the Stresa Conference, Mussolini had seemed no less anxious than the French to put a check upon German militarism. He still regarded himself, at that time, as vitally interested in maintaining the independence of Austria; and the days of the Rome–Berlin Axis were still undreamed of—at least, by Britain. With Italy's own emergence as an aggressor-nation, however, Mussolini had suddenly cast himself in a role similar to Hitler's own. And as Italy, unlike Germany, still remained a member of the League of Nations, he was to find himself faced at Geneva with the first retaliatory gesture offered against aggression since 1918.

When Lewis had been writing about 'obscure frontiers' to be defended, he could have thought of none more obscure than those between Eritrea, Italian Somaliland and Abyssinia. The admission of Abyssinia to the League of Nations in 1923 (under Italian sponsorship) had been opposed by Britain at the time. The various tribes within its frontiers were largely at odds with each other, and apparently agreed only in their practice of slavery and the castration of prisoners. As Winston Churchill was to remark, one could hardly 'keep up the pretence that Abyssinia is a fit, worthy and equal member of a league of civilised nations'. Yet when Mussolini had taken international law into his own hands and launched an old-fashioned imperialist foray into Abyssinia in defiance of the Covenant to which Italy had subscribed, the League reacted in a way that appeared to surprise him.

There was no great enthusiasm on the part of France for branding Italy as an aggressor and applying sanctions against her, as the Covenant of the League demanded. The initiative for that had come simply and solely from Britain, and the policy had been endorsed by the other member-nations with varying degrees of enthusiasm, if not downright reluctance.

Nor was Britain herself prepared to insist that the sanctions should really be made to bite: the Suez Canal was not closed to Italian troopships, and petrol was still made freely available for Italian planes and tanks. Never at any time was it suggested that Italy's defiance of the League should be met with military or naval force: the French fleet certainly had no intention of joining the Royal Navy in any such hazardous exercise. Why, then, had sanctions been resorted to at all, since they were necessarily ineffective, and did no more than antagonize an ally whose continued support had seemed so important towards keeping the peace of Europe? Why indeed? said Lewis.

Whatever reason really lay behind the British stand at Geneva, he insisted that one factor could be ruled out from the start: 'there is practically no one, outside of Colney Hatch, who believes that there is a spark of sincerity in the purely moralistic aspect of the dispute.'[19] Holding, as Britain did, the largest colonial empire in the world, it was hardly enough for Mr Eden to assert that colonial conquest was now 'anachronistic'. Who made the rules by which it had become 'anachronistic' so conveniently for ourselves? Was Britain perhaps afraid that the conquest of Abyssinia would lead on to an invasion of the Sudan—which would give Italy control of the headwaters of both the White and Blue Niles? Might it even lead on to an invasion of Egypt, once it lay between the pincers of an Italian Abyssinia and an Italian Libya? Was it the Red Sea route to India that Britain feared was being endangered? If so, the Government of India Act, passed by the same British Government in August, had been a strange way for them to strengthen our imperial hold on the sub-continent! None of these possible reasons could be sufficient in itself, Lewis felt. Was it perhaps Britain's interest in the Middle East oilfields that the trouble was really about? Did we fear that Mussolini would set himself up as the Protector of Islam—or even as 'mandatory overlord of the Jewish National Home'?

On balance, Lewis was prepared to favour the theory that the whole Genevan exercise had been in the nature of a dress rehearsal. It had been designed to test the effectiveness of League solidarity with a view to organizing punitive measures in due course against Germany. But in that case, as he failed to stress, nothing could have been better calculated to convince Hitler that the League was a nuisance which he could safely afford to ignore. In any case, how could the 'dress rehearsal' theory be squared with the open encouragement of Hitler which had been given by the Anglo-German Naval Treaty? Lewis confessed to finding the whole policy behind modified sanctions 'mysterious', but fell back upon his belief that once again it pointed clearly to 'interests pushing us towards a far more spectacular and comprehensive "kill" '.[20]

So once again we are back with the 'superior will' which had haunted his theorizing since *The Art of Being Ruled*. On the other hand, he was now prepared to exonerate the British Government of any deliberate Machiavellism: 'If a "Machiavelli" is at large, and pulling the wires, I do not believe he is to be looked for inside the British Cabinet.'[21] French beliefs to the contrary, no doubt, stemmed from the natural distrust of 'the Staviskified politicians of the Third Republic'.

But wherever the hidden pressure originated, there was no question in Lewis's mind that it was inimical to British interests. Back in the twenties, our government had been rightly suspicious of the League, and had refused to support the French—whose instrument it then was—in their attempts to rally support for 'the more bloodthirsty passages' of the Geneva Protocol. Now, it seemed, exactly the opposite was the case: Britain herself had begun to dominate League politics—but for whose ends? In Lewis's opinion, the only ends being served by League politics in 1935 were those of Moscow. So far as the democracies were concerned, the Covenant had merely become an instrument of repression, which could be used to enforce the Versailles writ to the last letter: it was the reactionary guarantee of an indefinitely extendable *status quo*. Or would be, if either Germany or Italy were prepared to accept it as such....

Admittedly, Italy had emerged at Versailles on the side of the victors: she had subscribed to the Versailles writ herself. On the other hand, she had reaped very little benefit from that writ. Unlike those of Britain and France, her colonial empire had not been extended by the addition of any territory—mandated or otherwise. As Mussolini saw it, the invasion of Abyssinia had been no more than a redressing of the balance. But at the same time it was a declaration to the world that Fascism was a new force to be reckoned with:

No one, I think, approves particularly of Mussolini's taste, or admires his idea as to *where* or *how* to start a war of liberation. His fellow 'fascists' in Germany certainly do not. That he was not guilty of an error of judgment, from the military stand-point—as was at first asserted—is now obvious, however. And that the industrious and ingenious Italian, rather than the lazy, stupid and predatory Ethiopian, should eventually control Abyssinia is surely not such a tragedy. But it is as a sort of war of liberation, that these events in Abyssinia and Geneva must, essentially, be regarded—as an act of national self-assertion rather than as an irresponsible predatory raid.[22]

Where the statesmen of the Great War had declared it 'a war to end war', Mussolini, being 'very rhetorical', had declared on the contrary that '*this* war of his is a war to bring war back into its own again—almost a war for war's sake'. That being so, one is only the more surprised that Lewis should appear to be condoning it. But who—or what—was it really a war against? Lewis believed that Sir Walter Citrine had probably put the case most succinctly when he had assured the T.U.C. at their Brighton conference that they 'will be defending Soviet Russia in defending Abyssinia'. Whatever that may have said for Sir Walter's reasoning, it goes a long way to explain Lewis's.

Quite certainly, the moral argument for sanctions was no more convincing to many Members of Parliament than it was to Lewis himself. L. S. Amery was particularly loud in his denunciation of the Eden stand at Geneva. Probably most of them felt that the watchful presence of Italian troops on the Brenner Pass was of far more interest to Britain than the con-tinuing independence of the Abyssinian tribesmen—or even the Negus himself. J. L. Garvin in *The Observer* described the publicity and the pressure with which Geneva had tried to deter Italy from her invasion as 'unheard of in the annals of statesmanship at critical times'. And though he condemned the Italian aggression in retrospect as 'unsuited to the ethics of the twentieth century', Winston Churchill remained tactfully silent about it at the time. As for the suggested imposition of *military* sanctions against Italy, George Lansbury preferred to resign the leadership of the Labour Party rather than compromise his stand for Pacifism; and there were many who regarded even economic sanctions as representing a highly dangerous precedent.

Yet Lewis need not have been so cursory in his dismissal of the 'moralistic' implications of British policy. Though it was generally loth to commit itself to 'moral' or 'ideological' positions, the National Government was sensitive enough to public opinion. And this had been made abundantly clear to them in the Peace Ballot organized by the League of Nations Union. The results of the Ballot, declared in June 1935, had shown over ten million voters out of eleven and a half united in what A. J. P. Taylor has called 'a ringing assertion of support for collective security by all means short of war, and a more hesitant support even for war'.[23] It was no accident that in their election manifesto the following November, the government had firmly declared that: 'The League of Nations will remain, as heretofore, the keystone of British foreign policy.' And when news of the cynical Hoare–Laval Pact leaked out shortly afterwards, with its promise of an 'accommodation' with Mussolini, public outcry drove Sir Samuel Hoare from the Foreign Office and replaced him by the pro-Covenant Anthony Eden in a matter of days. The power of 'moral issues' to unite public opinion was something which Lewis was apt to under-estimate. But no more convincing proof of that power need be looked for than the speed with which it enabled Baldwin to wind up the abdication of Edward VIII a year later.

There can be no doubt at all that public opinion was very much at the back of the stand which Britain took over Abyssinia. And it is worth remarking that it was the government, rather than public opinion, which quietly put an end to sanctions once the conquest of Abyssinia had been completed. For by then, the voice of Neville Chamberlain had made itself heard in foreign affairs, and appeasement was in a fair way to becoming the government way of life.

When *Left Wings over Europe* was being written, that policy had not begun to emerge very clearly, though sanctions were called off a month after it was published. To that extent, therefore, Lewis had successfully anticipated the new government line, though he could hardly claim to have influenced it. But far more alarming to Europe than the Italian victory in Abyssinia had been Hitler's remilitarization of the Rhineland two months earlier.

The abdication crisis had boiled up into a nine days' wonder and had been quickly disposed of to the satisfaction of Stanley Baldwin, Mrs Baldwin, the Archbishop of Canterbury, the editor of *The Times* and the British public—in that or any other order. The Press Lords, no less than Winston Churchill, had been unable to save Edward VIII from the moral indignation of public opinion. Laval had fallen from power in France shortly after and been replaced by a caretaker government under Sarraut. A month later the Franco–Soviet Pact had been formally ratified—and a week later again, Hitler had denounced the Locarno Pact: 35,000 German troops marched west to resume their interrupted Watch on the Rhine.

It has been variously argued that the British refused a French appeal for military aid to evict the German troops; that they had encouraged the French to go ahead with their own mobilization; that they had refused Litvinov's appeal for League Sanctions against Germany; that they had tacitly 'invited' the Germans to make the move in the first place; that they had offered to buy Germany off with the offer of at least one colony; that they had missed the one great opportunity of stopping Hitler when they had the power to do so; that they never had the power, but that all subsequent disasters had been made certain by their failure to make even an appropriate gesture.

The plain fact remains that there was no great inclination in Britain to take the German defiance very seriously. After all, the Rhineland was German territory: it was faced, in France, by the strongest military defences and installations in the world. The French had shown no great eagerness to assist Britain in imposing a decision by force upon Italy: why should Britain show any more eagerness to support France in the present instance? As the phrase went, the Rhineland was Germany's own backyard: she had every right to walk back into it. Furthermore, to confuse the issue thoroughly, Hitler had at the same time offered a twenty-five year Non-Aggression Pact to both France and Belgium, which Britain and Italy were invited to guarantee. He had even offered to bring Germany back into the League of Nations if the pact were accepted.

The response of the British press was mixed but hardly very

helpful. The *Daily Mail* declared that 'like a fresh breeze from the mountaintops' the German action had 'swept away the fog' and shown the world exactly where she stood. The country was solemnly warned against 'the Bolshevik trouble-makers', whose one aim was 'to involve the great Powers of Europe in a suicidal war'.[24] Indeed, for all the things that Lewis had said about the way that the Press Lords indoctrinated the public, the leader might well have been written by himself! The *Daily Telegraph*, on the other hand, regarded the German challenge as 'pointed, direct and deliberate, such as the signatory Powers of Locarno cannot possibly overlook'.[24] *The Times* and the *Manchester Guardian* sat side by side on the fence, drawing a careful distinction between the reoccupation of 'territory indisputably under German sovereignty, and an act which carries fire and sword into a neighbour's territory'. Along with the *Daily Herald*, indeed, they were agreed that the German offer of a twenty-five year pact should be carefully considered, *The Times* even hailing it as amounting to 'A Chance to Rebuild'. As on a more famous occasion later, the *Daily Express* assured its readers that Britain would not be involved in war—and on this occasion, at least, they happened to get it right. Nobody was.

In the House of Commons, opinion was almost unanimously in favour of caution and keeping Britain safely out of any further trouble: after all, sanctions were still in force against Italy. A month before the crisis arose, Lloyd George had expressed the opinion that Britain herself had been responsible for creating the atmosphere of fear against which Germany was bound to react. Now that she *had* reacted, he said it again—admitting that Germany had been rash, had been reckless, and had broken yet another treaty. Nevertheless, he felt, 'in a court of equity she would call evidence which any judge would say provided some mitigation of her fault'. At which point, *The Times* reported, there were (Cheers). (Lewis made a great play with *The Times* reports of both these speeches, which supported most of the arguments which *Left Wings over Europe* was advancing.) It was probably felt on many sides that if France felt herself in any danger, the Soviet Union would no doubt provide a sufficient guarantee of Hitler's good behaviour in the West. And if one of these days Hitler were to move East—in concert with Poland, perhaps?—Lewis probably spoke for the government side of the House at least when he enquired: 'What of it?'

What both Government and Opposition speakers knew equally well—whether they admitted it or not—there were very few British troops available for making a show of force in the Rhineland, even in *token* support of a French action. The fact that Hitler (as subsequently disclosed) had been prepared to pull back before the first sign of retaliatory action appears to have occurred to nobody at all! It does not even appear to have occurred to Churchill, who may perhaps have been misled by his own over-estimate of the degree of German rearmament at the time. According to his own account, the French had been told categorically by Baldwin that Britain could not support her if there was 'one chance in a hundred' of French intervention provoking a war. The French insisted that unless German provocation was stopped by force forthwith, war was inevitable in the near future. Churchill had apparently felt that the first move should be made by the French themselves: the danger, after all, was upon their own doorstep. But though his immediate reaction to the idea of intervention had been somewhat equivocal, he quickly came round to the French point of view— provided that intervention was decided upon by the League of Nations as a whole. This, he felt, was not a matter for one or two nations to decide among themselves. The spirit of Locarno was gone for good: the Stresa Front, intended to revive it, had fallen irreparably apart. All that remained was the Covenant of the League, and a policy of Collective Security in defence of it. Though he certainly did not speak for British opinion as a whole, within a month Churchill was calling loudly for 'the noble acceptance of risks inseparable from heroic endeavour— to control the hideous drift of events and arrest calamity upon the threshold'. His reaction to 'the hideous drift' was clearly stated: 'Stop it! Stop it!! Stop it now!!! NOW is the appointed time.'[25]

Unfortunately, Lewis was far from being alone in regarding Churchill as a 'firebrand', and his warnings against German rearmament as so many 'alarmist diatribes'.[26] A public opinion poll would probably have shown some three-quarters of the British people as sharing his suspicion. And Churchill's insistence upon Collective Security within the League was what Lewis remained at most pains to combat. Retrospectively, in

Rude Assignment and elsewhere, he claimed that he had been privately in favour of instant intervention over the Rhineland —in which Britain and France should have acted on their own initiative. If that was the case, talk of Collective Security caused him quickly to change his mind, for there is certainly no hint or suggestion to that effect in *Left Wings over Europe*, published three months later. The book is a vigorous defence of Hitler's entire policy up to that time, and accepts his proffered twenty-five year pact at something above even its face value. Lewis refuses to believe in the 'German menace' any more than Lloyd George believed in it. He believes that Germany's fear of 'encirclement' was behind every move she had made since Hitler came to power. He believes that Collective Security is no more than an instrument of Soviet intrigue at Geneva and that the Russians could hope for nothing better than to set Germany and Britain at each other's throats. He believes that should France and the Soviet Union dispose of Germany in the way they would like to do, the time must surely come when they would turn their attention to Britain also. And with Germany subjugated, Britain would find herself without a single friend or ally in Europe.

Lewis's belief that Hitler was only too anxious for cordial relations with Britain was not without its corroboration in *Mein Kampf* (if Lewis had got around to reading it) but his vision of Hitler as the misused suitor of Britannia is none the less amusing for that! One is glad to see his tongue thrust firmly into his cheek as he imagines the scene:

> Year in and year out, like a love-sick supplicant, Herr Hitler pays his court to the haughty Britannia. Every insult that can be invented even by the resourceful Mr. Churchill is tamely swallowed, every rebuff of Mr. Baldwin's, every sneer of Mr. Eden's, is meekly accepted, by this pertinacious suitor!
>
> When Britannia darkly conspires with France and Soviet Russia ... it makes no difference. There is no change in the attitude of Adolf. He just sadly shakes his head over all these heartless proceedings, of the siren of his predilection, and brings round his customary bouquet next morning. And if Britannia in a tantrum at his persistence ... flings back the posy at this old-fashioned—almost operatic—*inamorato*, he only picks it up, dusts it with a quiet, unaffected, pathos, and places it against his heart, under his rough homespun swastikaed tunic.

I am prepared to prophesy that when all the rest of the world has turned its back upon this unkind and greatly envied Mistress of the Seas, that the faithful Adolf will still be there—offering her his strong right arm (if she will not accept his heart and hand) for her defence against her enemies. And, still disdainful, it may be that Britannia will be compelled to accept.[27]

Only the genius of David Low could have done justice to an ironic vision—or an incredible delusion—such as that!

But apart from his complete misassessment of what Hitler really stood for—a misassessment which Lewis made in common with many of his political betters—perhaps the most surprising aspect of *Left Wings over Europe* is its complete reversal of all that Lewis had previously written on the subject of Internationalism. One can perhaps understand his refusal to accept the idea that peace is indeed 'indivisible': that the phrase should have been coined by the Soviet delegate to Geneva would be enough to blind him to its obvious truth. And that France should have sought for safety in a pact with the Soviet Union was perhaps enough to make him side with Germany in violent opposition to that pact. But it was not merely Soviet Communism, apparently, which Lewis had come to distrust. It was the whole Internationalist concept of which he had been so strongly in favour ten years previously.

Left Wings over Europe states the question bluntly: ' "Are you for the Super-state of Internationalism, or for the Sovereign State of non-International Politics?" '[28] And where he would once have answered 'For the former', Lewis is now constrained to insist that he is no less firmly for the latter. Internationalism is become for him the new heresy, the weapon with which Geneva and the League are seeking to destroy the very concept of sovereignty. For the arch-exponent of the self-sufficient, independent and sovereign state, clearly enough, is now Fascism. Therein lies the 'evil of Fascism' as the League—and Britain herself—had come to denounce it. But by sinking herself within the group responsibility of League politics, Britain is divesting herself of every last iota of her *own* sovereignty. She is subjecting herself to impersonal, centralized power in the same way that by learning to take their orders from Washington, the forty-eight States of the Union were surrendering their sovereignty in America. And as Lewis states emphatically at the start of *Left Wings over Europe*: 'As truly as Mr. Roosevelt, or Mr. Litvinov are *centralizers*, the writer of this book is the reverse. Centralized power—when it is human power—is for me, politically, the greatest evil it is possible to imagine.'[29] As exercised by Hitler, and dispensed throughout Europe in the making of his so-called New Order, centralized power was to prove itself *exactly* that. As exercised by Roosevelt in the United States, Lewis was later to find a great deal more to be said for it.

As we shall see, Lewis's renunciation of the Internationalist ideal was to be no more than temporary. It had merely been forced upon him by his desire to keep Britain out of dangerous entanglements in Europe. He was concerned, above all, to keep Britain out of war—whoever were to declare it, and whoever else were to be involved. Such a desire, it seemed, could not be squared with an Internationalism which carried with it responsibilities of the part towards the whole. And oddly enough, not even his predilection for authoritarianism could reconcile him to the prospect of subservience to the League: 'For, be it observed, no corporate state would be so corporative, nor any totalitarian state so thoroughly totalitarian, as the super-state envisaged at Geneva—a United States of the World, in short, controlled by a highly centralized internationalist executive.'[30] How far can a sudden back-somersault take one?

In *Rude Assignment*, Lewis dismissed *Left Wings over Europe* as 'quite unimportant'. He described it as 'a violent reaction against Left-wing incitement to war', which we can accept it as being—if we can first accept Lewis's identification of the Left-wing with virtually the whole of the political spectrum! He explained further, that he was then (1950) 'in complete disagreement' with much that the book had advanced, and had particularly changed his mind as to the evils of centralized power and the virtues of the sovereign state. By the time he wrote *Rude Assignment*, in fact, he had reverted to the Internationalist ideal which he first set out to promote in *The Art of Being Ruled*. He was not to renounce that ideal again.

NOTES

1. *Time and Tide*, 22.10.32.
2. The latter swing he denied in a letter to *New Britain*, 13.12.33.
3. *O-W S*, pp.53-4.
4. *M W A*, p.190.
5. Ibid., p.204.
6. Quoted Ibid., p.201.
7. Ibid.
8. Quoted in *The Anti-Appeasers*, by Neville Thompson, p.36.
9. *Time and Tide*, 2.3.35.
10. Ibid.
11. Ibid.
12. *Time and Tide*, 23.3.35.
13. *Time and Tide*, 9.3.35.
14. *Time and Tide*, 16.3.35.
15. *Time and Tide*, 30.3.35.
16. Ibid.
17. Ibid:
18. *Time and Tide*, 13.4.35.
19. *L W o E*, p.180.
20. Ibid., p.196.
21. Ibid., p.75.
22. Ibid., pp.164-5.
23. *English History, 1914–1945*, by A. J. P. Taylor, p.379.
24. *Daily Mail*, 9.3.36. These and the following editorial comments are quoted in *The British Press and Germany, 1936–1939*, by Franklin Reid Gannon, p.94ff.
25. *Step by Step*. p.19.
26. *L W o E*, p.25 and p.119.
27. Ibid., pp.330-1.
28. Ibid., pp.268-9.
29. Ibid., p.16.
30. Ibid., p.57.

CHAPTER 8

Ned and the Dead

The war in Abyssinia came to an end in May 1936 with the fall of Addis Ababa and the flight of the Negus. Sanctions against Italy were withdrawn by the League of Nations on 15 July, having achieved precisely nothing. Three days later, military risings in Morocco and Andalusia announced the outbreak of what was to become the Spanish Civil War. To those who knew anything about recent political events in Spain, the news was not altogether unexpected.

The troubled condition of the Spanish Republic in the years immediately before the war broke out had given Lewis the idea for one of his finest novels, *The Revenge for Love*. But by one of those infuriating delays to which authors are frequently subject, it was not to be published until the war had been fought for ten months and was in a fair way to being lost by the Republican Government. Not unnaturally, the appearance of a 'pre-Civil War' novel at that particular time was almost in the nature of an anti-climax. Its plot, which hinged upon a slight case of Communist gun-running (a single car-load of machine-guns), appeared somehow trivial when the International Brigades were defending Madrid, when Guernica had just been blown to bits by German bombers, and when Italian tanks and 30,000 Italian troops were battling (not very successfully) for General Franco.

Nevertheless, Lewis was right to regard *The Revenge for Love* as one of the most important and completely successful books that he had written. It is a brilliant novel of character, rather than a study of non-topical events. Its unheroical protagonist, the Communist agent Percy Hardcaster, is certainly among the best drawn characters that Lewis ever created. So are many of the others—the snobbish pseudo-Communist Gillian Phipps, her vulgarian lover Jack Cruze, and the tragic surrogates Victor and Margaret Stamp, whose love for one another invites the fates to exact revenge by their utterly pointless destruction.

Lewis was no lover of Communism, and he has much to say about it in *The Revenge for Love*: it is Communist intrigue on the Spanish border which provides the story with its frightening culmination. But here for once, Communism is accepted as a fact of life—and one which can even be treated dispassionately as the sincere faith of a professional revolutionary. Communism, to the working class Percy Hardcaster, is a lethal weapon to be used against the classes which he regards as his natural enemies: he knows its true potential and he is prepared to employ it ruthlessly. For the sham-Communism of the intellectuals, he has nothing but contempt—and it is a contempt which Lewis wholly shares. Professionalism of any kind, he is ready to respect: but the posturing of the fashionable amateur excites in him only hostility and disgust. To Lewis, as to the true Communist, the parlour pinks turned out by the public schools and universities of the thirties were just so many more Apes of God —the God on this occasion being Lenin. Their enthusiasms and allegiances were those of a social set rather than those of a social need. The true Communist was prepared to accept their services, while this could prove useful to the Cause: but ultimately they too were the enemy—and as such they would be treated when the time came. Which, says Lewis, it is only right and proper that they should be, if by their own stupidity they have helped to put themselves at risk.

Unfortunately, this cool appraisal of Communism in action was not always carried over by Lewis into his political pamphleteering. And if the uneasy prelude to the Spanish Civil War was to inspire one of his finest novels, the war itself was to give rise to perhaps his worst political squib. For if it is the privilege of every author to write one thoroughly bad book, Lewis availed himself of that privilege with *Count Your Dead: They are Alive! or A New War in the Making*.

Count Your Dead takes up the argument for an Anglo-German *rapprochement* where *Left Wings over Europe* had left off, using the issue of 'non-intervention' in the Spanish War as an additional ground for attacking British policy in Europe. Having already tried direct pontification to small purpose, however, Lewis this time tries a more oblique presentation of his case. For in *Count Your Dead*, he falls back upon the device of assuming a *persona*—that of an eccentric egocentric who goes by the name of 'Ned'. A three-part statement (of some eighty pages) in which 'Ned' explains his own standpoint serves to preface the main portion of the work—the supposed manuscript of some twenty-four 'Thoughts' which had been written down under his influence by a deceased friend, one Launcelot Nidwit. As Nidwit's literary executor, Ned purports to edit these 'Thoughts' and supplies occasional footnotes: the 'Thoughts' themselves are based upon conversations that he has had with Nidwit during the course of the war in Spain. The book was published in April 1937 and follows events up to the end of that February.

The ubiquitous Ned is a curious character, to say the least of him, and as cynical, hard-boiled, arrogant, snooty and 'naughty' as Lewis probably liked to imagine that he was himself. In the course of teaching his fatuous Nidwit to see things as they really are, to think for himself and renounce false doctrine as preached to him by the press and the politicians, Ned drives the poor fool to his death. As he himself puts it: 'He died, as a fact, from an overdose of the truth. This I myself deliberately administered. I foresaw that it would kill him. For I recognized that the amount of what-was-real that his system could safely absorb was strictly limited.'[1] The reader is invited to try the experiment for himself—though it is hardly likely that he will be tempted to *identify* himself with Nidwit, whom Ned dismisses contemptuously as 'the most consummate imbecile' he had ever encountered. And certainly, if any of Lewis's own acquaintances provided the general outline for the character, he must have been just that!

There is a curious reminiscence of the Pulley–Satters relationship in *The Childermass* about Ned and his disciple. But where Satterthwaite had been brilliantly drawn, one can only say that Launcelot has been drawn and quartered. As Ned explains him, he is the typical London clubman, and may or may not have been typical of the breed as it still existed in the thirties. (Maybe a similar exemplar may still be found lurking behind the leather in the Athenaeum—though it seems unlikely.) But perhaps his kind may be recognized in one of his 'typical' *obiter dicta*:

Germany *will* not accept Russia as a 'friend'. And we shall jolly well have to go to war with her again if she doesn't: that's all about it. Any fool can see that. That is the long and short of it. We cannot stand by and see one country treated by another in the way Germany does Russia—calling her a 'Bolshie' and all the rest of it! It's a bit over the odds. What have the poor Communists *done* after all to be treated in this beastly way? They would never harm a fly—at least not a British fly. And they drank the King's health in honour of Mr. Eden, didn't they, and have called one of their tube-stations after him. They can't do much more than that. They treat Russians a bit roughly sometimes, I'll grant you. But what are Russians after all but savages—half Chinks and dreadfully brutal, inclined to be Bolshie into the bargain. So it's only natural they should have to be a little severe with them, now and then. Besides, we don't always treat our *own* people so well as all that. One must see the other fellow's point of view. It's a good old British maxim.[2]

As will be seen, the Thoughts of Launcelot Nidwit—or his 'thinking aloud' as he likes to call them—are not of a kind that need to be taken very seriously. He is merely there as a foil for Ned himself—or perhaps one should say as a football.

Like the Lewis of that time, Ned is a convinced anti-Internationalist. He describes himself as a 'Tory-Bolshevik' or a 'Bolsho-Tory', being an 'anti-Russian Bolshie' and an 'anti-J. Bull Tory'. The Leader of the Bolsho-Tories, he explains, is Mr Baldwin—whom he feels free to criticize if only to prove that he is 'not the sort of man who could ever live under a "dictatorship"' —still less 'under the vile rule of some oppressive Fascist Caesar'.[3]

His main criticism derives from his belief that his Leader is clearly a Russophile. This would seem to be established by his Leader's continuing to maintain a close *entente* with France despite the existence of the Franco-Soviet Pact. To this, as a good Tory, Ned feels that he must take exception—also, he adds, as a good Bolshie. He wishes that Baldwin was not so much on the side of the arch-capitalists whom, as a good Bolshie, a good Tory and a good *democrat*, he loathes with 'a Baldwinian savagery' as so many 'dictators'. But then—what is one to expect? And quoting the *Evening Standard* to the effect that 'Mr. Baldwin as Leader of the House of Commons is a ruthless dictator',[4] he goes on to indict the parliamentary system itself—at least, when exemplified by the National Government of the time—as *'a fake antique'*. Baldwin himself he is forced to regard as something of a fake John Bull, and 'the "democracy" which he never tires of trumpeting' as a fake in itself. Government in Britain, in fact, is in the hands of 'a financial directorate', who are in business to hobble the world with 'Loan-Capital', as defined by Herr Feder, instead of enlivening it with 'Creative-Capital' as was (apparently) being done in Germany. As the spiritual home of 'Loan-Capital', London is continuing to connive at 'the conditions of "want in the midst of plenty" which prevail in every country today'. As such, it is even the spiritual sponsor of Marx and all his kind, since *'without* those conditions ... there would be no Communism'.[5] Which is no doubt the reason that there is such a strange affinity between the protagonists of Loan-Capital and the rulers of the Soviet Empire!

This is indeed in the nature of original thinking, though it has a familiar ring to it here and there. But it is perhaps worth remarking that while pursuing his friendly flirtation with Loan-Capital, Stalin was also busy purging those old-guard Bolshevik comrades of his who were rather less cordial in the appreciation of it—a fact which Ned fails to adduce in support of his unusual theories....

His attack on the non-freedom of life under democratic government, of course, is merely a repetition of what Ned might well have read in *The Art of Being Ruled*. But he is on rather newer ground when he proceeds to indict the British class system—or more specifically, the English variant of it. He is probably right when he complains that in no other country are the social barriers against the under-privileged so rigid and unscaleable. And with some irony he goes on to quote the *Manchester Guardian*—biased against Nazism as it was—to the effect that the society in process of formation in Germany was a truly 'classless' society. He is careful, of course, not to quote

some of the *other* things that the *Guardian* had recently been
saying about the joys of life in the Third Reich.

The one thing which Ned cannot understand about his
Leader, is why he insists on being so *beastly* to the classless
Germans. In particular, why must he always be so beastly to
the classless Führer? There is no doubt in Ned's mind that Mr
Baldwin is almost pathologically prejudiced:

> Germany is the arch trouble-maker. Everyone could sleep peace-
> fully in their beds; no one need have any arms or gasmasks; the
> world would be a Utopia; everybody would be *prosperous*; there
> would be no Distressed Areas; Mr. Baldwin could lay down the
> Premiership; King Edward VIII would never have met Mrs.
> Simpson; Mr. Roosevelt could give his undivided attention to
> 'the Forgotten Man'; there would be no influenza epidemic
> (which started in Berlin); the Thames would not heave with in-
> dignation and overflow its banks—*if it were not for Herr Hitler.*[6]

For this truly amazing situation, Ned can find no plausible
explanation: he can only rub his eyes in astonishment. But
such being his Leader's attitude to the Führer, and seeking as
he does to thwart all Germany's legitimate aspirations in
Europe, there can be small doubt as to the outcome. It will
almost certainly result in war—a war that, as far as he can see,
'would be an entirely purposeless one'.

All this appears no less deplorable to Ned than it did to
Lewis himself. Like Lewis's own, his interest in Germany had
always been slight. He had preferred the Latin mind to the
German mind. He was certainly not *pro*-German: he was as
little pro-German as he was anti-Semite, for instance.[7] But in
whose interest was it that Germany should be outlawed and
ostracized in the way that she found herself to be? Why was
the Soviet Union so much to be preferred as an ally?

There is no need to insist upon Ned's independent identity
any longer: obviously enough, he spoke very largely with
Lewis's own voice—a trifle more idiosyncratically, perhaps, but
mostly from the same inner convictions. Yet before we grow
too sceptical about their strangely similar protestations of im-
partiality and their mutual denials of any pro-German sympathies, it is worth examining just what could be said in favour

of those convictions. For whatever he was to become later, Hitler had certainly not become—for most people at that time—the incurably Bad Boy of Europe. His record, up to the Spring of 1937, had certainly been dubious, but it had not yet become utterly indefensible.

As Führer, he had made it abundantly clear that he was in no mood to accept the condition of Germany as he found it, or to abide by covenants which he felt had been wrongfully imposed on Germany by others. He had defied the Versailles Treaty by introducing conscription, by rearming generally (in naval terms, with Britain's express agreement), and by remilitarizing the Rhineland. Like Italy and the Soviet Union, he had flagrantly intervened in the Spanish Civil War, and (unlike Britain and France) had declined to intervene in the Abyssinian crisis. He had offered the democracies a twenty-five year Treaty of Non-Aggression—which he had only failed to implement, perhaps, on account of the Franco–Soviet–Czech Pacts which he denounced as 'encirclement'. He had admittedly threatened ultimate aggression in the East—since *Lebensraum* was necessary to the Reich—but had threatened nothing of the sort in the West. For Britain, as he had declared in *Mein Kampf*, he continued to profess the most friendly feelings: nor did the return of the German colonies appear to be too high a price to pay for continuance of them. So far as internal policy went, alone among the nations of Europe Germany seemed to be overcoming the problem of unemployment.

Unless one had an instinctive distrust of Hitler himself; unless one believed that he was secretly determined to push the world into war and impose his will upon all who could not stand up to him, there was as yet no reason to regard Germany in any way as a potential enemy. If one regarded the Soviet Union with suspicion; if one believed that the intrigues of the Comintern were indeed a threat to democracy everywhere; and if one regarded Hitler as Europe's strongest bulwark against the spread of Communism, there was every inducement to accept him as a potential ally. And a large proportion of the British press at that time were still prepared to do so sincerely —including *The Times*, the *Sunday Times*, the *Observer*, the *Daily Telegraph* and the *Morning Post*, quite apart from the *Daily Mail*, which had been so charmed by his irruption in the first place. Lewis was therefore far from being alone in his convictions.

There were many aspects of Nazism which revolted liberal opinion, just as there were many aspects of Stalinism which shook all faith in it as a better alternative. Hitler's rabid anti-Semitism was particularly distasteful, but was little worse than the anti-Semitism which prevailed throughout Central and Eastern Europe. His violent Russophobia seemed completely irrational, since Germany was committed to government on equally totalitarian lines, but it was acceptable to many who dreaded the spread of Communist influence: at least Hitler accepted Capitalism as a main prop of the Nazi way of life. As for his recent persecution of the Christian churches, this was only another form of the anti-clericalism which had been born in Paris and had found more recent expression in Moscow and Madrid. There were many people—both liberals and conservatives—who disliked all these aspects of Hitlerism, but were prepared to disregard them in the interests of international amity. There were even a few who were prepared to defend them.

But it was not so much because he believed in the virtues of Hitlerism that Lewis had adopted the line he did in the earlier thirties. If he was prepared to accept the Germans for what they were, it was certainly not because he did not know them. As already mentioned, *Tarr* had made perhaps the most telling analysis of the German psychology in contemporary fiction. Its anti-hero Kreisler embodied all the German traits which had made Nazism possible: he was not only the explanation of Nazism, he was its embodiment. The arrogance, the brutality, the callousness and the hysteria—all are there, as all were to be found in Hitler himself. And if Kreisler had been 'doomed evidently', Hitler was equally so—as Lewis subsequently admitted. But it was not with the Germanic qualities of Nazism that Lewis was then concerned. Nor was it with the unpleasanter aspects of life in the Third Reich—for these he did not have to share. The only question which had any weight with him was whether, on balance, Germany was less dangerous to Britain as an ally than as an enemy.

Count Your Dead was written, he states, in realization of the fact that the days of Palmerstonian diplomacy were past. Britain could no longer impose her will upon Europe: she must now accept Europe as she found it, and try to keep it roughly that way. To that end, concessions would undoubtedly have to be made, which meant that so far as Germany was concerned, appeasement would be the wiser course. Apart from which, it might even be regarded as a defensible course, since German demands to date had mostly been reasonable. Resistance to those demands would only provoke her to try and gain her aims by military force.

Like many other people, Lewis at that time believed the only real danger to lie in the disruptive ambitions of militant Communism. That the best guarantee against Communist imperialism could be found in a strong and vigilant Germany, was an opinion that he shared with most of the British statesmen of his time, although he did not appear to realize as much. What he did not share with the wisest of them was the realization that a strong and militant Germany posed a far more dangerous threat to peace in Europe than a militant Soviet Union. Stalin and what was left of Russian Communism, after all, were preoccupied with other matters: apart from the purges, there was the current Five Year Plan, upon the success of which the strength of the Red Army was ultimately dependent. The Soviet Union was not yet strong enough—even if it had wanted to do so—to over-run the rest of Europe. Germany under Hitler, on the other hand, was rapidly coming to the conclusion that she could.

As to the war in Spain, Lewis was just as convinced as Winston Churchill that it had been brought about solely by Communist intrigue and Russian intervention in Spanish domestic affairs. Franco's rebellion had merely forestalled a Russian-inspired seizure of power by the Spanish Communist Party. This may well have been the case; but as now seems probable, it was only with reluctance that Stalin agreed to Soviet intervention in the Spanish Civil War once it had actually broken out. There had indeed been political intervention by the Comintern, whose agents had been busy in Spain since the declaration of the Republic in 1931, and that must certainly have had his blessing. But it was not until the formation of the International Brigades, three months after the war broke out, that Comintern intervention could rightly be described as 'military'. As for direct military aid from the Soviet Union, this did not begin to arrive till later still. And though it must have been decided upon much earlier, Hitler and Mussolini had already made it perfectly obvious that neither had any intention of pulling out the troops, tanks and planes already in action.[8] Still less had they any intention of observing the Non-Intervention Agreement which they cheerfully signed along with the Soviet Union, France and Britain—and which Britain at least was trying to implement.

The fact probably was that in the summer of 1936, the Soviet Union was far more interested in cementing friendly relations with Britain and France than she was in endangering those relations by too ready an intervention in the Spanish War.[9] The Franco–Soviet Pact had been ratified that February, and it was still Stalin's hope that Britain could be induced to identify herself with its terms of mutual defence. After all, Spain was a long way from Moscow, and it was a great deal nearer home that trouble might be expected from German expansionism. The Spanish Communists could be left to take care of themselves, and as the driving force behind the *Frente Popular* they were well placed to do so—until German and Italian intervention had begun to weigh in the balance against them. Whether the Spanish Communists, without that intervention, would have been strong enough to put the Insurgents down, and then take over the government for themselves, is a matter for speculation. Quite possibly they might have been. But in the event, one thing is clear enough: the scale of Soviet aid was quite insufficient to save them from total defeat once Italo–German intervention had become a fact. And Stalin is not reported to have shed too many tears for them, once they had finally succumbed.

Feeling as he did about the menace of Communism, Lewis could hardly have been expected to accept this reading of events, even if the true facts had been readily available to him —which they were not. Even so, the account of the Spanish Civil War which he gives in *Count Your Dead* is biased, to say the least of it. And considering that he knew Spain reasonably well before the war, it is also rather misleading. So far as he is concerned, no parties were fighting in defence of the Republic other than the Communist Party. As for the disturbances which had torn the Republic apart for the previous five years—the church burnings and the horrible atrocities—these again are blamed *solely* upon the Communists. There is no suggestion that they might equally well have been laid at the door of the Anarchists (the F.A.I. and the C.N.T.) or even of the Trotskyists (the P.O.U.M.) who were all quite certainly involved in many of them. Yet in the report of the disorders and political murders in Valencia and Barcelona (which Lewis quotes from *The Times*) it is expressly the C.N.T. and the F.A.I. which the report blames for the troubles there. And while he himself declares that 'half the Spanish proletariat' are Anarchists, he draws no inference from the fact except that they will probably 'have to be wiped out by the Marxists' for that reason! As Nidwit sees it:

> on the whole Marxism is making a new man of the Spaniard. His 'rugged individualism' will be a thing of the past in twelve months' time. All the 'individualists' will be killed off ... and the rest, under a good stiff Red Terror, will toe the line. Probably Don Moses, or whatever Red Boss is there to do it, will have to pick off upwards of ten thousand pure Anarchists, perhaps more. Anarchists have to be killed just like vermin. If you want law and order, there's nothing else to be done with them, our Communist friends say. Then things will be nice and quiet.[10]

If the 'thought' is Launcelot Nidwit's and the irony Lewis's own, the sentiment would seem to have been shared by the Insurgents. Only the Insurgents, of course, would have included the Communists in the general massacre, just as the Communists would have included the Insurgents....

According to Lewis, all that the wilder Insurgents ever indulged in was a little mild retaliation:

> When the troops of the Legitimate Government vacated the town of Ronda, the Rebels who had had the impudence to drive them out found five hundred corpses, most of them with toothpicks stuck in their eyeballs and their tongues sawn out (and most of these were not Fascists, only not manual workers). One or two English newspapers had a spasm of reactionary indignation. It was rather funny to watch.
>
> But luckily before that wave of namby-pamby sentimentalism could go very far, it was reported that Franco had started a few reprisals. In a mild way, it is true. He hadn't the guts to do it

properly, and use toothpicks. And he respected his enemies' testicles.

Violence breeds violence in the long run—as a tactless police-man who kicks his captive in the stomach usually finds. In Badajos a lot of men who had been picking off Moors from roof-tops got the goat of these bloodthirsty Blackamoors, who, when they sur-rendered, put a bullet in them, to teach them not to snipe once the battle is over.[11]

Nidwit's 'snipers' were the estimated 2,000 defenders of Badajos who were rounded up and massacred in the bull-ring. How Lorca was killed in Granada has never been quite established—or why. No doubt it was in reprisal for something serious—as with the other 5,000 killed there. Or the 7,000 killed in Navarre, or the 9,000 in Valladolid or the 20,000 in Seville or the total 200,000 estimated to have been executed by the Insurgents up to July 1937.[12]

Whichever side might have claimed the greater diligence in the way that it conducted 'reprisals', there cannot have been very much in it either way. It might have been wiser for Lewis to admit that the appalling savagery of the Spanish Civil War was attributable first and foremost to the inbred cruelty of the Spaniard himself, and that it had little to do ultimately with Fascism or Communism or Anarchism. That cruelty, after all, had long been exercised in the name of the Catholic Faith—most notably, perhaps, in the Low Countries, in Mexico and in Peru. It had given birth to that most Spanish of all institutions, the Inquisition, which had popularized the *auto-da-fé* as a wel-come alternative to the perpetual bull-fights. Perhaps Lewis *did* realize that something more than mere politics was involved in the Spanish war; for at least he accepted the Peninsula as a further extension of Africa, and admitted that Europe—as we like to think of it—ends at the Pyrenees....

But though the manner in which it was fought out might be regarded as peculiarly national, the ideologies at issue gave the Spanish Civil War an almost universal significance. It has been said that no war in modern history divided opinion in Britain more sharply or more vehemently. Lewis can hardly be blamed for taking sides in an argument which was embroiling the whole country. The concept of General Franco as 'a gallant Christian gentleman' had been presented to him by a well-known Conservative Member of Parliament. The sinister role of 'Señor Don Moses Rosenberg' had been discovered for him by J. L. Garvin of the *Observer*—and any resemblance to the Soviet Ambassador to Spain, Marcel Rosenberg, was largely coincidental. One is not surprised to find 'Ned' accepting Garvin's assurance that Don Moses 'is the real master of the camarilla called the "Spanish Government"', and indeed there is nothing about the Spanish War in *Count Your Dead* which J. L. Garvin might not have written for Lewis, the political slant of the *Observer* being what it then was.

Once again, in fact, Lewis was ignoring the validity of a middle way. Those who were unwilling to commit Britain to a policy of out-and-out aid to Franco were automatically in favour of a Communist Spain. Those who viewed the prospect of a victorious Rome–Berlin–Madrid Axis with dismay (most notably, the Popular Front Government of Léon Blum) were working hand-in-glove with the Soviet Union to encircle Germany! The fact that the British Government was working—hopefully but quite unsuccessfully—to enforce the Non-Intervention Agreement which it had tried to impose upon reluctant neighbours, was dismissed as clear evidence of their connivance in clandestine intervention by the Soviet Union and France herself. And the fact that so-called Non-Intervention was operating overwhelmingly in favour of the Insurgents was conveniently overlooked!

We can appreciate why Lewis's predisposition in favour of his Christian gentleman should leave him strongly critical of the way that the war was being reported by correspondents writing from Madrid. One can understand why he should be exasperated by pro-Republican sentiments as expressed in debate by British Members of Parliament. ('It is common knowledge that eighty per cent of the present members of the House of Commons would vote for Communism in Spain, if it lay between Communism and Fascism.'[13]) One can see why it should annoy him that there were far more British volunteers fighting in the International Brigades than with his friend Roy Campbell (in the *requetés*) on the side of the Insurgents.[14] Indeed, it would have been surprising otherwise.

But one finds it harder to understand why he should feel that the National Government of Mr Baldwin (Ned's respected

Leader) was working implacably to secure a victory in Spain for World Communism—even to the point of conniving at and condoning political atrocities.[15] Quite obviously both Mr Baldwin and Mr Eden were pursuing the old-fashioned British policy of sitting on the fence while events took their appointed course. No doubt they would have been more enthusiastic about the Republican cause if it had not been so openly dependent on Communist support. They would probably have been more sympathetic to the Insurgents than they were, if Franco had not been so obviously dependent upon the Axis powers. But things being as they were—and Mr Baldwin's lips being sealed as usual—they were content with trying to maintain some sort of balance between the two sides, while committing Britain effectively to neither. In this, of course, they succeeded in rousing not only the wrath of the Garvin–Lewis faction: they angered the liberal Opposition faction even more.

The fact was, however, that for Lewis—as for everyone else in Europe—the war in Spain was merely an embittered prelude to something far less localized and far more catastrophic. Apart from questions of legitimacy, humanitarian values, religious allegiances or even a fondness for lost causes, reaction to the war in Spain was generally indicative of reaction to something else. For most people, it was not so much a question of who should govern Spain: it was far more a question of who should govern Britain—or rather, in alliance with whom Britain should still attempt to govern herself. Europe was being cleft down the middle, and soon survival would require a taking of one side or the other—alliance with the Left or the Right. The only other course was a taking of no side at all: the sort of isolationism that was being preached by Lord Beaverbrook and Viscount Rothermere. But apart from their lordships, very few people were quite convinced that isolationism was viable; and the course of events would seem to suggest that in the modern world it no longer was.

So we return to the real point at issue: where did Britain's interest lie? Not in alliance with Communism, says Lewis, and not in further antagonizing the Axis powers. That way lies nothing but disaster. For unlike the Axis leaders themselves, he is convinced that a Second World War can result in nothing but a victory for World Communism. The possibility of an

Axis victory—in despite of an Anglo–Franco–Soviet alliance—is something which he never even considers. Nor does he once consider the likelihood of the war being *started* by one of the Axis powers: it is always them—and more particularly, Germany—against whom a war is about to be launched.

The message of *Count Your Dead*, therefore, is that Britain should play no part in launching such a war; that she should refuse to play the Soviet game in alliance with pro-Soviet France; that she should cease to align herself with the Communists in Spain against Franco's crusade for law and order; and that she should cease to bully the Axis powers whenever they strove to assert their legitimate rights.

That message was certainly not acceptable to Left-wing opinion in Britain at the time; but the fact remained that Britain did not have a Left-wing government—despite Lewis's belief that Stanley Baldwin was the spiritual comrade of Harry Pollitt. To the Left-wing, it seemed that the National Government was in fact pursuing exactly the policy which Lewis demanded that they should. There was *no* disposition to conclude an alliance with the Soviet Union on any terms, nor was one ever concluded until the Soviet Union was itself attacked in 1941. There was *no* alignment with the Communist side in Spain: the policy of Non-Intervention, which Britain was doing her utmost to implement, could lead to nothing but a victory for the Insurgents—as it ultimately did. There was *no* serious attempt made to deny the Axis powers anything that they could get away with, as Britain's acceptance of the *Anschluss* and her part in negotiating the Munich Agreement would shortly make depressingly plain.

But it was not merely with what he supposed to be Britain's foreign policy that Lewis found fault. In *Count Your Dead*, as elsewhere, he continues to blame the National Government for its utter failure to deal with the problem of unemployment:

> By common consent all issues except those of Foreign Policy have been banished from our political life. This suits everybody. Mr. Attlee likes it because *he* doesn't want to discuss Distressed Areas, or anything of that sort. Mr. Baldwin likes it, because *he* doesn't. And both are in hearty agreement that since the nationals of all other countries are more interesting than those of our own, and that only a 'Fascist' is a 'nationalist' (for Mr. Baldwin means

no harm by the use of the word 'national' in *National Government* and everyone knows it) that Foreign Affairs are the only affairs worthy of a wise man's attention.[16]

That the plight of the Distressed Areas was due to the anomalies of the monetary system was an idea that Lewis shared with many other intellectuals—most notably, perhaps, with his friends Yeats, Eliot and Pound. (Joyce, of course, was interested only in linguistics.) He believed, as they did, that the economics of the thirties were far too 'conservative' in their approach to poverty (as indeed they were) and that 'it is thanks to the toughness of the cortex of "conservative" England that the maggots inside are enabled quietly to gut the country'.[17] Main maggot at work in the soft centre, he believed, was 'Loan-Capital'—of which Mr Baldwin himself was the subservient if unwilling tool. Lewis is even persuaded that 'after he has gone I am sure that he believes that some lovely William Morrisish sort of Webb-like Soviet will take his place'.[18] But, says Ned–Lewis, 'Marx with his dreadful plan for helot states is *not* the only solution. My leader [Mr Baldwin still] would excommunicate me if he could hear me, but Fascism is at least a better solution than that. I will be thoroughly naughty, and say that Fascism might be a very good solution indeed.'[19] We are to understand by that, no doubt, the 'modified form of Fascism' which *The Art of Being Ruled* had once suggested 'would probably be best' for the Anglo-Saxon countries.

With that 'naughty' suggestion before us, it is inevitable that we should wonder whether, in fact, Lewis himself was not the Fascist that he always denied being. ('Fascism is a revolt of the People. A revolt against debt. I am no Fascist. But I love Freedom. Also I hate Usury.'[20]) Yet we must be careful not to fall into Lewis's own mistake of presuming that a measure of agreement—on specific points—constitutes whole-hearted acceptance of a political creed on *all* points. Unwilling as he might have been to admit it—along with Baldwin and Chamberlain, Attlee and Churchill, Lewis clearly remained in the middle—right of centre maybe, but none the less in the middle. He would commit himself to *neither* extreme.

As already noted, he was of the opinion that 'to get some

sort of peace to enable us to work, we should naturally seek the most powerful and stable authority that can be devised'.[21] That the 'stable authority' of the Soviet Government under Stalin had come to fill him with horror, he made abundantly clear. That Mussolini's brand of 'stable authority' had failed to impress him for very long, we are at liberty to deduce—his opposition to sanctions over the Abyssinian war notwithstanding. (That, after all, he shared with Chamberlain, Amery and large sections of the British press.) And that his initial interest in Hitlerism had stemmed from a belief that here at last might be the 'stable authority' which he had anticipated, we may take for granted. In fact if a Hitler had not been forthcoming, at some stage Lewis would probably have been tempted to try and invent one. (He later gave it as his opinion that Hitler *had* been invented—but not by him!)

He had not been alone in championing the early intransigence of Hitler: that had been championed by Vernon Bartlett and many other liberals, insofar as it called attention to the injustices of the Versailles *diktat*. Many British statesmen of the time had been willing to excuse it; and at most, it was the methods by which Hitler achieved his ends—rather than the ends themselves—to which exception had first been taken. As for the policy of appeasement, which Neville Chamberlain was to substitute for the wary non-committalism of Stanley Baldwin and the League-mindedness of Anthony Eden—that was acceptable to the majority of politicians and (almost certainly) to the majority of the electorate. At least, it was acceptable until the rape of Czechoslovakia in March 1939 dispelled the last illusions about Munich.

Lewis was unusual only in his conviction that Fascism had an answer to the problems of poverty no less than to the anomalies of uneasy peace. Yet there was, after all, some reason for that optimism as well. For although it had been largely by Hitler's programme of massive rearmament that German unemployment had been cured, an equally massive expenditure on public works had certainly contributed to the cure. (That the *Autobahnen* were built with a view to military needs is really beside the point.) A similar programme of public works under the New Deal was rapidly coping with the effects of the Depression in the United States. And many more people than

Lewis were angered by the fact that only in Britain was almost nothing at all being done to cope with the miseries of poverty and unemployment. If economic stagnation was the price that had to be paid for democratic government, then might not the price be too high?

It was the posing of that particular question which had divided intellectuals during the early thirties. Many, like Auden, Spender and Day-Lewis, had thought to find a better alternative (theoretically) in Communism. Others, like Sir Oswald Mosley, after failing to win parliamentary support for a forthright economic programme, had turned to the flashier showmanship of Fascism. Mosley had quickly been joined in that political blind alley by all who liked donning their black shirts and raising their right arms in the usual rituals of xenophobia. But Lewis had not been one of them. As an individualist, he preferred to remain on the outside, where he was free to look in and carp.

In his capacity of individualist, it is worth remembering that Lewis did indeed contribute an article to the first issue of the *British Union Quarterly*, which was dated January–April, 1937. This was entitled *'Left Wings' and the C3 Mind*, and explained his function in life as being 'not to teach Communism, Fascism, or Democracy, but to whirl a bullseye round upon all that its ray will reach'—the C3 mind in Britain being then in the ascendant. As the article is now hard to come by, it might be worthwhile giving the drift of it—for it must have caused many a simple Blackshirt to scratch his baffled head! (It is not recorded whether Lewis was asked for a further whirl of his bullseye: if so, he does not appear to have come up with it.)

Politely declining the Editor's invitation to criticize the Fascist movement in Britain (which had been done by others), Lewis launches one more attack on the one-sidedness—or left-sidedness—of contemporary literature and journalism in Britain. For supposing that he were to say 'something very nice about Fascism, just for fun, and *pour changer un peu*', then he knows only too well that 'ninety per cent of the Public would stamp and snort, in imitation of its morning paper'[22]—the remaining ten per cent, perhaps, being readers of the *Daily Mail*. The Marxists, he feels, have had it their own way uninterruptedly for eighteen years, and he sees it as everybody's business, 'whether he be a "Fascist" or merely an open-minded citizen, with a taste for liberty', to try and redress the balance. This he proceeds to do, in much the same terms as in *Count Your Dead*, which he was busy writing at the time. Non-Intervention is decried as a convenient cover for French and Russian military aid to Spain; 'Moses' Rosenberg is back on the job; and even T. S. Eliot is lined up among the Left-wingers since 'his slight aversion to Communism is counterbalanced by a more recent aversion to Fascism'.[23] (In the days of the New Party, Eliot had spoken well of Mosley's programme: he had rather withdrawn support of late.)

In a plea for objectivity among intellectuals, Lewis then indicts almost all his distinguished contemporaries from Virginia Woolf to Philip Guedalla and from Sir James Barrie to Bertrand Russell as being 'all upon one side'. As he protests, 'were everything in the Fascist philosophy demonstrably false and absurd, that would still not absolve our intellectual giants from their duty to denounce all that is false and absurd in all that is not Fascism, or rather in all that is anti-Fascism'.[24] In point of fact, many had consistently done so: all that they seem to have been united in decrying was the Franco rising in Spain. And that, after all, did not necessarily align them with either Stalinism or the Comintern....

'I am the last person to set myself up as a model of what is *objective*,' Lewis concedes. 'Yet in spite of myself, almost, I am objective, I am detached, if I compare myself with say Trotsky or Baldwin. For I am not a politician.' And he goes on to explain that while he is himself an anti-Marxist, that does not leave him in anybody's pocket: as he sums it up, 'the *beaux yeux* of a possessing class play no part at all for me, except to *repel*'.[25]

There, at least, one can accept his assurance without reserve: he had certainly not ingratiated himself with the 'possessing class' either by his novels or his pamphleteering! And just to show what he thinks of the exactions of the Rich, he moves on to a spirited defence of the rights of the Poor. He admits that Left-wing sympathies are generally to be traced back to the same ideals as his own, but believes that Left-wing sympathizers have 'got their terms of reference wrong'. For while it masquerades as 'the principle of the Poor against the Rich, of the Little against the Big', he contends that Marxism represents no more than the exercise of an unlimited power. How does it come about, he wonders, that the only two countries in 'alliance' with the Soviet Union are 'the two greatest landowning, imperialist States of the world, France and Great Britain'?[26] For while Capitalism can cheerfully ally itself with Communism, 'all the impoverished communities, or the small peasant States, dread and oppose it'.

Without going into possible reasons for Britain's (as yet non-existent) alliance with the Soviet Union, one can agree with much that he says in denunciation of Soviet tyranny—without finding Fascist tyranny very different in kind. But it is in the platform that he creates for the British Blackshirt that one can find the clearest indication of what Lewis understood by 'Fascism'—and what he had once hoped to find in a 'modified form' of it for Britain:

> You as a Fascist stand for the small trader against the chain-store; for the peasant against the usurer; for the nation, great or small, against the super-state; for personal business against Big Business; for the craftsman against the Machine; for the creator against the middleman; for all that prospers by individual effort and creative toil, against all that prospers in the abstract air of High Finance or of the theoretic ballyhoo of Internationalism.[27]

To that statement of allegiance, William Morris himself might almost have subscribed, and it is no surprise to find Lewis informing his Blackshirt sternly: 'You stand to-day where Socialism stood yesterday—for the Poor against the Rich.'

In Lewis's listing, it is to be noted that the small trader is now grouped with the peasant and the craftsman as a repre-sentative of the embattled lower orders. The 'small man' of *The Art of Being Ruled* has been demoted from his anti-social en-clave in the *middle-world*: perhaps as a sign of the times, he now finds himself rated among the under-privileged. But it is the working class—the industrial working class—which provides Lewis with his most illuminating thought of all:

> Even if the workmen throughout the world could bring about to-morrow the full international order, 'world-revolution', it would from their standpoint be a folly to do so, for that would

be the *last* revolution. And it is self-evident that the threat of revolution is better than the reality, for on that throw the workman would be staking everything, and if he lost—that is to say if he got *the wrong revolution*—he would lose everything. Then he would have nothing left to bluff the Rich with. And, depend upon it, the Rich (in whatever disguise) would still be there. The Rich are always with us![28]

The Rich are always with us indeed! In one particular disguise, they have even tried to engraft Fascism upon this country.... And as Lewis so aptly puts it: 'The danger for the Poor has always been that the Rich or some creatures of the Rich, would insinuate themselves into the struggle and just take over the Poor Man's eternal campaign for better conditions, and run it for him.'[29]

Perhaps, after all, it is not surprising that no further contribution from Lewis appeared in the house-magazine of the British Union....

NOTES

1. *C Y D*, p.2.
2. Ibid., p.258.
3. Ibid., pp.13-14.
4. *Evening Standard*, 19.1.37.
5. *C Y D*, pp.18-19.
6. Ibid., p.76.
7. Ibid., p.78.
8. It will be remembered that Italian aid had been promised to Franco immediately after the rising, and German military transport planes had actually flown his Moorish troops onto Spanish soil for him.
9. This point is well argued by Hugh Thomas in his monumental history, *The Spanish Civil War*, p.283ff.
10. *C Y D*, p.202.
11. Ibid., p.206.
12. These figures are quoted in *The Spanish Civil War*, p.223.
13. *C Y D*, p.222.
14. It is interesting that in 1944, Lewis could write to Mrs Roy Campbell from Canada: 'The best Catholic opinion now—and I speak from very near the horse's mouth—is that the *requetés* were on the wrong side in the land of the flowering rifle.' *Letters of W L*, p.374.
15. *C Y D*, p.236ff.
16. Ibid., p.51.
17. Ibid., p.30.
18. Ibid., p.82.
19. Ibid., p.83.
20. Ibid., p.276.
21. *A of B R*, pp.369-70.

22. *The British Union Quarterly*, January–April, 1937, p.22.
23. Ibid., p.28.
24. Ibid.
25. Ibid., p.30.
26. Ibid., p.31.
27. Ibid., p.33.
28. Ibid.
29. Ibid., p.32.

CHAPTER 9

In Search of Mr Bull

All in all, the thirties were still proving unpropitious for Lewis as a writer. *Left Wings over Europe* had run to a second printing in August 1936, but his satirical novelette *The Roaring Queen*, which should shortly have followed it, had been suppressed before publication—once again on the grounds of possible action for libel. Its tone was broadly farcical, if not downright slapstick, and to compare it with *The Apes of God*, as has been done disparagingly by some critics, is simply to compare *Mac Flecknoe* with *Absalom and Achitophel*. Its principal target was the late Arnold Bennett, who is lampooned as Samuel Shodbutt, dispenser of the ineffable Book of the Week Award. But while Bennett had been safely dead for some five years, no doubt his soul went marching on in the literary world of the time. As for the other characters in the skit—Mrs Wellesly-Crook the hostess, Lady Saltpeter and her nympho-daughter Baby Bucktrout, Donald Butterboy the award-winner elect, Mrs Rhoda Hyman the established plagiarist, M. Jacques Jolat the French critic, and the rest—there would certainly have been plenty of literary figures around ready to identify themselves with the mannikins that Lewis was ridiculing. As he remarked in a letter (which he may or may not have posted!) there might even have been some 'either with a grudge against the author, or with a keen business sense and desire to turn an honest penny', who would have been ready to claim damages.[1] That being so, Lewis had demanded an *absolute assurance* from his publishers that there was nothing in the book that they would not be prepared to 'stand by'. Such an assurance, we must presume, was not forthcoming—which was a pity, perhaps, for there is much in the book which is rollicking good fun, if nothing more.

As already mentioned, untimely publication had left *The Revenge for Love*—one of Lewis's undoubted masterpieces—more or less unsaleable a year later. And though he continued to regard it as 'a first-rate peace pamphlet, which would have resounded in a smaller, more instructed, society like the hammering of an alarm-gong',[2] *Count Your Dead* was hardly a book to increase his reputation at the time, or perhaps even subsequently, though it would be easy enough to accept it as a clanger. To the relief of his faithful admirers, it was to be followed up six months later by a far better written and highly enjoyable piece of autobiography, *Blasting and Bombardiering*, one of the books by which he is best remembered today.

As it was wholly retrospective, harking back to the days of the First World War and its immediate aftermath, *Blasting and Bombardiering* need not be considered here. Its brief description of Lewis's few days in Venice shortly before the March on Rome, when 'the hoardings, lavatories, and railway stations had everywhere chalked slogans—"Death to Mussolini!" and counter-claptrap', is no more partisan than he assures us his attitude had been at the time. In those days, he explains, as regards Communism or Fascism he had no opinions to offer one way or the other. The 'pickets and posses of militant black-shirts, fascist bands, with clubs and knives' which clattered about him on all hands were no more than 'the modern equivalents of the "prentices of London": cobblers, barbers, watchmakers and young watermen'.

If anything, he admits that the war as he remembered it had left him 'a straight "leftwinger", as it would now be called'. And it was shortly afterwards that he had written *The Lion and the Fox*, in which that attitude is reflected. The first stages of the Fascist Revolution in Italy had left him 'without the least suspicion of anything unusual being afoot', and while he was far more politically conscious when he had his first sight of the Nazi Revolution in Germany, he avoids the temptation to elaborate upon it. All he admits is that if he had ridiculed what he saw in the Berlin of 1930, and had 'assured the public that Hitlerism would be as dead as the Dodo within six months', he would have been complimented on his 'penetration and sense of reality'. And he concludes with a certain sarcasm: 'A pity we should always want to hear what corresponds to our wishes and prejudices!'³—a thought which might well have been turned against him by his critics of the time....

As it was, events in Europe were still moving inexorably on towards the Second World War, a war which Lewis had never ceased to denounce as an eventuality to be avoided at all costs. Stanley Baldwin had been succeeded as Premier by Neville Chamberlain, as Anthony Eden was later to be succeeded as Foreign Secretary by Lord Halifax. The Rome–Berlin Axis had become a menacing reality, and after joining Germany and Japan as a signatory of the Anti-Comintern Pact in December 1937, Italy in turn had withdrawn from the League of Nations. In February 1938, the future course of German aggression was clearly indicated by the *Anschluss*, which at last brought the Nazis to power in Vienna. The anti-Jewish terror which followed was quite in the worst tradition of beastliness that prevailed in Germany itself.

Perhaps it is worth remarking that by 1938, thanks to the Nazi war upon Loan-Capital, income from capital and business in the Third Reich had risen by 146%—against an increase of 66% in salaries and wages. As remarked by William Shirer (from whom the figures are quoted) 'a sober study of the official statistics, which perhaps few Germans bothered to make, revealed that the much maligned capitalists, not the workers, benefited most from Nazi policies'.⁴ The benefits to be derived from such policies were soon to be extended in many new directions.

By the time of the *Anschluss*, Lewis was engaged upon one of his most amusing and provocative 'essays'—a study of English society and the English national character, *The Mysterious Mr Bull*. As such, the reader has his solemn assurance that 'there are no politics, party or otherwise, in this book'—but perhaps that was a little too much to be expected. The fifth of the seven parts into which the work is divided gives a thirty-seven-page consideration of John Bull's *Foreign Policy*; and once again, needless to add, Lewis is found in opposition to that policy as he sees it. But there is a noticeable shift of emphasis in the arguments which he puts forward; and in that, the work might be said to foreshadow the change in his political thinking which the events of 1938 were to bring about.

He is still of the opinion that the policy of Collective Security, with its concomitant fondness for the imposition of sanctions under the Covenant of the League, is 'bellicose', and remarks drily that his own views on the subject are fairly well known. But he goes on to add: 'These views I have modified of late,' though he still regards 'a *status quo* policy, involving a major war, as stupid'.[5] In what way, then, had his views been modified? Principally, perhaps, in that he is beginning to revert to his old belief in the virtues of Internationalism, though he is still not convinced that this was synonymous with the policies of the League of Nations—at least, not as those policies had recently been interpreted by British statesmen. 'Nevertheless,' he admits for the first time, 'I am genuinely sorry not to be at their side. For the international idea is the right idea, in the abstract. Only some guarantee there must be that it would not, like the old Liberalism, work out in the interest of the shark, the crook, and the money-dictator.'[6]

He reiterates that the days of Palmerstonian diplomacy are long since past, and that Britain can no longer afford to indulge in it. Yet Palmerstonian diplomacy was what Baldwin and Eden had been trying to perpetuate in an epoch where 'all the motives and interests standing behind policies' were entirely different. And it is at this point that he brings John Bright into the argument, by way of questioning whether Palmerstonian diplomacy had been economically defensible even in its own day. By way of proving that it had not, he quotes from a speech in which Bright had reviewed British foreign policy as he found it in 1858:

'I believe that I understate the sum,' said John Bright, 'when I say that, in pursuit of this will-o'-the-wisp, the *liberties of Europe*, and *the balance of power*, there has been extracted from the industry of the people of this small island no less an amount than £2,000,000,000 sterling.'[7]

In a listing of the various treaties and guarantees to which Britain had committed herself in Europe over the years, Bright then explains where the two thousand million pounds had been invested—and Lewis is not slow to point out that it is precisely the same sum which Neville Chamberlain had proposed, in 1937, to invest in re-armament against a threat to the balance of power in Europe by Germany and Italy. As for the need of such an investment, he quotes Bright again as being very much of his own way of thinking:

'The more you examine this matter the more you will come to the conclusion which I have arrived at, that this foreign policy, this regard for *the liberties of Europe*, this care at one time for *the Protestant interests*, this excessive love for *the balance of power*, is neither more nor less than a gigantic system of outdoor relief for the aristocracy of Great Britain.'[8]

Only now, says Lewis, it is not the aristocracy—'the Great Whig families'—which reaps the benefit of British intervention in European affairs: it is rather 'the great lords of Business and Finance', who were dispossessing the aristocracy even before John Bright's time, 'though it still succeeded, before it quite passed out, in getting in another war or two, such as that little masterpiece, the Crimea'.[9]

It is amusing to find Lewis falling back upon the arguments of the Manchester School in an effort to prove how the British were being bled white by 'Business and Finance', but politics (and Lewis's thoughts on them) are apt to come up with such anomalies. As he sees it, had John Bright been able to foresee the entanglements in which Britain was to find herself involved in 1938, he would have felt that the 'Whig Oligarchs' of his time had been outdone. And it is certainly interesting to speculate what he would have felt about the British guarantees to Poland and Romania which were to be offered so impulsively by Neville Chamberlain one year later....

National Government foreign policy, Lewis thinks, was wrong because it was completely out of date. It was a continuation of a policy laid down by the Whig territorial magnates a century before, which had been attacked in its own day by both John Bright and Disraeli, though from opposite sides. Interference in Europe, under the guise of maintaining a balance of power, had resulted only in a succession of wars—and could result in nothing else for the future. Certainly, nobody could suggest that those wars had benefited the British people as a whole. Today, says Lewis, we have no John Bright to stand up and enquire for whose profit those wars were being undertaken. Right and Left were united in their determination to pursue them. Yet would it not be better to let the war brewing in Europe between the Nationalist and Internationalist blocs begin without us? Why were we so anxious to participate? If we were so anxious to interfere, would it not be more sensible merely to re-arm against the victors—if any remained a danger to us?

There is still a great deal of wrong thinking to be found in *The Mysterious Mr Bull*, leaving John Bright out of the question altogether. Even if he had been able to agree that a balance of power in Europe should be maintained at the expense of the British taxpayer, Lewis is still unable to see just how much the balance had recently been disturbed. He is still far from convinced that Germany had become 'the strongest power in sight'—and was, in fact, the power with which a balance would have to be struck. Such an idea is still dismissed as so much war-mongering, since 'Germany's situation offers too many glaring weaknesses and inadequacies, to convince anyone but the ignorant, or the self-deluded'.[10] Perhaps it was lucky that everyone in Britain was not so self-deluded as he was.

But *The Mysterious Mr Bull* is rather more significant for what Lewis is now prepared to say about the political thinking of the Left. He had long complained that between the policies of the National Government and the Opposition, there was virtually no difference which could be discerned. Indeed, this had been one of his chief jibes at the parliamentary line-up in his time—that it was almost as single-minded as the dictatorships which it was always denouncing. Who could say that the voice of opposition was to be heard in the land, when on a subject of such vital importance to peace as British interference in Europe, both sides of the House of Commons thought as one?

But while he cannot accept the standpoint of the Tories, the attitude of the Left is beginning to make more sense to him. Whether their policy was wise or not, the Labour Party was bound to adopt an anti-Fascist attitude for obvious reasons:

They observe on all hands, in states where authoritarian régimes have been set up, the independent workers' organizations liquidated. A philosophy of force, and in some cases a philosophy of imperialist conquest, is announced as superseding the era of democratic and humanitarian ideology. How could they as typical Western democrats, be otherwise than extremely disturbed?

Very naturally their foreign policy is ideologic; it is directed implacably against those foreign governments which liquidate trade unionists, and say: 'L'État c'est Moi!'[11]

This attitude, Lewis is prepared to respect though he can still not bring himself to share it. At the same time, in another context, he admits that 'The essential Englishman can only feel deeply upon a moral issue. No intellectual issue touches him at all.' And while ideological issues may not always be quite the same as moral issues, he comes very near to admitting that in this particular case they may be—at least, so far as Left Wing thinking is concerned.

But what could be said of the Tories' attitude towards war? As the spokesmen for free enterprise and management, they could hardly claim the same solicitude for the future of the working class in Europe, having shown far too little sympathy for it at home. Their interest, surely, was far more in the profits of war-making than in its ideological aspects. 'For few people are so simple as to suppose that all these tremendous sums of money are being spent for *us* ... especially seeing that even the most paltry sums are refused us, when we mention the "distressed areas", or draw the attention of our rulers to any of those things which disgrace this very wealthy country, and make a mockery of all our humane pretensions.'[12]

But if he finds it difficult to see the Conservative clubman as 'the friend of the poor and humble', Lewis has little more to say for the Labour Party itself. He accuses it of being 'as blandly callous to the interests of the Poor and the distressed, as is the smuggest, most bridge-playing and golfing, of "Madames"'—indeed, he is far more appreciative of such far-left rebels of the time as Sir Stafford Cripps. They at least, he feels, would seem to be aware that 'what we name, generically, "English liberties" are the liberties of the Common People'. And however mistaken he thinks that Cripps himself may be as to foreign politics—'if he did not stand up for the forgotten man, in England, who would, of equal abilities?'[13]

Lewis's identification of himself with the cause of the Common Man might seem a trifle unconvincing in itself, if it did not come in the context that it does. So far, we have only quoted from the book on the subject of foreign policy, but with that *The Mysterious Mr Bull* is concerned only incidentally. As explained, the book is predominantly a consideration of English society and the English character, and its account of what goes to make up an average Englishman is one of the most entertaining and disrespectful things that Lewis ever wrote. Furthermore, in his destructive analysis of the English social system—which he carefully distinguishes from the Scottish or the Welsh—he makes it perfectly clear that his own sympathies are far more with Hodge than with his Masters.

John Bull himself, he believes, is an abstraction which does not really exist. Or rather, he is a composite made up of three irreconcilable elements—the average Englishman, the Englishman of the ruling class, and the empire-building Englishman—the last of whom he describes as being more properly thought of as a representative of John Company, and one who has 'far less to do with John Bull than the Comintern has to do with Russia'.

The pedigree of this tripartite hero he traces back to the Celts—by way of the Normans, the Danes and Norsemen, the Anglo-Saxons and the Romans—in much the same terms as Defoe's *True Born Englishman*. Though himself a representative of the Celtic fringe (with Cambrian, Irish, and Scottish elements in unequal parts) it amuses him to stress that racially the English are predominantly Germanic. He even reminds us that the word 'Welsh' derives from the Anglian *welisc*, and that the *Welschere* of modern Germany are her traditional enemies, the Italians.

From his admixture of the Celtic (Brythonic), the 'Celtiberian' (Goidelic) and Teutonic stock, the Englishman emerges as a 'blend of neolithic dago and Low German'. Little remains—if anything—of the Roman; Norsemen, Danes, Angles, Jutes and Saxons were all Teutonic cousins; and though they were French-speaking by 1066, the Normans were of course cousins again. All but the last named went to the making of the English average; but it was with the Normans that the forebears (and later, the pattern) of the English ruling class arrived.

Lewis decides that it is from the very nature of the admixture that the English derive their obsession with 'class' and their

almost total indifference to 'race'. In support of this, he quotes
Defoe's dictum that 'the Englishman is the mud of all races'—
most part of the mud having arrived from the estuary of the
Elbe. Racial feeling he finds far stronger among the Irish, without committing himself to any inference from the fact. But he
suggests that it is the Englishman's habit of making fun of
himself that is one of his most engaging traits, and that when
he is no longer prepared to do so—and becomes as nationalist
as everyone else—his end will be near.

Mainly Germanic as he is by extraction, the Englishman has
very little of the *Blutsgefühl* which so distinguishes his continental kinsman. Indeed, being the mongrel that he is, any
such sense would be sadly misplaced in him. But then, says
Lewis, why should he need it? Had not his Dutch critic Dr
Renier, in *The English: Are They Human?* called attention to
the Englishman's unshakeable conviction that Englishness implied an absolute superiority over everything which was *un-*
English—a conviction which carried with it a certain *noblesse
oblige?* And he goes on to wonder whether it was not this very
fact which had made Nazi racialism so odious to him:

> For (may he not argue) had the German, in fact, an 'absolute
> notion of his superiority over all that is not German,' would he
> not be ready to foregather—just as he would himself—with the
> humblest of Galician Jews? His great aversion for the racial-pride
> of the Nazi can be accounted for quite satisfactorily upon these
> lines.[14]

On the subject of race, indeed, Lewis is persuaded that while
the Germanic part of John Bull may be the larger part, it is
only his Celtic strain which can account for the fact that he is
'superior' in anything at all. Like other near-Celts before him,
Lewis has small regard for the Saxon as such: 'in the scale of
civilization,' he feels, 'it would be difficult to go any lower.'
Even composite Englishness is tolerated by *professional* Celts
only because it stands for wealth—or did at one time. As for the
professional Irish, they no longer even tolerate it: they have
taken themselves off. (Ulster was not proving particularly Irish
at that time.)

What are the characteristics of Bullism, therefore, by which
the breed may be recognized? To begin with, there is John

Bull's celebrated stupidity (this Lewis feels he has done his best to correct), which goes along with a certain uncanny 'wisdom' by way of compensation. Though he prides himself (for the most part) on being manly, John Bull is essentially unwarlike—which is greatly to his credit. He is the reverse of boastful, and experiences a fanatical aversion for every form of ostentation. 'The Jingo-Briton,' says Lewis, 'is a vulgar foreign import-ation.' And whatever else you may say about him, John Bull is anything but vulgar. There is a certain sphinx-like quality to his face, for which discovery Lewis is again indebted to Dr Renier. As the first clean-shaven personage in modern Europe, he is apt to fiddle with his face for lack of a better camouflage. But having no emotions to hide, he is really in no need of hairi-ness—which Lewis decides that he finally discarded when it began to get caught up in his machinery—like Mrs Bull's ex-crown of glory. (One wonders whether industrial accidents are on the increase among the bullocks of today.)

So far as his cooking goes, John Bull is certainly hard on his vegetables, which his climate grows to perfection; but even at its worst, his cooking is 'a dream of delight compared to the German or the Swiss'. As to the English climate itself, Lewis has no more to say for it than he had in *BLAST*. It is respon-sible, in its vaporous muzziness, for a general blurring of hard outline defined by more classical skies, and this is no doubt responsible for much that is muzzy in English thought, since 'the eye, and its habits, has a great effect upon the psyche closeted at the back of the eye'. But while he regrets that the feminine softness of English perspective may be 'hostile to the hard, the classical, the emphatic', Lewis is ready to admit that there are compensations to be taken into account: 'You pay a terrible price for it, but you get delicious effects in these watery islands: the liquid brilliance of John Constable, or the velvet opacity of the Whistler Nocturne, are worth a good many colds in the head.'[15]

Not that John Bull has any great feeling for art himself: he probably regards a cold in the head as far less dangerous. Lewis is forced to concede that his standards of art have always been pitiably low. He reports him as having an instinctive distrust for anything remotely pertaining to the intellect, and deeply resenting anything which he regards as 'clever'. Indeed, he subjects all forms of 'cleverness' to 'the sort of semi-ostracism that overtakes those guilty of what is known as "bad form" (a sporting expression)'. For John Bull, art is really another name for gamesmanship, and as Lewis puts it bluntly: 'Cricket and Painting cannot co-exist within the boundaries of the same State.' To make all finally clear, he explains that 'the Royal Academy is Cricket. All the rest of art is not.'[16] One is left to wonder whether Constable himself, while batting for the Royal Academy, was ever forced to appeal against the vaporous muzziness on the grounds of bad light....

But however deficient John Bull may be in intellect, Lewis is ready to credit him with a great sense of style. Nor does he feel that this is confined to what he regards as the upper classes (of which more later): he finds it among all classes without distinction. Whether his sense of style and his stupidity are merely opposite sides of the same coin, Lewis is prepared to debate. But style, says Lewis, John Bull undoubtedly possesses. He sees it, admittedly, all too often as 'a veneer of languor—as a trick, for evading the issue—as a receipt for passing off ignorance and laziness as ability and judgment'. And it has worked out, in a sense, as 'the apotheosis of the Amateur'. As such, it is naturally most cultivated among the Apes of God. But style, for what it is worth—and Lewis has an obvious respect for it—is certainly to be found among the English.

The strange thing, of course, is that occasionally even the dullest and most phlegmatic nationalities will come up with an outstanding genius. Even the Dutch ('without doubt the most stupid people in the world') produced their Rembrandt, as the English ('the next most stupid after the Dutch') produced their Shakespeare. And while they have made many attempts to prove that Shakespeare was no more than a pseudonym for some scion of the nobility, no Englishman has yet been so bold as to suggest that he was actually a foreigner. (Matthew Arnold, of course, had suggested that he was a Celt who had strayed over the border from Cambria, but Lewis had dismissed that little heresy in his diatribe on Celticism in *The Lion and the Fox*, where he had gone so far as to say that no such thing existed.) Shakespeare, says Lewis, was *undoubtedly* a John Bull; and goes on to make the case that only a nation of John Bulls could possibly have given birth to him: 'If it is *intensity* you want, you can only get it—only grow it, so to speak—in a dull and brutal bed.'[17] A second-best bed indeed!

For that very reason, he suggests, France has nothing equal to offer. The general landscape may be more elevated, and peaks of a kind may be in far greater profusion—if they are peaks—but that is as far as it goes. 'There are "giants", certainly, but nothing record-breaking, after the fashion of the English national poet, or the misty colossus of painting produced by the Dutch.'[18]

Turning to the Jews, Lewis finds that it is very much the same thing—only more so. 'The average Jew is twice as intelligent as the average Englishman. Indeed, with the Jews, mental endowment seems to be distributed evenly throughout the race to a remarkable degree.' But outstanding talent is not to be nurtured in a bed so stimulating. An occasional Heine is the most that they come up with on the cultural front. Musical as they are—and perhaps because of that very fact—they have no Mozarts or Beethovens to their credit, though many a Mendelssohn and many a Bloch. Even so, as Lewis hastens to add, they are apt to excel 'in certain well-defined directions, like science (Freud), romantic politics, or in the uninspiring fields of economic theory'.[19]

So far as his well-known sense of humour goes, Lewis is prepared to accept John Bull at his own valuation. After all, like a sense of style, humour can be used as some form of insulation against unpalatable facts; and as such, it has been much cultivated by John Bull's daily press. But sense of style notwithstanding, John Bull's sense of humour does not extend to satire. For satire, Lewis sadly notes, John Bull has absolutely no appreciation whatever. Indeed, he positively resents it—not least of all, when it is directed at himself. It is quite obviously, so far as he is concerned, a matter of 'bad form', and by no stretch of the imagination could it be described as 'cricket'. By way of explaining the matter, Lewis points out that 'to start with, "satire" most definitely *does* something to somebody else, whilst "humour" is rather a something done to himself by the man in question. The essential thing about English humour is that you should not take *yourself* seriously: it is not directed outward, but inward.'[20] Having thus got back to his old preference for the objective rather than the subjective, Lewis politely refrains from pushing it any further. The satirist is a mechanic rather than a metaphysician, and there are times when his art may be salutary: but he is prepared to admit that the satirist may also be something of a butcher, and he would not recommend full-time satire as a calling for any mother's offspring. He will only defend the art—such as he understands it—'as one might defend, against the Christian Scientist, the calling of the surgeon, or, against the anti-vivisectionist, operations upon the living dog'.[21] Coming from The Enemy, this modest apology for satire is at least calculated to appeal to the Englishman's sense of humour.

But it is not merely a dislike of satire that Lewis remarks in his subject: John Bull has an instinctive dislike of being reminded of anything which he would prefer to ignore. This applies to far more than his own shortcomings: it applies to a great deal with which he might be expected to be vitally concerned. If it is possible to disregard anything which he finds unpleasant, for the most part John Bull simply does not want to know. Being stupid and slower on the uptake than most people, half the time he is not sure what his own government is up to; and in case he would not approve of it, he generally decides not to enquire. As for the idea of him trying to impose his will upon half the world, and building up an immense Empire in his own image—that, says Lewis, is all wrong. That was another John Bull altogether—or rather, it was a handful of unEnglish military adventurers, masquerading as John Bull while he was not looking.

In a highly amusing rewrite of imperial history, Lewis maintains that as regards every extension of the Empire, it had been 'in the teeth of the utmost opposition on the part of the home government that these territories were brought under our unwilling sway'.[22] India had been created as a commercial empire by an independent trading company with its own private army, and later extended by such untypical eccentrics as Napier. The Cape Colony had been settled by the out of work and the starving, who had been shipped away south by John Bull as the only means he could think of for getting them safely off his hands. The fact that 'thousands of charming Kaffirs, who had never done any harm to anybody, were slaughtered by this out-of-work rabble' was deplored no less by John Bull than by any-

one else. As for the convicts who were shipped off to Botany
Bay, they had been guilty of very much the same sort of thing,
and had embarrassed John Bull even more by colonizing
Australia. (New Zealand, of course, had been wished onto him
by the everyway unreliable Scots—again while he was thinking
of something else.) Whatever had accidentally happened in
Egypt (for John Bull's feelings about which, see Wilfrid Scawen
Blunt), General Gordon had 'undoubtedly shortened Glad-
stone's life' by trying to secure control of the Sudan for the
City. And the same sad story had gone for one new slab of
territory after another: try as he would, as a Little Englander,
John Bull had been unable *not* to acquire an Empire. All
which, Lewis admits, may sound highly funny to the foreigner
—but seen as an average native of these islands, John Bull is
far too gentle and kindly to indulge in any such brigandage. He
is, says Lewis, 'rather unenterprising than otherwise; stay-at-
home. A quiet chap'.[23] The almost indecent haste with which
he has off-loaded his Empire over the last few years would
seem to support this estimate.

Thus far, Lewis has been considering John Bull only in
general terms: the characteristics discussed were common to
both the classes into which—according to Lewis—he had divided
himself. But when he comes to consider the two classes in
themselves, the picture of John Bull begins to fall apart. To
start with, 'half of him will scarcely speak to the other half—
or only when strictly necessary, and with a wounding con-
descension'. For examined separately, in neither half can Lewis
find the least resemblance to the portly yeoman-figure of *Punch*
and the cartoonists. Whatever he may be as a class-complex,
therefore, Lewis comes to the conclusion that John Bull as the
world imagines him is virtually a myth.

But is he? In dividing him up between only *two* classes—the
ruling and the ruled—Lewis is once more making his old mistake of failing to recognize the significance of the middle. Because he equates the middle with the mediocre, he prefers to
deny it an identity of its own. It is certainly not possible to
identify more than the *upper*-middle class with any ruling
caste—either on the grounds of wealth or political influence.
But it is no more possible to identify the middle and the *lower-*

middle classes with the working class: they remain far too obstinately a society unto themselves. As such, they continue to make up a sizeable buffer between the ruling class and the vast majority of the ruled. It is, indeed, in their own medial stratum that the truest likeness to John Bull is to be found, since they provided his archetype in the first place. And often as Lewis decides that he is a 'myth', he continually returns to his concept of John Bull as an identifiable type: the average Englishman. It is surely worth remarking, furthermore, that the average Englishman can be identified with no extreme politically: he is neither a Fascist nor a Communist—he is something infinitely more numerous and more important than either.

Though he continues to think in terms of his extremes, however, Lewis has again some salutary things to say on the subject of English class-consciousness. There is no other country in the world, he reiterates, where the class barrier is maintained so rigorously as in England. In his own estimate, while this is to the detriment of seventy per cent of the English people, it is to the great advantage of the remaining thirty per cent. For that 'upper class' he has little but contempt: they are a pseudo-caste, a class of usurping interlopers in whom can be found very few of the better qualities which dignify the majority which they patronize. And though he finds their social 'superiority' as much of a myth as John Bull himself, their stranglehold on English society is something which he attacks in no uncertain terms.

In extraction, of course, there is no particular 'difference' between the two classes he differentiates: one is as English—and as average English—as the other. The one-time aristocracy, with what remains to it of its Norman blood, has been effectually 'bridled and bitted' for the last hundred years and is being steadily squeezed out of existence by death-duties and punitive taxation. As a ruling caste, it had shown no ability to protect itself against the rising power of business wealth; and what Lewis regards as far more serious, had proved 'quite incapable of supplying the leadership required of it by the English nation'. Having won out in its struggle for power against the monarchy in the seventeenth century, it had proceeded to lose out in the nineteenth century to the rich bourgeoisie. But the vast majority of the English people, Lewis insists, lost out at the same time:

> To explain what has happened, it is sufficient to point out how the original 'lower class' has been deliberately kept intact, *psychologically*—in spite of the fact that the original 'upper class' has been destroyed. But in order to keep the 'lower classes' in a semi-idiot subjection, there has to be at least a simulacrum of the aristocratic class—an 'upper class' in the old and traditional English sense—on top.[24]

Having neither tradition nor birthright to distinguish them, nor old estates to give them a local standing, the new 'upper class' had to look for an image elsewhere. As a result, the educational system of the country was pressed into service to create one for them. With Dr Arnold's regimen to guide them, the public schools quickly adapted themselves to turning out the sort of 'gentlemen' who could take over from the landed families that their fathers were ousting from political power. The public schools created a voice and they cultivated a manner and an insolence; they moulded their pupils into an exclusive club, for membership of which they alone were eligible. And by the spread of so-called popular education ('the cruellest sham of all, in the "democratic" repertoire of deceit'), it was assured that the voice and manner required of all club-members should be made accessible to no one else. As Lewis had complained in *Count Your Dead*, accent can be used among the English as an offensive weapon—and frequently is. Acquisition of a 'right' accent is certainly an open sesame to life among the privileged. For the substitute-aristocracy has locked the patent of its nobility deep within its larynx, and by their vowels shall ye know them.

No such imposition of a substitute ruling class would have been possible, Lewis is convinced, if the older aristocratic tradition had not dated back to the Dark Ages. The Norman nobility, engrafted upon Saxon England by William the Bastard, had been distinguished not only by its own language, but also by its superior culture and refinement. It had awed the humbler Saxon by the mere parade of its attainments. From that day to this, instinctive respect and a sense of awe have survived—but the Norman superiority has not. Even when the ruling-caste had lost its language, the tradition of its 'foreign extraction'—

and hence of its essential 'difference'—persisted in the average mind. When in course of time it was itself dispossessed by the sham-aristocracy of wealth, the substitute ruling class 'had to *pretend* that it was foreign still, in order to be sufficiently impressive'. But its only 'difference' consisted in the amount of money which it commanded. It seemed 'different' from the average merely because it had been trained to appear so—and because it could afford to be so.

As for the vast majority of those over whom the new rule had been established—like their original masters, they in turn had been dispossessed. Even before the Industrial Revolution, they had become a class without property, a proletariat rather than a peasantry, a class of wage-slaves rather than a class of independent small-holders. In that, they were unlike the majority of the French, among whom property—as Hilaire Belloc had pointed out—was far more widely and more equitably distributed. Tied as they were to the industrial machine, and with social machinery discriminating so heavily against them, the working class of the thirties had little chance in England of enjoying the better things of life. As Lewis sees it, the working man of his time was not merely a second-class citizen: his life was little better than that of a helot. And as a dissident member of the ruling class which he blames for thriving upon the helotry, he makes it clear enough where his own sympathies lie: 'I would for my own part,' he admits, 'far rather have been born a straight slave, in a Greek or Roman city-state, than have been born a member of the British working-class.' And having drawn a withering picture of the injustices of the class system—to say nothing of the economic anomalies from which it derived—'all this taken together,' he concludes, 'if I had had to support it, would have made me a far redder "Red" than any I have yet encountered'.[25]

This little aside might have come straight out of *The Art of Being Ruled*, where it would have seemed entirely consonant with a great deal more that he was thinking at the time. But coming as it did immediately after the anti-red diatribes of *Count Your Dead*, it rather suggested that Lewis's later allegiances were beginning to change. There is no attempt to ally himself with the *cause* of the under-privileged: he has other causes which engage him too fully. He is still girding at the

shams and shortcomings of 'democracy' which have reduced
the John Bull of legend to the fecklessness of Strube's 'Little
Man'. He is claiming that even when England's wealth was the
envy of the world, 'a majority of the English nation were worse
off than the nationals of any other white community'. But he
is also now admitting that 'an Englishman, if he escape the
hypnotism of democratic mass-rule, can still be freer than men
can be in most other places'.[26]

He is still persuaded that the foreign policy to which the
country had been committed would lead it before much longer
into a disastrous war. At the same time—and for the first time
—he is prepared to admit that 'Great Britain feels itself threatened, as it has not done for a very long time'.[27] And while he
does not necessarily share that feeling, he is at least prepared to
accept it as sincere in those who do. Apart from the international alliances which they have entered upon as a result of
that threat, there is also discernible among his countrymen 'a
veritable renaissance of something that, with the Englishman,
takes the place of nationalism". And once again he strikes a
distinctly new note in his comment:

> If all the symptoms of nationalism that we are at present observ-
> ing are 'Left-wing' nationalism, there is nothing surprising in
> that. The Left-wing are for better or worse, and whether you like
> it or not, the most vital part of the country. And therefore when
> the country is vitally stirred, it is its 'Left-wing' circles that are
> stirred.
>
> The majority of the nation is lethargic. That I have called the
> Big Soft Centre; which will go wherever it is pushed. The Right
> Wing just sits tight, hanging on shortsightedly to its money-bags.
> All the best brains are on the Left.[28]

This is indeed a new view of the political scene, and one
which Lewis would have been unlikely to come up with a year
earlier. But the political scene, after all, was changing, and even
while he was writing *The Mysterious Mr Bull* the future course
of events in Europe was beginning to declare itself. The initiative clearly was no longer being taken by Britain—whether or
not it ever had been. Even Lewis was beginning to wonder
whether the plans for another European war were not being
hatched elsewhere. That being so, he may well have felt that it

was time for him to come in from the cold. English democracy
might have its exasperating sides, which he could never accept
willingly. But a simple fact remains: 'We all not only belong
to a nation, willy-nilly, but we all of us need a nation: to transport us to our individual goal.'[29] And from the days of *BLAST*
onwards, Lewis had always been far too much of an intellectual
John Bull to have sought his goal anywhere beyond the English
Channel.

This side of the Channel, he still has his own particular part
to play. It is the part of the critic rather than the part of the
leader; but so far as the argument goes between what is and
what ought to be, there is no doubt upon which side he will be
found. He is with Godwin in being 'as tolerant of social compromise as it is possible to be'. He is one who favours the
tabula rasa—the clean break and the new start—in both art and
politics. He believes in the scrapping of all outworn institutions,
in the correction of the illogical and the redressing of the unjust. He declares that he would assist at the general bonfire
forthwith—if it were not for one thought: 'just the same sort
of people who brought into being and handed down to us the
nonsensical system we have got would be employed in the
erection of the New Jerusalem.'[30] And harking back to *The
Caliph's Design*, in which he had speculated about the building
of an ideal city, he admits—again for the first time—that there
are, in fact, no easy answers:

> Once one has recognized quite clearly that there are insuperable
> difficulties—difficulties inherent in the semi-animal, irrational,
> basis of human life—to dreams of theoretic political perfection:
> that there is a great *non possumus* at the bottom of all our
> intellectual planning and plotting—a perfectly insurmountable
> *organic* snag, as if the foundations of our proposed City-Beautiful
> turned out to be not rock, as we had naively supposed, but some
> disintegrating living substance—once one is entirely satisfied as
> to that, as a *concrete* architect one's occupation's gone.
> One knows from that moment that one will never build again,
> except in one's dreams.[31]

He had confessed very much the same thing the previous
November (1937) in a letter to the editor of the 'Wyndham
Lewis Double Number' of *Twentieth Century Verse*: 'I could

build something better, I am sure of that, than has been left us by our fathers that were before us. Only I know this is quite impossible.' And he notes, by way of explaining his changing political position: 'I have learnt my lesson, and, in spite of being the pure revolutionary, I am a bit of a realist too.'[32]

There are indeed no easy answers. The world will be changed only in its own good time and in its own good way. Nevertheless, change it undoubtedly will. And with change in mind, there are both times and places where the revolutionary will find the portents more propitious than usual. As to times, the Industrial Age is itself a kind of revolution, for it *exacts* the New: 'It is a force that will split and tear the Old like a wind, or burst a dam, if the Old is too obstinate.'[33] As to places: 'You may have an upheaval in these islands before long, and it may take a socialist form. Indeed, I believe that it *must*, for only the "Left-wing" can command the requisite amount of moral stimulus.'[34] And whether there is a touch of Moody and Sankey to them or not, something of Pym and Penn, of William Morris, William Godwin, John Bright and the Tolpuddle Martyrs has to be there 'if you are to get the Englishman's fighting glands to function properly'. To succeed in England, change must *depend* upon a moral stimulus, for that is the only stimulus to which an Englishman will ever respond. To try and stir him with an idea or an ideology is to waste one's time, if not to invite reprisals. For whatever is left of his original nature, the Englishman at least survives as a moral animal.

And although he can find no evidence for the survival of John Bull as he once imagined himself, for the average Englishman Lewis retains a high regard. But his regard is not for the Englishman as the foreigner is apt to meet him, either on the world stage of diplomacy or in the popular press. No more is it for the Englishman who tries to perpetuate the *status quo* on the walls of his Royal Academy:

I see, rather, a picture of a man who is civilized and friendly to a fault: who is content to live beside other men without over-reaching them, and who esteems a neighbour for his gentle qualities rather than for those attributes that give people power over their fellows: who hates violence with an almost morbid distaste (our prize-ring notwithstanding): whose word is his bond, and who rates honesty so high that he almost invariably sends the wrong man to jail, so great is his haste to be done with a rogue; who is as sensitive where it concerns others as where it touches only himself: who is a patron of lost causes; who is so kind to beggars that the latter swarm at every street corner: so affectionate towards animals that in England there is almost a dog for every man, and a couple of cats for every woman: who never boasts—though his Press belie him morning, noon and night with their unspeakable vain-glory: who is so truly unassuming and ready to give up his place to another, that every impostor has been mistaken for him in turn—since his high places have been occupied by same: so that, in fine, Mr Bull, after all these centuries, is the least known of all the peoples of Europe.[35]

NOTES

1. *Letters of W.L.*, p.240.
2. *R A.* p.211.
3. *B and B*, p.234.
4. *The Rise and Fall of the Third Reich*, by William Shirer, p.264.
5. *Mr Bull*, p.178.
6. Ibid., p.182.
7. Ibid., p.186.
8. Ibid., p.191.
9. Ibid., p.194.
10. Ibid., p.204.
11. Ibid., p.177.
12. Ibid., pp.195-6.
13. Ibid., pp.199-200.
14. Ibid., pp.81-2.
15. Ibid., p.90.
16. Ibid., p.172.
17. Ibid., p.118.
18. Ibid., p.117.
19. Ibid., p.118.
20. Ibid., p.146.
21. Ibid., p.145.
22. Ibid., p.239.
23. Ibid., p.243.
24. Ibid., pp.270-1.
25. Ibid., p.280.
26. Ibid., p.97.
27. Ibid., p.234.
28. Ibid., p.234.
29. Ibid., p.265.
30. Ibid., p.230.
31. Ibid., pp.232-3.
32. *Twentieth Century Verse*, Nov./Dec. 1937: *A Letter to the Editor*. Also quoted in *Letters of W L*, p.246
33. *Mr Bull*, p.262.
34. Ibid., p.235.
35. Ibid., p.287.

CHAPTER 10

The End of the Hitler Cult

While *The Mysterious Mr Bull* was printing, the British people —and Lewis personally—had been deeply shocked by the sudden eruption of the Munich Crisis. The hysterical abuse which Hitler had hurled at President Beneš from the Berlin Sportpalast had left his world audience in small doubt as to the paranoid savagery which was soon to be launched against all Europe. To Lewis himself, the broadcast came as a sickening revelation: for the first time he recognized the tiger he had been trying to ride. He resigned for good any lingering hope he may still have had that British 'understanding' could maintain even precarious peace with a military power which was so clearly hell-bent for destruction—its own, and that of any nation which happened to stand in its way. Hitler's ultimatum to Czechoslovakia could not be excused as a 'reasonable demand' by any stretch of the diplomatic imagination. It was obvious that he would not be bought off for long by a mere handing over of the Sudetenland: even if that sufficed for today—tomorrow, the world.

It would have been some salve to our national pride, in retrospect at least, if the British liberal press had at once united in deploring Chamberlain's surrender at Munich. But in point of fact, that was not immediately the case. *Reynold's News* and the *Daily Worker* were alone in denouncing it for what it certainly was—a gross betrayal of a friendly nation in the face of a brutal military threat. This was obvious enough to the neutral countries, who were not themselves directly involved. It might well have been clear to the British public, if war nerves had not been quite so taut at the time. But with gas-masks being distributed, trenches being dug in Hyde Park, and the air-raid sirens being tested out—it was understandably difficult for most people to think very clearly at all. To the man in the street, peace was simply preferable to war—particularly when it could be bought at someone else's expense. And if he had taken the same line at the time, Lewis would have been in step (for once) with public opinion. As it was, the Munich Crisis was a manifest proof to him that his whole attitude to Germany would have to be re-thought. As he was to explain in *Rude Assignment*, it was as a result of Munich that he wrote *The Hitler Cult and How it will End* in which he freely admitted how far at fault his judgment had been, no matter how well-intentioned his motives. It has even been claimed for him that he was at work on the book some time before Munich gave it an added urgency. At least the book made clear that at long last Lewis had begun to take the true measure of Nazism—and all that it boded of evil for Europe. Unfortunately, once again delays in publication ensued: by the time *The Hitler Cult* appeared, the Second World War was three months old. A book which had been conceived in a spirit of prophecy had to adapt itself as best it could to events that had already occurred.

More unfortunately still, now that his understanding of the situation had changed so radically, a cheap edition of *Count Your Dead* nevertheless appeared on the market. Its derisory jibes at the *Sunday Referee* and Madame Tabouis for wrongly forecasting an imminent German invasion of Czechoslovakia was rather untimely in the very month (March, 1939) when German tanks went rumbling into Prague. And 'first-rate peace pamphlet' though he believed it to be, there was no longer any belief—even in Lewis's mind—that peace was possible for many months longer. Plans for war were already being worked out by Hitler and his General Staff in their final details: all that remained was for the appropriate moment to occur and the necessary 'issue' to be arranged. Nor was there any doubt as to where the blow would be struck when the moment arrived. Whether or not it was 'to go and fight for the Prudential Insurance Company's mines in Poland' (as *Count Your Dead* had suggested),[1] it was obvious enough that under the terms of her new Polish guarantee, Britain would be firmly bound to declare war on

Germany if and when Poland was invaded. The guarantee may have seemed to Lewis as unwise as it did to many others at the time; but the guarantee was there to be honoured, and unless Britain was to admit before the world that her word was as worthless as Hitler's own, honoured it would have to be. Six months remained to her before the issue was put to the test.

Meanwhile, and before Lewis had been able to find a new publisher for his later thinking on the German menace in Europe, he was at least able to make clear his thinking on a related subject—the unhappy lot of the Jews. The treatment to which all German and Austrian Jews had been subjected by Nazi tyranny had been decried by liberals and men of goodwill throughout the world. The Nuremberg Laws of 1935 had merely been the first of the punitive legislation which had dispossessed them, and which had as its aim the complete exclusion of the Jewish race from the Third Reich. The *Kristallnacht* pogrom of 1938, which followed upon the assassination of vom Rath in Paris, had been merely the latest and most murderous attack to be launched against them physically.

To survive the Nazi persecution, as many German and Austrian Jews as could escape sought sanctuary abroad. Many of them had been admitted as political refugees into this country, where their increasing influx had excited much sympathy, but also, as was to be expected, a certain resentment in some quarters.[2] And although the British are rarely guilty of turning resentment into action, they undoubtedly have a tendency to express prejudice by social discrimination—as any West Indian or Pakistani would be ready to testify. While this could rarely be said to amount to downright anti-Semitism, it certainly qualified for Lewis's own description of 'a pinch of malice'.

Perhaps because he had come to realize just how wrong he had been in his original belief that Hitler himself was *not* anti-Semitic, Lewis felt himself impelled to speak up on behalf of the Jews as they were becoming increasingly known to the British. His short treatise *The Jews, Are They Human?* appeared in March 1939, having been written after his first draft of *The Hitler Cult* had been finished, but the publication of which it anticipated by some nine months.

The title, as Lewis pointed out in the foreword, was in no way intended to be disparaging: it merely repeated the question which Dr Renier had recently asked about the English themselves. And the whole import of the work was to prove that the Jews—if anything—were perhaps inclined to be *too* human. As a race—or perhaps one should say, as a fraternity—they shared all the virtues on which the English prided themselves. As for their less engaging characteristics, these were generally to be blamed first of all upon the adverse conditions under which they had long been forced to live. Their Christian overlords had no such excuse to offer for themselves: in their case the failings were innate, and frequently more blameworthy.

An occasional pinch of malice notwithstanding, Lewis had always been scrupulously fair to the Jews in all his books. Even in his most sustained attacks upon what he regarded as false doctrine—as in the case of his favourite adversary, Bergson—he had never been tempted to bring race into the argument. He had spoken in very friendly terms about many Jewish intellectuals, and when he found occasion to mention the Jewish race as such, it had always been in respectful terms. In *Doom of Youth*, the Jews had been 'an ancient and exceptionally gifted race';[3] in *Left Wings over Europe*, they had been 'that redoubtable and often scintillating people'.[4] In *The Mysterious Mr Bull*, as already noticed, he had found that 'the average Jew is twice as intelligent as the average Englishman',[5] and in *Hitler* the average Jew could 'make rings around' the average German 'in all that universe that is not war, or mechanical technique'.[6] Even the egregious Ned in *Count Your Dead* had 'often felt compassion for the Jew' until he had come to identify him with the Left-wing intellectual.

Indeed, it was only once or twice, when Lewis had tended to identify the Jews with the financial stranglehold of Big Business, or (ironically enough!) with Communism in the Soviet Union, that he had indulged even his *pinch* of malice. And compared with the frequent fistfuls indulged by some of his intellectual contemporaries, the pinch had been minute indeed!

The Jews, Are They Human? made amends for it none the less. The book is written in no spirit of partisanship or emotional involvement: it is 'a work not of love, but of reason'. Lewis feels that too much had been written about the Jews in a spirit of common humanity, and far too little on the grounds of common sense. His appeal, therefore, is to the intelligence rather than to humanitarian feeling, though 'it is extremely un-intelligent, it is as well to remember, not to be humane'.[7] He is no more 'pro' Jewish than he is 'pro' anything else. Once more he reserves the right to stand outside the question at issue, and examine it independently.

In the emotional climate of the time, this attitude was salu-tary. Impassioned partisanship has a way of creating its own form of backlash. Lewis, then, has no harder word for anti-Semitism than that it is 'unintelligent', and only when he has carried his argument through to its logical conclusion is the anti-Semitic diatribe dismissed contemptuously as 'ugly non-sense'. There is no more attempt to sentimentalize the Jew than there had been in *Paleface* to sentimentalize the Negro. He is clinically examined, with all the warts that are sometimes wished upon him, and it is only upon an overwhelmingly favour-able balance that he is accepted. But once he has *been* accepted, Lewis will allow no reservations.

As for the persecution from which the Jew was currently suffering in Europe, 'it is infinitely regrettable that the middle-European should have exhibited so extreme a departure from the human norm'.[8] But this, after all, was something to which the Jew had grown accustomed over the last 2,000 years. And by way of putting the matter in proper perspective, it is pointed out that the Jew in flight from persecution 'is a purely Christian phenomenon'. The only answer to which, perhaps, is that some countries are more 'Christian' than others....

It is not necessary to examine Lewis's balance-sheet in detail. As he says, the British themselves have mistreated many people besides the Jews: apart from what we have done to various races up and down the Empire, in Britain itself we have built our ghettos—only here, we call them slums. He remembers 'that hideous Victorian saying, "The Poor are always with us!"' without apparently remembering its Jewish origin. As for the slum-dwellers themselves—who is to draw distinctions of misery and ugliness as between Whitechapel and Battersea? He admits to disliking the Jewish bumptiousness and swagger, but realizes that they inevitably go with 'that Chosen People feeling'; and having accepted our own religion at his hands, to dislike the Jew himself is to dislike Jehovah, 'the God to whom we pray when we enter our churches'. The fact that God had never chosen *him*, on the other hand, does not bother Lewis in the least: he prefers to remain an outsider. He would certainly not like to be a Jew, since he would not care to have behind him 'so many martyred generations'. But the Jew himself does not bear grudges; he is 'the human being *par excellence* perhaps'. In his almost pathetic desire to be friendly, 'he is as anxious to forget the horrid past as we should be to atone for it, if we consulted our humaner feelings'.[9]

In character, the Jew tends to be feminine—receptive and parasitic as all women are—but like women, he is practical and gifted with a hard business sense. If he succeeds in business rather better than we do, let us remember that the rules of the game were invented by us and not by him. One is hardly justified in resenting the fact that he can perform our own kind of juggling tricks better than we can. The Jews, after all, were not in any way responsible for Poverty in the midst of Plenty: that was the handiwork of that ferocious individualist, the Western European. And in a summing-up which ought to be better known, Lewis adds:

> The terrific usurious system of bank-capital, that fairyland of Credit in which we wander like herds of lost souls at the present day, *is all our own doing*, or the doing of men of our own race. Aryans like ourselves conceived it and established it; and it is better that we should realise that, and not blame it onto somebody else. It is important that we should realise what follies, and what crimes, *we* are capable of. Otherwise those crimes and follies are liable to be indefinitely repeated, if a scapegoat can so easily be found.[10]

It is a pity that this thought did not have wider circulation among those 'credit cranks' that Lewis had always been so chary of joining.

All in all, Lewis finds that in his aptitude for hard work, his business ability, his intelligence, his taste and his 'gift of intellectual sympathy', the Jew had indeed qualified for 'full partnership in a concern in which he plays so important a part'—namely, British social life. His contribution to British culture had been noteworthy—not least in that it had tended to disrupt our narrow and bigoted insularity. There must be no more suggestion of according him merely an 'inferior status'. Everything should be done to eradicate from our minds all our in-built prejudices and outworn superstitions about him. To that end, the Jew himself might contribute by relaxing, so far as he could, 'that religious and nationalist organization that is Israel'.[11] For the very concept of 'the Jew' is anachronistic—in the same way that 'Frenchmen', 'Italians', 'Germans', or 'Englishmen' are anachronistic to a good European. As a citizen of the modern world, the Jew—*qua* Jew—is just as obsolete a concept as the old John Bull himself. It was high time that both of them became assimilated.

As for what can be done to relax 'the religious and nationalist organization' that is Christianity:

> We must make up for the doings of the so-called 'Christians' of yesterday—who degraded the Jew, and then mocked at him for being degraded. We must give all people of Jewish race a new deal among us. Let us for Heaven's sake make an end of this silly nightmare once and for all, and turn our backs upon this dark chapter of our history.[12]

It would indeed be pleasant if we could. . . .

As the book in which he finally renounced Hitlerism and all its works, it is a pity that *The Hitler Cult and How it will End* should suffer from being such an ill-fitting assemblage of separate parts as to be almost a palimpsest. If we accept Lewis's assurance that it was written 'at the time of Munich', this can obviously apply only to certain sections of it. In others, there are quotations from the press dated April 1939, when he was clearly trying to bring it into line with later events. Following that partial revision, the manuscript must have gone to the printers, as there is no further updating to cover the events of the summer. The day before war was declared on Germany by Britain, Lewis had sailed with his wife to North America; but in an attempt to make the work appear less painfully out of date when it appeared, a few minor alterations to the text were made in London while it was still in the proof stage. The latest of these is a mention of 'October 1939'—a rather ambiguous reference to Russian moves in Poland and the Baltic States.

Needless to say, the result of such haphazard revision must

have been highly confusing to anyone who read the book when it was published that December. The occasional updating would lead him to infer that the book embodied Lewis's considered response to the war itself—which was certainly not the case. Indeed, there are many plain indications in the text that war had *not* broken out when it was being written. Many passages would surely have been couched in far stronger terms if it had.

As it emerged, the book does at least prove that Lewis's eyes had been opened to the true nature of Hitlerism some time before he found himself at war with it. His one-time 'neutrality' on the German question is formally disavowed: 'the time has passed for that, and it could no longer serve any useful purpose. To-day, to be neutral is to be anti-British. Further,' he adds significantly, 'it is to be anti-European culture, as I understand it.'[13] He defends his former 'neutrality' firstly on the grounds of having been wrong in his estimate of Hitler, and once again on the grounds that falling foul of Germany had always seemed to him the shortest way into another World War. To warn his fellow-countrymen of such a disaster had seemed to him his first duty as a writer on foreign affairs; and he freely admits that to this end he had indulged in 'efforts at "appeasement" beside which those of Mr. Chamberlain pale in comparison'.[14]

This merely amounts to Lewis's admission that, like the British Government itself, he had wholly misjudged Hitler's military intentions in Europe. A large proportion of the British people had been guilty of the same mistake—not least of all, those who had been loudest in their defence of the Munich betrayal. To do him justice, Lewis had not been a party to that: while he seemed to have no strong feelings about the independence of Czechoslovakia (never having been there), his only word about Munich was that—as another British humiliation—it had been 'unedifying'.

But however many people may have agreed with it, there can be no denying that Lewis had been dangerously naïve in his estimate of the German menace throughout the decade. He had not taken the threat that 'heads will roll' very seriously, when Hitler had uttered it in September 1930. He had disregarded the message of *Mein Kampf*, which he admits to having read 'all through' only recently. He had misjudged Hitler's potential for 'sustained nonsense', and unlike certain 'warlike persons', had certainly not recognized him as 'a potential Tamerlane'. For while he had been right in his insistence upon the hold which Hitler exercised over the German people, he had failed to realize what that hold would make possible: for that, he suggests, he would have had to be 'a very exceptional seer'. He emphasizes that at no time had he personally succumbed to Hitler's influence or extolled National Socialist doctrine: as an observer, he had merely explained both as best he could. Having pointed out that Hitler had been the natural answer to Versailles, he had believed that the best way to draw the teeth of Hitlerism would be by removing the injustices which Versailles had imposed upon Germany. This, admittedly, had led him to support a certain measure of German rearmament. But who, he wonders, 'could have foreseen the lightning recovery of that unpleasantly resilient country?'[15] And who could have foreseen what use of limited rearmament Hitler would promptly have made?

It has to be remembered, of course, that *many* people had foreseen these things—and not merely those who 'perhaps with the intuition of the quarrelsome' had recognized 'another of their kind'. Some of them, like Frederick Voight of the *Manchester Guardian* (who had taken issue with Lewis over his first published articles on Hitler, back in January 1931) had foreseen *exactly* what Hitler intended, and had never ceased to warn the world of the danger and evils which he represented. Others, like Winston Churchill (who had been dismissed by Lewis as a warmonger), had consistently called attention to the speed and nature of German rearmament—in which he had even been seconded by Viscount Rothermere, to give his lordship due credit. Indeed, it was Lewis's long failure to realize what Hitlerism really boded for the world, which had left him out of step with most of the writers of his time. Having been right in his guess that Hitler would succeed to power, he had allowed himself to accept the fact as a good and reasonable thing.

Even in *The Hitler Cult*—presumably that part of it written before or at the time of Munich—he is still apt to underestimate Hitler's true capacity for harm. He still tends to be lulled by 'that platitudinous exterior': while Hitler is no longer to be regarded as 'papier mâché', Lewis can still not accept him as 'an iron Chancellor'—nor does it seem likely that he will prove so troublesome as Napoleon, 'for there is little of the Corsican tough in him'. He is 'no bona-fide brute', like Bismarck; and his model, Frederick the Great, has about as much in common with him 'as the Duke of Wellington would have with Lord Nuffield'—a disarming comparison! He still sees Hitler as something of 'a twentieth century German Don Quixote', the English being 'one of this deluded man's biggest and most dangerous windmills—alas!'[16] He condemns Hitler for 'petty and stupid malignity in his pursuit of the Jewish Minority' in Germany, which he finds 'an extremely ugly mark against him',[17] and he admits that Nazi anti-Semitism is 'new in degree, if not in kind'. He despises Hitler as a *destroyer of culture*, in which he lumps him along with 'the "geniuses" who invented the Yellow Press', and he speaks up at last for the German intellectual, 'since he, poor devil, if he remains inside the Reich, cannot answer for himself'. National Socialism he now denounces as 'a pernicious racket, that has got entirely out of hand',[18] and goes so far as to hope that 'something a bit superior to a Nazi' will be found by way of a Nietzschean higher being, 'if we are not all to perish in a series of senseless wars'.[19] So far as Hitler's ambitions are concerned:

> The changes Herr Hitler desires seem to me to be dull changes —a mere shift in the balance of power, so that Germany took the place of England as the political boss of Europe.... I could not myself take an interest in such a meaningless change-round as that—quite apart from the fact that as an Englishman I should not relish it, and that it would be a change for the worse.[20]

All of which, one may assume, would have been expressed in rather different terms if it had been written after the complete destruction of Warsaw....

Obviously, it was a serious disservice to Lewis that *The Hitler Cult* should have been published in that historical context. There is a great deal in the book which bears witness to a far more radical re-evaluation of recent events than these random quotations would suggest. Whatever the injustices of Versailles had been, would a victorious Germany in 1919 have imposed any less onerous terms on a defeated France and Britain? Lewis agrees that her handling of the Russians at the dictated peace of Brest–Litovsk hardly suggests as much. Nor, if the Versailles

Treaty had been hers to impose, would she have 'sat idly by while England, clause by clause, tore it to shreds'.[21] That the German people—no less than Hitler himself—worshipped violence, wanted mastery rather than equality, and so far as war-mindedness went, were 'unteachable', he now ruefully admits: 'for if the last war did not open their eyes nothing will.'[22] The post-Bismarckian German middle class, in 1914, had 'staked all upon a great war and lost'. Given the opportunity, they were obviously prepared to do so again.

Only this time, with Hitler to lead them, their imperialist ambitions stretched vastly further. So far as Hitler himself is concerned, Lewis assumes—this time, quite rightly—'that a Germanic hegemony in Europe, from Gibraltar to the Carpathians, from the Baltic to the Bosphorus, is now his aim'.[23] (Perhaps it would have been wiser to substitute the Urals for the Carpathians and the Persian Gulf for the Bosphorus.) But it is with no apparent sense of incongruity that he comments: 'Now that the restraints have been removed, now that arms are in its hands again, which it brandishes fiercely at all and sundry, one begins to wonder how one could ever have felt a sympathetic twinge for such a monster as Grossdeutschland.'[24] To which Lewis's critics of the thirties might well have answered, 'One does indeed. . . .'

But it is in its new approach to British foreign policy during the thirties that *The Hitler Cult* is most remarkable. It is now clear to Lewis that as a result of what she chose to regard as British 'encirclement', Germany was far more concerned to humble Britain than she was even to defeat France. Without British aid, France was in no position to withstand the combined might of the Axis, as she was very well aware. (Though Lewis does not mention it, Sir Norman Angell had long since stressed the fact that France herself had been technically defeated in World War I: victory had been finally won for her only by her allies.)[25] But if Britain had emerged as the true object of German hostility, she had really only her own irresolution to blame. Chamberlain's policy of appeasement had certainly failed: what policy *vis à vis* the dictators would have been more effective?

Once again, Lewis considers the three alternative policies which presented themselves to Britain in the earlier part of the decade. The Left-wing had been in favour of resisting aggression from the beginning. What he calls 'Fascist' or 'Fifth Column' opinion had been in favour of 'compacting' with the aggressors —believing that this would be in Britain's own interests. 'Isola-tionist' opinion had been in favour of Britain's remaining strictly neutral and leaving aggression to take care of itself. This last, it will be remembered, was the policy which Lewis himself had originally advocated, though his 'isolationism' had clearly been compromised by his desire for an 'understanding' with Germany—an 'understanding', we are to presume, which did *not* imply any 'compacting' with her. Such a policy would seem to have roughly coincided with appeasement as under-stood by Chamberlain and Halifax, whatever they felt about their obligations to France. But as Lewis sees it, appeasement had been nullified by the policy of 'interference' which had been followed earlier during the Baldwin–Eden days—what he calls 'a dubious mixture of all three policies'.[26] Interference itself had foundered upon its unsuccessful attempt to impose sanctions against Italy, the only result of which had been to drive Italy into the arms of Germany. 'Even to-day,' Lewis protests, 'most Englishmen do not admit that. Yet the outcome of Sanctions stares them in the face. Sanctions = Axis. It is as simple as that. And the Axis is no joke at all.'[27]

Lewis's chief objection to the Baldwin–Eden policy was that it represented a fundamentally *bogus* Left-wing attitude. It was bogus because it was neither one thing nor the other—neither the true Nationalism of a National Government nor the Social-ism of a true Labour Opposition:

> I am not suggesting here that the Baldwin Government should have approached the problem of Abyssinia as Nationalists. A crude Nationalist would be impossible in England to-day. What I am suggesting is that that Government should not have mixed up Socialist and Nationalist politics so inextricably as to cancel out both one and the other, and to alienate for ever Nationalist England's trusty friend, Italy. Sanctions was to no purpose, from the purely Socialist angle, for the sanctionist policy was not car-ried through to the bitter end. From the Nationalist angle it was fatal.[28]

Lewis confesses that his new sympathies lie 'with the parties of the Left', and their criticism of National Government policy he finds 'on the whole well-founded'. But he finds himself torn between what he regards as 'the specific interests' of the country to which he belongs, and 'those abstract, non-national interests—those of absolute justice—which the Left parties represent'.[29] Nevertheless, he attempts to assess—as a historian —what Britain's policy against the Axis might have been in terms of national expediency. She had, over the decade, been faced with five international crises—over Manchukuo, Abyssinia, Spain, Austria and Czechoslovakia.

Nothing much could have been achieved against the Japanese in Manchukuo, he believes, without the co-operation of the United States—which was not forthcoming. Denied that co-operation, the Royal Navy might well have lost half its strength in Far Eastern waters without having anything to show for it. (After Pearl Harbor, even with American co-operation, they quickly did.) As to intervention in Spain, we had made victory certain for Franco without having necessarily intended to do so. We had certainly failed to gain any advantage from his victory. We had tolerated Hitler's and Mussolini's intervention on his behalf in a way that had excited nothing but their derision:

> But let us all the same *suppose* that Great Britain had acted rationally, and with proper vigour and sunk all the pocket-battleships, and 'barred' Spanish waters to Axis shipping for the duration of the Spanish Civil War. We should have all become the best of friends. Both the Germans and Italians would have understood that perfectly.
>
> To have allowed the guns to speak was our obvious cue.... Instead we have employed the debased language of evangelical commonplace, which has only earned us their anger and contempt. At the time of which I speak we enjoyed a great superiority in Force. It was most disastrously inconsistent not to use it. For either we eschew Force altogether, or else we are not ashamed to employ it.[30]

As regards the invasion of Abyssinia, there again Britain might have acted decisively—if she was going to act at all. If she had done so, no Axis would have come into existence, for 'it would have been perfectly easy to blow Italy out of the Mediterranean and bring Mussolini's head on a pike to London'. But while we could quickly have won a shooting war, we had preferred to suffer a heavy diplomatic defeat. By doing so, we had acted in nobody's interest but Hitler's. We had made him a valuable present of an estranged ally, and from that time the *Anschluss* had been inevitable.

There is certainly something rather comical about this *post facto* Palmerstonianism—though there is a good deal to be said for the argument itself. But one can't help wondering how Lewis-the-pamphleteer would have reacted at the time, when the guns began to loose off. 'How to make a war about Nothing', would have been the very mildest way that he might have expressed himself! One can think of many things he would have been far more likely to say....

Nevertheless, times change opinions. And it is in his attitude to the diplomatic defeat of Munich that Lewis departs from his earlier stance most noticeably. By then, he feels, Britain was only too ready to make Hitler a present of the Sudetenland— 'and all that lay behind it'. For he believes that Stalin was probably right in his guess that the Western powers were secretly hoping that if the way was laid open for Hitler into Ruthenia, he would be 'really beautifully placed to make a piratic grab at the Ukraine'.[31]

Things, of course, had not worked out that way. Instead, following on the 'liberation' of Slovakia, and the total absorption of Bohemia and Moravia, Ruthenia had been handed over (for the time being) to the Hungarians—and Hitler had begun to show more interest in Danzig, the Polish Corridor and Romanian oil. In a manner which had been described by Robert Boothby as 'reckless, even desperate', guarantees against German aggression had promptly been extended by the British Government to Poland and Romania—and even, for good measure, to Greece. The first two of those three guarantees Britain was in no position to implement without Russian assistance. But no great anxiety had been shown by the British Government to ensure that assistance by treaty or negotiation: discussions in Moscow had been conducted half-heartedly at far too low a level. In the event, no promise of assistance had been forthcoming. Before Lewis's proofs were being finally updated, Britain was faced by a Nazi–Soviet Pact, and found herself at war with Germany over the invasion of a Poland she could not even reach by bomber.

That Lewis had been in favour of an Anglo-Soviet *rapprochement* while it was still possible, *The Hitler Cult* makes perfectly clear. Whatever he thought of Communism, by the spring of 1939 he could see the Soviet Union—at last—as a necessary ally in any confrontation with the Axis powers: 'The natural alignment is England, France, and Russia—with the United States hovering bellicosely in the background, and backing the Western *bloc*, if not with men, with material of war.'[32]

British negotiations with Moscow had begun in April 1939, but even before that, Lewis believes that Stalin must have lost all faith in an effective alliance with the West—particularly so, after the Munich Conference which he was not even invited to attend. But could nothing more have been done to win Russia's trust while there was still time? Lewis clearly thinks that something could, and blames the British Government for a totally wrong approach to Moscow. It was still behaving, he feels, as though it was in a position to bargain and impose conditions, whereas there was little enough that it could offer which was much to Russia's advantage. If the Kremlin was to be in any way impressed, it was high time that the condescending manner should be abandoned. He is not suggesting that Mr Chamberlain should 'get himself up in a cloth cap and a choker', though it might bode rather better for the Distressed Areas if he were to do so! But the simple fact remains that 'Russia is many times the size of England, and will be there after our empire is only a memory. And the "Russian steam-roller" should obviously be approached hat in hand, or with the circumspection of a Pekinese encountering a St. Bernard.'[33]

Lewis's whole attitude to an Anglo-Soviet alliance had changed—so much so, that in support of it he now found himself in agreement not merely with Lloyd George, but even with Churchill himself! To certain of his critics, this sudden switch in his political thinking seems to have come as a matter of some surprise. It need not have done so, even if Cobbett and others had not set him an earlier example in the way of reversed political opinions. The fact was, that under pressure of events, Lewis was merely reverting to older ways of thought—most notably, to his earlier Internationalism. In considering a situation which had resolved itself in a way that he had not expected—and had certainly not desired—his response to that situation had been forced to adjust itself. In the new context, even the doctrine that 'Peace is indivisible' is one that he is prepared to accept.

As regards the attitude of the United States, which he recognizes as being of the first importance, he admits that while President Roosevelt seemed only too anxious to support Britain against the Axis powers, the American people were still highly suspicious of all European entanglements. They were even more suspicious of Britain herself—combining as Britain did, imperialist traditions, an unAmerican class-consciousness, and a trick of defaulting on repayment of her war-debts. Perhaps the only hope of active support from that quarter lay in the fact that, like the British, the American is 'incapable of remaining morally detached', and war in Europe was clearly going to be fought on a moral issue.

But facing the facts as he finds them, Lewis is none too happy about Britain's prospects in the war when it breaks out. Both America and Russia remain as imponderables; yet without the support of the one and the neutrality of the other, the democracies stand a very good chance of being defeated. There is the chance that the Germans may choose to wage a limited war against France, protected as she was by her Maginot Line, at the same time launching an *un*limited war against Britain. There is always the possibility that France might be overwhelmed and compelled to sue for peace. Would Britain then be prepared to fight on against Germany on her own? If so, she might easily find herself starved into submission, unless America decided to intervene. Either way, the chances of a British victory were slight, and the price to be paid for it might well prove it a Pyrrhic victory at best. In a limited war, where the full force of Germany was hurled against us while France stood idly by, Britain might well lose everything.

Lewis is not always right in his predictions, by any means, but he is right occasionally. He is right in supposing that Britain would be forced to violate neutrality in an effort to deny Germany access to Swedish ore. (We did so by mining Norwegian waters in 1940.) He is wrong in supposing that the state of Czechoslovakia would ever be reconstituted. He is right in declaring that the Soviet Union 'would prove the grave of Fascist hopes much more effectively than Madrid, if Hitler were ever so stupid as to try his luck there'.[34] In which incomprehensible comparison we have a typical instance of the mixed-up patch-work-dating which is to be found throughout the book!

Needless to say, Lewis is no more of a strategist than he was a practical politician. His guesses are mostly made on the basis of wrong or insufficient information. It is quite pointless, there-fore, to read him as a sort of Nostradamus: that he was no 'very exceptional seer' he must surely have proved to himself, during the thirties, let alone to those who were apt to take his political pamphleteering over-seriously. His guesses are interest-ing to us because they are the guesses of a creative mind; but that does not make them any more trustworthy. Like Bernard Shaw, no doubt, Lewis reserved the right to be completely wrong—so long as he remained completely readable. But there is no doubt at all that he had an unusual ability to draw useful inferences from what he was able to study at first hand. And while he may not have known his Nazis, he certainly knew the British people. Critical as he had been of them on occasion, his good opinion of their better qualities emerged refreshingly in *The Mysterious Mr Bull*. What he was to say of them in the closing sections of *The Hitler Cult* is equally reassuring. Though they might be 'psychologically unprepared' for total war, he knows that they could be relied upon to withstand the horrors of any *Blitzkrieg*. There would be as many 'Old Bills' in Toot-ing Bec and Downing Street, he decides, as ever there had been in Flanders. And they would be as rich as ever in 'the old Pickwickian philosophy'.

Perhaps *The Hitler Cult*, therefore, is more interesting for what it says about Britain than for what it says about Nazi Germany. By the end of the book, Lewis has found himself largely in agreement with Dr Beneš, that the one great weak-ness of democracy is its lack of any real faith in its own principles. In Britain also we had tended too long to steer by 'utilitarian opportunism'—or rather, that was what most of our leaders had tried to steer us by. As for the British themselves, Lewis still growls that they are only too ready to be ruled in a 'slovenly manner'—though he agrees that this leaves us free of the rigours endured by the peoples of what he now calls 'the high-tension states'. He agrees also that rulership, as practised by the dictators, can be a far worse hazard than 'slovenly' government. There is nothing for John Bull to envy about the Spartan régime of the robots beyond the Rhine: his strength is certainly not to be sought in a regimented Strength through Joy. The end-product of the Hitler Cult he dismisses as 'a Sunday School of sunburnt state-paupers, armed to the teeth'. And thinking back to what he had seen of life in the Third Reich, he ends on a newly philosophic note: 'The mere thought of Hitler's Germany almost reconciles one, does it not, to our ramshackle civilization?'[35]

That 'almost', of course, is obligatory. For while Lewis has finally washed his hands of Hitlerism and all its works—which are certainly in no further need of 'expounding'—he is still unready to maintain that avoidance of a greater evil means tacitly to accept a lesser. And like Blake before him, where social justice and principles are concerned, he is unwilling that the sword should sleep in his hand.

For while he believes with Beneš that the coming war is not to be fought in a 'crusading' spirit—our society being what it is —he is at least anxious about its final outcome. Always granted that Britain wins through to enjoy it, the peace that follows the war must have something better to offer mankind than peace had had in the past. If Britain is indeed to be on the Christian side of the issue, the fact remains that she is still 'too imperfectly Christian' to make the fact as meaningful as it might be. And it is this thought which leads Lewis to make what is perhaps the most striking suggestion in the book:

> *Now we are at war, every soldier should go into battle with a charter of new liberties in his pocket.* A solemn promise from his rulers of a new deal for him and his children. They should be handed to every conscript, as he is called up. Then, indeed, we should be on the side of the light.[36]

Such a charter, Lewis maintains, could have been exacted by the Trade Unions and the Labour Party as the price of their support for conscription and the war effort. The wish for such a 'new deal' he sees as being shared 'by every intelligent man, whether he belongs to a political party or not'—for it requires neither Communism nor Socialism to bring it about: 'it is now only plain common sense.'[37] In the event, something very near to such a charter was implicit in the Beveridge Plan, which was presented as a blueprint for a Welfare State in 1943. As we know, that was to receive a very lukewarm endorsement from the Churchill government—and the electorate was to draw its own conclusions from the fact when the war ended. If the post-war Welfare State as it emerged was not exactly what Lewis's charter of liberties had implied, it had at least been inspired by the same ideals.

As for the Internationalism to which Lewis had reverted even before 1939, the closing sections of *The Hitler Cult* preach it again with all the persuasiveness that had been found in *The Art of Being Ruled*. Though it was vastly to be preferred to the German alternative, the British concept of Empire was not enough for him. The British knew well enough that they lived —as a people, and from day to day—not as the builders of an Empire, but rather as a small and overcrowded nation. That, no doubt, was why they were so paradoxically anxious to guarantee the freedom of nations even smaller—to support which, in a world dominated increasingly by giant states, only the role of a mock-Leviathan would seem to fit us. But ultimate survival could not be expected from any such self-inflation: our Empire itself was far too unstable. At best, it amounted to little more than a world-wide archipelago, every section of which was to some extent vulnerable. At worst, it provided Hitler and other imperialists with something of an alibi for conquests of their own.

A likelier hope of survival might lie in a federation of the Western democracies and the United States, if the parties to such a federation could be induced 'to abandon their national sovereignty, pool their resources, have a common Parliament and armies under one direction'.[38] Any such federation, Lewis is now prepared to support—for something, at least, of national identity might be preserved in such a merger. And in the teeth of his own beliefs of two or three years ago, he admits that 'if we could all of us have made up our minds to that earlier we could have avoided a general war'.[39]

But a balance of power, even between giants, is not the final answer, as the dangers of the Cold War were to remind him ten years later. Like peace itself, humanity should be indivisible:

> *The whole earth* should be the only giant! I cannot be interested
> myself, I confess, in an Empire that is smaller than that. Is not a
> *world-state*—one and indivisible—on the political plane, what
> monotheism is on the theological? Over against a plurality of
> 'sovereign states', is it not what a high-god is over against a
> multiplicity of deities? That is probably what the sincerest of
> those who supported the *Société des Nations* struggled towards.
> Though how vain to have done so, without first eradicating from
> the famous covenant clauses penalizing so intolerably the
> vanquished in a general war![40]

It was at least a *different* mistake which was later to hobble
the effectiveness of the United Nations....

NOTES

1. *C Y D*, p.80.
2. One remembers the would-be witticism of the cockney bus-conductors,
for example: 'We are now approaching Hampstead—please have your pass-
ports ready.'
3. *D of Y*, p.121.
4. *L W o E*, p.258.
5. *Mr Bull*, p.117.
6. *Hitler*, p.137.
7. *The Jews*, p.9.
8. Ibid., p.17.
9. Ibid., p.12.
10. Ibid., p.92.
11. Ibid., p.107.
12. Ibid., p.111.
13. *The H C*, p.vii.
14. Ibid., p.viii.
15. Ibid., p.27.
16. Ibid., p.62.
17. Ibid., p.97.
18. Ibid., p.23.
19. Ibid., p.130.
20. Ibid., p.135.
21. Ibid., p.28.
22. Ibid., p.42.
23. Ibid., p.191.
24. Ibid., p.192.
25. *Time and Tide: Foreign Affairs Supplement*, 6.4.35. The article had
been commented upon adversely by Lewis in a letter to the editor.
26. *The H C*, p.137.
27. Ibid., p.140.
28. Ibid., p.141.

29. Ibid., p.139.
30. Ibid., p.182.
31. Ibid., p.99.
32. Ibid., p.146.
33. Ibid., p.161.
34. Ibid., p.225.
35. Ibid.. p.254.
36. Ibid., p.184.
37. Ibid., p.221.
38. Ibid., p.239.
39. Ibid., p.241.
40. Ibid., pp.206-7.

CHAPTER 11

Western Man Goes Cosmic

Unlike that of certain others, Lewis's abrupt departure for
North America in September 1939 was not a planned escape
from the coming war—despite the pains he had been at, over
the last few years, to prevent that war from involving Britain.
But having undertaken the trip as a portrait painter in search
of commissions, he was to find himself marooned on the American continent for the full duration of hostilities in Europe. And
that the exile was anything but a happy one, emerges clearly
enough from his correspondence and the autobiographical overtones of his later novel *Self Condemned.* Perhaps it is not
surprising that the Second World War spanned the least
creative years of his life.

After their arrival in Canada, Lewis and his wife crossed into
the United States, where his first painting commission awaited
him in Buffalo. With its largely Polish population, the reception
in that city for the visiting Englishman would no doubt be
cool, so shortly after the death-agonies of Warsaw. But as no
more commissions were to be found there, the Lewises moved
on to New York, where at least they had many more friends. It
was there or in Connecticut, over the next few months, that
Lewis wrote up his impressions of America during the period
of the 'phoney war': they were published in New York the
following August as *America, I Presume.*

While it is little more than a pot-boiler, the book at least takes
a shrewd look at the American social scene, which Lewis was
able to study with the same amused detachment that he had
devoted to life among the mountain tribes of the High Atlas.

In writing it, he once again assumes a *persona*—this time, that of one Major Archibald Corcoran, an ex-army 'pukka sahib' who is over in America on a lecture tour in that capacity. While not so exasperating as 'Ned', Archie Corcoran is quite as fatuous as Launcelot Nidwit; and one is relieved to find that his narrative slips out of character for most of the book's 300 pages. But despite its 'pukka sahib' overlay—or what passes for such —the tone of the whole work is unmistakably Lewis's own. (So much so, in fact, that on one or two occasions we find him blandly quoting Lewis—without acknowledgment!) But slight as the book is, its keen observation is in the old Lewisian tradition. In particular, his descriptions of the middle class American at home are happily accurate; and there is one excursion into Canadian gothic—*I Dine with the Warden*—which is in his best satirical vein. But though he draws some amusing comparisons between English and American manners, and many astringent comparisons between their respective snobberies, there is nothing in the book which could really be described as 'political'. Even his discovery that 'since the war started Mr. Neville Chamberlain has rivalled Herr Hitler in unpopularity in the United States' is hardly significant: so had President Roosevelt, in many Republican circles. Lewis's growing respect for Roosevelt and the New Deal is tactfully kept out of the account: it reveals itself only in his correspondence.

As to the future of Anglo-American relations, there is little that such a book could do to define them usefully. For the most part, Lewis finds that the natives are friendly. Often enough, they find him funny—as he finds them funny in return. He is well aware of the distrust and antipathies which often divide the average American from the average Englishman. But what of that? '*Understanding* does not involve anything embarrassing or emotional: just a fair measure of give and take. Understanding is not love. Perhaps, indeed, it precludes love.'[1] Luckily, 'understanding' involved far less for Lewis in relation to America than it had in relation to Germany; and in this case, something nearly akin to love was to be born of it in the long run. For of one thing he was quite certain from the outset: whatever happened during the present war—whether America were to be drawn into it or not—'it is of vast importance that the English-speaking peoples of the world should act in harmony'.[2] That thought was to occupy him till long after the war was over.

It is implicit, for instance, in the pamphlet which he published the following summer in Toronto—*Anglosaxony: A League that Works*. Lewis had retired to Canada following the expiry of his American visa the previous autumn, and it was there that he was mostly to be immured for the next four years. The *Anglosaxony* pamphlet had been commissioned by the Ryerson Press, of which Dr Lorne Pierce was Editor-in-Chief. Though written primarily as wartime counter-propaganda, Lewis insisted subsequently that 'much of the argument has a validity beyond the special pleading of the moment'.[3] One is happy to accept this, for the pamphlet goes a long way to correct the balance of Lewis's political writing throughout the thirties. Though it is only seventy-five pages long, therefore, *Anglosaxony* is important. Unluckily, it is one of the hardest to come by of all his political works.

Writing as he was mainly for a Canadian audience, Lewis could assume that few of his readers would be familiar with his earlier pamphleteering. He was therefore under no great necessity of explaining the apparent shift in many of his political ideas. Even so, just to be on the safe side, he concedes that his previous works had sometimes been misunderstood:

> When people wish to be offensive about somebody, they call him a 'red' or a 'fascist'. (Which term they employ depends upon circumstances.) As for a long time a certain coolness existed between Stalin and myself, I have not been spared the epithet 'fascist'. But fascism—once I understood it—left me colder than communism. The latter at least pretended, at the start, to have something to do with helping the helpless and making the world a more decent and sensible place. It does start from the human being and his suffering. Whereas fascism glorifies bloodshed and preaches that man should model himself upon the wolf....[4]

It may have taken Lewis rather longer than some people to 'understand' Fascism, but once having reached that understanding, he had no further use for it even as an intellectual concept. In all fairness, it had never been more to him than that.

Anglosaxony is written in three parts, of which the first is mainly a defence of the democratic ideal against critics of both the Left and the Right. As so much of Lewis's distrust of democratic government derived from its failure to provide for the needs of the under-privileged, it may well be that the generally higher standards of living which he found in Canada and the United States—those parts of them that he visited—had convinced him that democracy and poverty need not necessarily be synonymous. In any case, the welcome absence of a British-type class-structure, even when replaced by one based simply on affluence, had apparently been something of a relief to him. But whatever the reason, it was from Canada that he first spoke up in full appreciation of the democratic system and democratic institutions.

It is a truism that one tends to undervalue what one is taking for granted; and it may well be that Lewis would have spoken up for democracy far sooner, if he had ever been forced to live under anything else. What he now says in defence of it, indeed, he may well have neglected to say before simply because, as he might have put it, 'every fool knows *that!*' But when he is taking his first look at British democracy from outside Britain (to which he was desperately anxious to return) distance had not so much lent enchantment to the view—rather, it had let him see the view for the first time in a proper perspective.

Where Fascism amounts to a religion, he now sees, democracy does not: but it is founded upon Christian ideals which he finds a welcome antidote to Fascism's law of the jungle. Under a democratic government, the State is there as a convenience for the individual: under Fascism, the individual is no more than an expendable unit in the totality of the State. Lewis no longer finds it necessary to 'expound' Fascism to the reader, since 'what the fascist does is quite sufficient explanation of what he is'.[5] (This cogent phrase he had obviously inherited from Hulme.) And while democratic government may be 'ramshackle', it is at least a 'well-meaning institution': if it does not always live up to them, its ideals are worthy. Its freedoms may be only comparative, since absolute freedom is an abstraction; but democratic government can ensure far more freedom for the individual than any alternative known to us. And though it may be attacked sometimes for its 'uncertain muddled outlines', that freedom is of the first importance. The Left-wing dissident may combine with the Fascist in asserting that democracy 'is in practice merely an attractive word to disguise the unattractive fact of plutocracy, which is what in fact our system is'.[6] But while he agrees that such dissidents may represent a 'sincere minority', nevertheless, Lewis declares, they in no way represent 'the average attitude' of the society which they are criticizing. And where he would once have dismissed this 'average attitude' as uninformed, he is now prepared to accept it with respect—where the society itself is worthy of respect.

Over the past decade, he feels, democratic society has paid more attention than perhaps it need have done to Left-wing intellectual opinion; but since the outbreak of the war, this has been noticeably on the wane. The Russian version of Communism is hardly to be taken very seriously in the light of recent events in Poland, Finland and elsewhere. (The Nazi attack on the Soviet Union had not been launched when he was writing.) But on whichever side the dissident intellectual might be found—with the Nietzschean supermen or the Leninist reformers—he had never yet succeeded in converting the majority of people without a resort to force. Lewis admits that he had once been a 'theoretician' himself, an advocate of the *tabula rasa*. But he has abandoned that position, as he no longer believes it is tenable: 'We cannot build up from the base, politically; all we can do is to alter as we go along, adapt, and, as we believe, improve.'[7]

This, of course, he had already admitted in *The Mysterious Mr Bull*: it is wiser, as he now sees it, to be practical than to be a perfectionist. Even so, he would still add a warning:

> Before, however, turning our backs—in the name of common sense—upon the dreamland of the theoretician, with his blueprints of the perfect society, let me say that we should be unwise entirely to forget it. If it is true that it has been a happy hunting ground in recent years for great numbers of ambitious nobodies (who cared about as much for the working man as they did for the dinosaur, or as the Kaiser for his cannon fodder) it is, all the same, the homeland or trysting-place of the saints and the philosophers. If we are compelled to admit that it is impracticable for us to mass-migrate to it, let us not forget it altogether.[8]

In short, while we should be rash to exchange our democratic

system for any other, we should still be ready to improve that
system in any way we can.

For the chief advantage of democratic government, as Lewis
has come to realize, lies in the fact that it *can* be improved.
Democracy in its essence is optimistic: it invites change and
improvement where Fascism does not. Democracy does at least
'leave the road open for an advance in the right direction'.
Totalitarianism, on the other hand, 'closes that road for good'.[9]
It treats all such democratic ideals as freedom, justice and social
equality as unrealizable—and even as undesirable. In doing so,
it may claim to be sweeping away a certain amount of pretence,
but is that a wise thing in itself? Lewis does not think so: 'Provided our pretensions do not go so far as to suppose ourselves
capable of ethical feats to which only a saint could aspire, a
moderate amount of illusion is an excellent thing'. There is
certainly nothing to be feared of aspiration.

But it is when he moves on to the subject of how the democratic ideal has evolved among the Anglo-Saxon people that
Lewis really gets down to his new thesis. For over-simplification
though it may seem, he is now prepared to maintain that
'Democracy is merely a name for the Anglo-Saxon peoples,
and their traditional way of behaving'.[10] He agrees that such
an identification would not have been possible in the days of
nineteenth century jingo-imperialism. 'Democracy' was as bad
a misnomer for that as it had been for the slave-societies of
Athens or the Roman Republic before Caesar. But that idea of
a pseudo-democracy had surely been repudiated for good. The
anomalies to which it had given rise had been weighing increasingly upon the conscience of society; and the British, at
least, were clearly determined that they should be done away
with to make room for something better. Indeed, that was the
very reason why Britain had embroiled herself in what could
only be described as an ideological war. And whether the ideals
for which she was fighting would be 'on the ascendency in the
years immediately succeeding it, will depend upon the extent
to which the Anglo-Saxons have coloured with their personal
ways of thinking the world-tide—the great will to social re-
adjustment, which the next peace will see at its flood'.[11]

Even so, while equating democracy with the Anglo-Saxon
tradition, Lewis is careful to underline the fact that this is in

no sense to give it a nationalistic slant. We had no desire to impose our own brand of democracy upon others—provided they did not try to impose their alternative systems on us, and 'do not insist upon their right to commit murders every night in their own house, while we neighbours have to lie awake and listen to the screams of their victims'.[12]

The short second section of *Anglosaxony* is devoted to Lewis's account of *How Fascism Began*, and contains nothing of any great moment. But it is for the last of its three parts—that devoted to *Sea-Power and Universalism*—that the pamphlet is perhaps most original. Even as far back as *BLAST*, the sea had been a factor in British life which Lewis had been prepared to bless. But now he goes so far as to credit the sea with having given birth to Anglo-Saxon democracy no less than to Aphrodite herself. Sea-power and sea-mindedness, furthermore, he regards as linked to the cult of Internationalism, in the same way that the land-mindedness of the Nazi—his obsession with *Blut und Boden*—is symptomatic of his myopic nationalism. The 'maritime universalism' of British sea-power, resented so violently by Goebbels, is something which Germany can never forgive: it is also something which she can do nothing to contest. Not even the Italians had thought of exercising sea-power beyond the Mediterranean—the *mare nostrum* in which we had disputed it with them so successfully. As for the Japanese, with a fleet built to operate in Far Eastern waters, they 'remained the Malay pirates that they have always been—seamen not looking essentially beyond the waters in which they have operated since the dawn of history'.[13] Only Britain and America have made it their business to sail the seas of the world and control them—since the seas are what both live by. Britain and America are the cosmopolitan powers of the sea: the other nations are continental powers controlling merely their own coastal waters. These two kinds of seafaring, Lewis describes as being 'as different, one from the other, as chamber-music is to a symphony written for a great orchestra'[14]—one of the few musical comparisons in which he ever indulged himself.

Sea-mindedness, admittedly, is only a minor aspect of the 'universalism' or Internationalism for which he believes the world will be waiting when the war is over. But it goes with the outlook of which Internationalism will be born. And being a prerogative of the Anglo-Saxon powers—with which he has already identified the truest essence of democracy—Lewis decides that both are likely to be formative influences in the shaping of the future World State. As to the World State itself: 'In this war the curtain may not fall upon anything as satisfactory and conclusive as that. But all of us feel that the present struggle with the Dritte Reich will at least be the prelude to some such consolidation of life on our planet into one political organism, in place of many'.[15] Needless to say, if Lewis had realized while writing that, how the Soviet Union was to emerge from the war as one of the victors, he would not have felt quite so sanguine about *one* political organism. . . .

As it was, he leaves no doubt that in such a consolidation he sees the only hope of lasting peace. And while they will be no more than participants in a World State, he makes a strong plea that the Anglo-Saxon powers should seek to infuse it with the character of their own democracy. It will have to be an *improved* democracy, purged of any taint of racialism or class-snobbery, and even be put forward as 'an antiseptic, sweet-smelling, blue-eyed version of communism'.[16] (That, after all, might better recommend itself to the under-privileged nations than what they had come to mistrust as 'bourgeois' democracy.) Since the Anglo-Saxon genius is flexible rather than hidebound, and their democracy is adaptable, this could very easily be done. But in whatever way we choose to adapt it, the democracy which we offer to the peoples of the world must retain its essential character:

> No one will ever offer them anything half as good. If they are such fools as to think otherwise, we can do no more about it. The Anglo-Saxon has played his part. And then Anglo-Saxony *is* a League of Nations that *works*. Our parliaments, our *gemots*, are in full working order. Leagued as we are together, we comprise by far the greatest political force in the world. Let others join us if they feel so inclined. That, I submit, should be our attitude.[17]

Such a peroration certainly strikes a new note for the author of *The Art of Being Ruled*, but the note has a curious ring of sincerity to it. Lewis's sub-title—*A League that Works*—had been wished upon him by his publisher, and he makes what he can of it. But it was not merely the British Commonwealth that he had in mind when he coined the word 'Anglosaxony'. For while the United States were in no 'league' with the Commonwealth at the time, he makes it plain that he expects them to be drawn into war on the same side. A composite Anglosaxony, in fact, is what he would dearly like to see established as a power for good in the world—the first step towards his idea of the World State which he hoped to see built up very much in its likeness. And as the major partner in such a composite, it is to the United States of America that his thoughts were to turn increasingly over the next few years.

In one of his letters to Lorne Pierce, Lewis makes it clear that the thinking behind the last section of *Anglosaxony* chimes with a concept of the American columnist, Dorothy Thompson. In a recently syndicated article, she had apparently referred to the 'Cosmic virtues' of the American people: 'and it seems to me,' Lewis writes, 'that the English, owing to their seafaring habits, possess, in their different way, those cosmic virtues too... More and more it becomes apparent that we the island-nations, with our sea-power, will be the *outsiders*, in the coming years: I mean that of the big power-groups that are in process of formation, we are the inhabitants or controllers of the great ocean wastes, outside the old continental nucleus.'[18]

As we know, *outsideness* was a state which Lewis was very ready to accept. Indeed, it was the state that he had sought to maintain and propound throughout his writing life. But it was Dorothy Thompson's mention of 'Cosmic virtues' that was to suggest to him the theme of his next book, *America and Cosmic Man*. It was to be a case of slow gestation, for while Lewis mentions the work in 1943 as having been in hand 'for some time', it was not finished until three years later. As it was then rejected by the American publishers to whom it had been offered, it had to wait a further two years before finally appearing in England in July 1948.

As already mentioned in a footnote, a section of the work had been published in *The Sewanee Review* under the title of *The Cosmic Uniform of Peace*, and this article might fittingly be regarded as Lewis's farewell to North America. For before it had appeared, in the autumn of 1945, the wartime ice-pack had finally broken up, and along with his wife, Lewis had thankfully returned to a London from which he had been cut off for the last six years.

Read in conjunction with the letters which he was writing at the same time, the article provides an interesting proof of the distinction Lewis was still apt to draw between what might be called the concept and the everyday reality. In a letter to Allen Tate, who had accepted the essay for *Sewanee*, he confesses that life in America had appalled him by its blatant commercialism. As for New York, he feels that he will never lose his terror of the city. Yet the theory which he is evolving in his essay—that America represents a way of life for the future—fascinates and even excites him: 'The destiny of America is not to be just another "grande nation": but to be the great big promiscuous grave into which tumble and there disintegrate all that was formerly race, class, or nationhood.'[19]

Lewis's ready acceptance of this idea as something right and proper in itself is strangely at variance with the attitude of Henry James, whose thoughts on the subject in *The American Scene* he had discussed in *Men Without Art*. Where James had likened New York to a 'cauldron', Lewis had seen it as a 'Melting-pot'; but from their identical concepts of the city, they had drawn very different conclusions. What had been for James the tragic end of an older way of life ('what type, as the result of such a prodigious amalgam, such a hotch-potch of racial ingredients, is to be conceived as shaping itself?') this had seemed to Lewis rather the coming to birth of a new and sounder society. The rootless nature of American society had filled James with dismay: it filled Lewis, on the contrary, with admiration. It is a surprise to him, he says, that 'the bluff of the *rooted* boys has never been called'. And he contends that 'No American worth his salt should go looking around for a root. ... For is not that tantamount to giving up the most conspicuous advantage of being American, which is surely to have turned one's back on race, caste, and all that pertains to the rooted state?'[20]

It might be argued, of course, that the average American tends to seek for his roots in affluence—often enough in the 'great tough clamorous abyss of Dollar madness' to which Lewis had been objecting. But so far as theory goes, he identifies the American as one who has uprooted himself by design: he is a man who has rejected an older way of life and opted, of his own free will, for a life which he believes to be better. That life, which is the abnegation of every idea of nationality in the European sense, offers the immigrant something which can be offered by no other country on earth, 'for in becoming an American, it is not a nationality that is being assumed, but a new way of life, universal and all-inclusive in its very postulates'.[21]

But how is a similar supra-national unity to be promoted upon a world-wide basis? Will the peace to which war has given place in Europe produce that desirable result? If men could only be inspired by a will to achieve their own salvation, it certainly would: world peace would replace with a single cosmic uniform the many uniforms in which they had been so madly slaughtering themselves. But is it reasonable to blame the stupidity of continuing national-mindedness upon the stubbornness of the mass of men? Lewis will not admit this. Harking back to his old argument—that freedom and irresponsibility are commutative terms—he points out that it is not in the nature of the majority to be concerned with reform and change. Rather it must inevitably be to their leaders that one must look for political initiative. And if one begins to wonder how much longer it will be before we arrive at 'the only logical thing, one society, for one poor little earth', it is not among the conservative masses that the answer is to be sought: one must address oneself to the Management. For they alone have the means of achieving the world unity which we all desire.

Nor is Lewis by any means convinced that such unity can be looked for in the United Nations Organization which had recently been created:

At the moment at which I write it is proposed to reassert the sovereign rights of all nations, irrespective of size or other limitations. We should of course, instead of this, be insisting upon small states merging themselves into larger units, not the perpetuation of insignificant politics, the accidental creations of a world very different from ours. To go into a conference insisting that Russia and Santo Domingo possess the same voting power, as we did at San Francisco—so that two Santo Domingos outvote the Soviet Union—is as dangerous as it is silly.

While many people must have agreed with Lewis on this, his next point was rather more questionable:

> The fact that the Soviet Union is rapidly absorbing a number of small states, which ought to be a matter of general satisfaction—for it is a step in the right direction, i.e. political monism—is instead a subject of scandal and reproach. A world-state can only come piecemeal. It will never be the result of a fiat.[22]

The fact that any such 'absorption' of smaller states must inevitably lead to an ultimate confrontation between rival 'monisms' appears to be a hazard which Lewis had already resigned himself to accept. 'In the end,' he supposes, 'one monster will gobble up the other. Then there will be one political body there, throughout the world.' Which monster it will be —the United States or the Soviet Union—he leaves us to conjecture. Nor does he attempt very accurately to prophesy the date and nature of that final Armageddon, but derives wry comfort from the fact that whatever happens meanwhile, 'the era of great wars will end when a projectile is produced so powerful that it will wipe out the Bronx or Brooklyn at one blow'.[23]

Even before the essay was published, two such weapons had been dropped on Hiroshima and Nagasaki. And as Lewis was to realize yet again, his vision of world unity and peace was no nearer at all.

As already noted, it was three more years before the ideas put forth in *The Cosmic Uniform of Peace* were finally expanded into the book *America and Cosmic Man*. In that work, Lewis is no longer prepared to look for easy answers. Confrontation between the two great 'monisms' was an all too ominous fact. For what it is worth, he gives it as his opinion that an atomic war appears to be 'almost inevitable'. He assumes—correctly—that the bombs dropped on Japan in 1945 are 'no doubt already poor things to what are at present at our disposal'. And while never himself having been what could be called technically a pacifist, he wonders whether the time has not arrived when it would be legitimate to say: ' "From this point on all men who are not violently against what is known

241

as 'war' are insane, and the term 'pacifist' has no further relevance?"'

But that speculation comes only at the end of the work: for the most part, *America and Cosmic Man* is concerned with the nature of American democracy, and the formative influences which have made it what it is. Most notably, the book is an affirmation of Lewis's new belief that in the multi-racial structure of American society, with its concept of *e pluribus unum*, we have an impressive prototype of the world society of the future.

To many readers the theme may have seemed almost academic at a time when the Cold War was occupying so much of the news. Czechoslovakia also had recently been 'absorbed' by the Soviet bloc: the Berlin airlift was at its height, and the outbreak of another major war in Europe seemed only too probable. Cosmic man may well have seemed even more of an abstraction than usual, when the survival of *any* kind of man was becoming increasingly uncertain.

Perhaps it was not surprising, therefore, that the book was not very highly spoken of by some of the English critics.[24] Their reaction was only in line with the latent hostility, noticeable in many quarters, to America herself. The much-advertised American loan had just been exhausted, without bringing any lessening of wartime austerity to the British people. America had appeared to thrive on a war which had reduced Britain to the status of a poor relation. And to hold up the affluent American as a model to all future generations—at a time when bread and shoes were still on ration in British shops—was hardly likely to win the sympathy of the average British reader.

But *America and Cosmic Man* is nevertheless a work of considerable interest, and undoubtedly of the greatest relevance to a proper understanding of Lewis's later political thought. It is certainly one of the most perceptive books written about the Americans by an Englishman, and one which it is easy enough to appreciate today. As Lewis explains, it is not designed to 'sell' America to the English: it merely calls our attention to something of great significance which America had taught him to understand. That understanding, he declares furthermore, will influence everything that he thinks and writes henceforth. For it had turned him from 'a good European into an excellent internationalist'.

Once 'Western Man' was the object of my particular solicitude. He was ailing, in fact in a decline—it was denied me to foresee what would so shortly befall, and I sought to heal and reinvigorate him. He was of course past help, and now is dead.

He only breathed his last a short while ago, but to me he seems as far away as Cromagnon Man. I cannot regret him, I find, in the slightest degree. I feel no loyalty towards him. All my loyalties today are for a far more significant and imposing person, namely Cosmic Man (or 'Cosmopolitan', as they would have said in the last century). This man I have seen and talked with in America. So I know what he will be like when his day comes, and he is everywhere.[25]

Like another traveller before him, Lewis felt that he had seen the future—and it worked!

In tracing the origins of American democracy, Lewis has some illuminating things to say about the two opposing principles which he finds behind it—the centralizing authoritarianism of Hamilton and the decentralizing libertarianism of Jefferson. For Hamilton he can find kind words, despite the fact that he regards his open predilection for monarchy as an unforunate aberration. Indeed, in his declared insistence upon 'Authority', and his belief in the need for 'a political and social élite', Hamilton's ideas bear a strange resemblance to Lewis's own. As for Jefferson, with his ideal of 'the less government the better', Lewis notes a popular tendency to equate him over-closely, perhaps, with what we now regard as the democratic process. His idea of democracy 'contains much more that is anarchical than democratic, in the stricter sense'. And beside the bright flame of Paine's libertarianism, that of Jefferson is apt to appear a little smoky. In any case, for him, the need of America was for a pastoral society rather than for urbanization: if it had rested with Jefferson, the future of the Republic would have been agricultural rather than industrial. Yet it is to what he calls the 'beautiful polarity' of Hamilton and Jefferson that Lewis ascribes the balance which America now holds between the needs of the State and the rights of the individual.

It was in the personality and policies of President Franklin Delano Roosevelt, Lewis thinks, that the polarity found its most effective expression. It will be remembered that in *Left Wings over Europe* he had denounced Roosevelt (along with Litvinov!)

as a 'Centralizer', and complained that 'Centralized power—when it is human power—is for me, politically, the greatest evil it is possible to imagine'.[26] Whatever he had 'imagined' it to represent, however, observation of the reality had impressed him very differently. He had reverted to his earlier Internationalism before ever he had returned to the States in 1939, and after having studied their impact at first hand, had quickly reversed his opinions of both Roosevelt and the New Deal. In a letter to T. Sturge Moore, dated 15 July 1941, he admits to having been 'very impressed by the intelligence and humanity of Mr. Roosevelt, as observed at fairly close hand,' and goes on to say: 'His "new-deal" might extend—though not of course directed from or imposed from any centre—to all corners of the earth. A "new-deal" in some form or other is sorely needed, in almost every nation, where industrial technique has outstripped social organization, and made a nonsense of government on the old lines.'[27] A year later, writing to Naomi Mitchison, he is even more enthusiastic: 'For life on this continent, unpleasant as it has been, has given me a close-up of Roosevelt. All the hostility I felt for the *centralizer* I no longer feel. If you are a really *global* centralizer, as Roosevelt is, then it is a different matter. And perhaps you have to get outside of Europe to see *the earth*.... Decentralization, upon so small a planet, is an absurdity.'[28]

It must now be perfectly clear that Lewis's ideas upon authoritarianism meant no more to him than a firm preference for *effective* government. When 'Ned' was naughty enough in *Count Your Dead* to suggest that Fascism 'might be a very good solution indeed' for the economic ills of Britain in the thirties, he had really been saying no more than that a government which resolutely did *something* about those ills might be better than one which happily did nothing at all. In Roosevelt's administration, Lewis found a government which had resolutely done a very great deal. As a President, he rates Roosevelt himself as 'one of the most dazzlingly successful' that America had elected. Under his New Deal, he feels that the United States had 'moved forward a century or so'. Most important of all, so far as Lewis is concerned: 'Within a decade this new bureaucratic power had put the big-business world under its spell. Could Roosevelt have lived a few years longer the New Deal might, for better or for worse, have effected a complete break in American tradition. They might have rewritten the Constitution—not of course torn it up—so that it harmonized with contemporary economic conditions.'[29]

Though the means which Roosevelt had been sometimes forced to employ—like his packing of the Supreme Court—had not been so 'democratic' as they appeared, the fact remained that the results had always been beneficial to the majority. More significantly, even when his actions had been most authoritarian, the average American had felt no loss of his political rights. This, of course, was fully in accord with what *The Art of Being Ruled* had advocated as the best and most effective way to run a modern state. And it is interesting to find Lewis now confessing that the best balance yet between firm government and individual freedom had been struck by a democratic rather than a totalitarian régime.

While never belittling his shrewdness as a politician, it is as an impresario that Lewis finds Roosevelt most intriguing. He had shown a remarkable aptitude for surrounding himself with technical experts and administrators who knew far more about the actual processes of government than he did himself. His 'brain trust' had been given its head to create the New Deal in his name—while, typically enough, he himself remained no party to it. In effect, after all, the New Deal was itself unconstitutional—and as President, it was the Constitution that he was pledged to uphold. After his particular contribution had been made, therefore, nearly every prominent New Dealer had been firmly (and not always quietly) removed from the political scene. The team may always have been changing, but never since Jefferson had such encouragement been given to so many talents. Never since Hamilton had there been so convinced an exponent of centralization, though the unorthodoxy of Roosevelt's economic thinking might well have reduced Hamilton to despair. First of all Roosevelt's virtues, in Lewis's eyes: 'No contemporary statesman was so confirmed an internationalist. He, more than any man, was in the secret of the peculiar destiny of his country.'[30]

That the average American should be totally unaware of that destiny, Lewis is again the first to agree. The average American is quite sufficient unto himself, and the recurrent phases of

American Isolationism bear witness to his essential reluctance to become involved in matters which do not concern him. Even so, his destiny—whether he likes it or not—is to be the catalyst that will break down the barriers of world society, just as he himself had once been broken down within the American Melting-pot.

Nor is it really a matter of what the American has already done to change the world, though most of it has been for the better. It is really more a matter of what America has done to him herself. For alone among the countries of the world, the United States were born of idealism and optimism: their creation was 'an act of faith in tomorrow', and the act is renewed by every immigrant who reaches their shores. For as Lewis was not the first to have remarked, 'America is much more a psychological something than a territorial something'.

Of that psychology, and the outlook to which it has given rise, Lewis is wholly appreciative. He admits that there is a strongly anarchical strain in much that makes up the American tradition and way of life. With his old distrust of political chaos, he himself is anything but an anarchist; but he can still approve of a libertarianism which derives no less from Jefferson than from Proudhon. He is even prepared to concede that in a well ordered society, 'there must not be too much order: better chaos than that'. And he admires the rebel that is in every American, no matter how firmly he is tied down by sumptuary laws or bureaucratic red tape, for in that rebelliousness is the seed of individuality. As for the pursuit of happiness, he is prepared to accept it as an end in itself, and will certainly defend it against any imposed canons of austerity, whether Marxian or whatever. For while he feels that complete anarchy is the philosophy of Paradise rather than of any earthly society, 'theoretically it might quite well be the philosophy of the cosmic society of the future—or some democratic régime, with a generous admixture of anarchy'.[31]

But it is the social characteristics of Americanism which impress Lewis most deeply. The American still enjoys a strong and natural feeling of 'brotherly love' for his fellow-men, which may well hark back to the early Quakers and Puritans whose influence can still be traced throughout the country. It is precisely this 'beautiful impulse to befriend' and 'to treat all men as brothers' which Lewis finds most inspiring and surprising about American life. Often enough it may be related, perhaps, to the 'frontier spirit', which persists long after 'The Frontier' has ceased to have any meaning. The American's rootlessness—his freedom from all restraint of place or tradition —and the gregariousness which goes along with it, have left him better fitted to mix in with his neighbours, and made of him in consequence a better citizen than most people. It is this fact, Lewis decides, which makes of American society 'a sort of communal pooling of all the cordial reactions of man'.

As for the mixed nature of American racial stock, even the amalgam represented by John Bull himself is poor by comparison. Every nationality in Europe, every race under the sun, every shade of colour and every variety of faith have been poured into the crucible. In its ameliorating chemistry, the world has merged all that it has to offer of difference or degree: yet the process is still no more than a beginning. America is merely the start of a new relationship between the world and those who inhabit it—no more than a trial run. 'There is new man there you do not find anywhere else. He is not Cosmic Man yet, of course, he is innocent of the notion, even, of a cosmic culture. But he is moving towards that end, by reason of the logic of his position in time and space.'[32]

Not that Lewis denies America her share of faults and imperfections: a fair proportion of *America and Cosmic Man* is devoted to examining them. Culturally, he regrets that America has as yet very little to show for herself, though he believes that a cosmic culture will probably precede a cosmic society, and to that America will doubtless contribute in time. But meanwhile, White America at least is virtually in the grip of a cultural ice-age. Commercialism—whether in Carthage or in Manhattan— is totally allergic to the cultural impulse; and nowhere else on earth, Lewis admits, does commercialism reign so squatly and so bleakly as it does among White Americans. On the economic front, despite the brilliance of her scientific and technological achievement, America's financial system continues to creak along as though the days of the ox-drawn waggon lingered on. For that reason, if for no other, America still suffers like the rest of the world from all 'the horrors of peace'—poverty, disease, injustice, intolerance and violence. Even socially, it seems, the

American amalgam still leaves a great deal to be desired. Most notably, America is to be blamed for the discrimination which she continues to exercise against the Jews, and for her total failure to integrate the Black American, whose plight in or out of her ghettos Lewis deplores as utterly indefensible. And remembering the misunderstanding to which *Paleface* had once given rise, he goes out of his way to set that particular record straight:

> American civilization as we know it owes more, probably, to the Negro than to anybody. The coloured people are the artistic leaven; out of their outcast state they have made a splendid cultural instrument. The almost solar power of their warm-heartedness has been a precious influence; their mirth, too, which explodes like a refreshing storm, often making these house-serfs the only sane thing in the White household. Yet everybody knows how they are requited by their fellow-citizens for their enormous gift to America.[33]

The dark laughter has obviously begun to reverberate through Lewis's subconscious; and so long as he does not have to listen to it, perhaps, he is now prepared to accept even American jazz. (The jungle tom-toms have at least successfully put down the Irish bagpipe—except on St Patrick's Day.) He has the highest hopes of what may lap over into America from China and Japan, whose arts are among the greatest that he is prepared to recognize. But now that the Cosmic Melting-pot is well and truly on the boil, even the American Indian becomes a worthy and necessary ingredient. After all, Diego Rivera, a Mexican Indian, has already frescoed Detroit with the one great glorification of American industry—it having taken an Indian to 'understand the tropical shapes of the great steel labyrinths'. Rivera, Orozco, Siqueiros and their compatriots he regards as the 'best North American artists'. (It is worth remarking that much of Lewis's own painting would not look out of place in their company, e.g. *The Armada* or *The Surrender of Barcelona*.) And when 'the Indian culture of Mexico melts into the great American mass to the North, the Indian will probably give it its art as the Negro has its music'. Mexico City, in fact, appeals to him as 'the future Paris of the New World'—and if only the Papacy could be persuaded to establish itself in Quebec....

After all, America has always been built from the outside—
'many different peoples and cultures converging on it'—and it
is this centripetal force which has become America's greatest
strength. If the synthesis is not yet complete, it has long since
passed the point where anything could be done to arrest it: the
future has already been assured. For America is the one place
on earth where the Greek ideal of Cosmopolis is in course of
being achieved. More important, the American Union is the
one area on earth which is a triumphant renunciation of the
Platonic heresy—austerity-ridden sovereignty dwelling in fear
and mistrust of its every neighbour: 'so grim, and cruelly dull,
a pattern of a state could never have occurred to him had Plato
lived in a world in which state-sovereignty had been abolished,
or had never existed.'[34] For within the American Union, it has
been proved that neighbouring states *can* live in amity, one
with another. There is no enmity there between Athens and
Sparta: states' rights have been subordinated to the welfare and
strengthening of the whole:

> To what conclusion can it lead, except to a deep conviction of the
> inexplicable folly of these ancient states over here, which persist
> in their murderous habits, and, as a consequence, sink into misery
> and ruin? In the forty-eight united states of America we have the
> model and exemplar of what is required everywhere. In the fact
> that great numbers of people of different nationalities can live
> side by side, without interfering with one another, we have the
> proof that it is not the *people* who are responsible for the inces-
> sant disputes and armed conflicts. All that is necessary is *one*
> government instead of many. It is as simple as that. How right
> Lincoln was to fight to the death for that. The end of state
> sovereignties would not resolve all the problems of human life.
> But the difference would be so enormous that anyone might be
> excused for thinking of that to the exclusion of everything else.
> No official of U.N.O., however the Charter may read, should
> admit any other thought to his head.[35]

Whatever Lewis had once had to say about national sovereignty in *Left Wings over Europe*, he is now unsaying with a
vengeance! But America in herself is not the answer to the
problem that he is trying to solve. Happy as the relations between his forty-eight states may be, there is still the obstinate

fact to face of the sovereignty of the American Union itself. There is also the uncompromising sovereignty of the Soviet Union with its fifteen republics, to say nothing of the sovereignty of the People's Republic of China and the possibly foreseeable United States of Europe.

Lewis is firmly convinced that 'Were all the facts put before them without bias, a referendum of the inhabitants of the earth would tomorrow produce a vote quite overwhelmingly in favour of a world government.'[36] He is resigned to the fact that no such referendum will ever be held—though he is now prepared to bring even Rousseau to his support in arguing that it should be.[37] But perhaps we may be forgiven for questioning his assumption. Supposing that a world referendum were resorted to as a necessary and feasible thing—can we be sure that it would be 'overwhelmingly' in favour of anything at all? Leaving political pressures out of the reckoning, far too many prejudices, fears, jealousies and superstitions are abroad in the world to cancel each other out. Human psychology being what it is, the sexes balance out no more equally than the 'ayes' are balanced out by the 'noes' on any general issue. If any world authority is ever confirmed in power, as Lewis himself regrets in another context, it will have to be by courtesy of the old antinomy of squabbling national managements.

If for no other reason, Lewis is anything but hopeful that his vision of World Government will be achieved in the near future. That would be far too much to expect—whichever way 'the inhabitants of the earth' might feel about it. 'The chastest of women,' he says bitterly, 'could be thought of much more easily succumbing to lascivious advances, than could powerful states be imagined parting with their precious sovereignty.'[38] And seeing things now in rather better perspective than he once did: 'to merge Wall Street and the Kremlin seems, for a start, a sheer impossibility.'

So he is back once more with the fear that the Bomb will prove to be the only effective catalyst. A World State may conceivably be *blasted* into existence, but who will be left alive to enjoy the fact? In any case, the cost might well appear to be excessive—whether Cosmic Man resembled his American prototype or not. It is to be hoped, therefore, that common sense will prevail. For of one thing we may be reasonably certain: a world divided as ours is will not remain divided and quiescent indefinitely. 'A very few years of no-change-for-the-better and you have atomic war.'[39]

Lewis was to return to the theme in *Rude Assignment*, two years later. For that work was not only to complete the intellectual autobiography begun in *Blasting and Bombardiering*: it was also to comprise his last important political testament.

NOTES

1. *A I P*, p.204.
2. Ibid., pp.211-2.
3. *The Cosmic Uniform of Peace*, by Wyndham Lewis: *The Sewanee Review*, Autumn 1945, p.507. Subsequently the passage was reprinted in *America and Cosmic Man*, p.154.
4. *Anglosaxony*, p.35.
5. Ibid., p.6.
6. Ibid., p.8.
7. Ibid., p.72.
8. Ibid., p.13.
9. Ibid., p.17.
10. Ibid.. p.20.
11. Ibid., pp.23-4.
12. Ibid., p.30.
13. Ibid., p.56.
14. Ibid., p.59.
15. Ibid., p.61.
16. Ibid., pp.74-5.
17. Ibid., p.75.
18. *Letters of W L*, p.289.
19. *The Sewanee Review*, Autumn 1945, p.509.
20. Ibid., p.519.
21. Ibid., p.520.
22. Ibid., p.511.
23. Ibid., p.513.
24. When published in America the following year, the reception was more friendly. A highly appreciative review by David T. Bazelon appeared in the *Partisan Review* (August 1949), for example, where Lewis was not normally given very cordial treatment.
25. *A C M*, p.219.
26. *L W o E*, p.16.
27. *Letters of W L*, pp.292-3.
28. Ibid., pp.328-9.
29. *A C M*, pp.55-8.
30. Ibid., p.57.
31. Ibid., p.199.
32. Ibid., p.184.
33. Ibid., p.186.
34. Ibid., p.171

35. Ibid., pp.219-20.
36. Ibid., p.220.
37. 'Jean-Jacques Rousseau's insistence that no government deserves the title of "Popular Government" unless the people participate directly in the law-making and *not through delegates or representatives* should command attention. In societies so large as ours it is only by the Referendum that direct popular action can be compassed. Without that, Democracy is an anachronism.' Ibid., p.34.
38. Ibid., p.220.
39. Ibid., p.224.

CHAPTER 12

The Circle Rudely Squared

The Britain to which Lewis returned in 1945 was a very different place from the Britain he had left in 1939. Nor was this any great surprise to him: he had already resigned himself to the fact that so far as the national economy was concerned, the only result of World War II could be crippling insolvency. If German militarism had achieved no more than that, at least it had been able to reduce Britain to the condition of a 'bankrupt slum'. And that was the condition in which it seemed to be on his return—though the blame could not be put entirely upon the Germans. It seemed to him, rather, that postwar economic chaos 'is what the Socialist Government of England inherits from generations of men who have put class before country, but were too stupid to keep healthy and intact the milch-cow of their privileged order'.[1] The chaos was little more attributable to wartime disruption than to post-1931 National Government misrule—to say nothing of pre-1931 misrule by every political party. In this analysis, quite a number of people were ready to agree with him.

Lewis had always been a professed believer in 'some form of Socialism'—no matter under whose auspices it was being applied. During the war, he had found the Beveridge Report 'cheerful reading': its promise of a post-war Welfare State appealed to him as 'the minimum requirement', and he had expressed the hope that the 'progressive' parties in Britain would stand by the report and 'not allow the smallest fraction of it to be whittled away.'[2] Obviously enough, the 1945 electorate had been very much of his own opinion. And on his return to London, Lewis had continued to side with certain Left-wing friends in their belief that peace in Europe would bring 'social justice and the destruction of much nonsense.'[3] He was even prepared to be doctrinaire: 'In orderly progression let us hope all necessary measures of nationalization will be carried through, and exploitation of the people (us and the rest) be made impossible.'[4] As for the Labour Government that he found in office—as already noted, he was prepared to greet it as 'the best—or at least to start with the most promising' government that Britain had ever known.[5] When he later found cause to complain of the deadening effects of austerity from which the country continued to suffer, it was not so much Socialism that he blamed as the inefficient and unimaginative way in which it was being introduced. Here again, there were many people ready to agree with him.

But it was not really the 'stern ordeal' of living under a severely regulated economy which concerned Lewis as a writer during the later forties. The long delay in publishing *America and Cosmic Man* was bridged by a brilliant series of art criticisms which he wrote for *The Listener*, and by the writing of an autobiographical *apologia*. This was originally to be called *The Politics of the Intellect*—a title used earlier for the last chapter of *The Art of Being Ruled*. It was finally published in November 1950 as *Rude Assignment*, and a second impression was called for two months later. Lewis described it as *A narrative of my career up-to-date*, and in its completion of the story partly told in *Blasting and Bombardiering*, it is one of the most readable of his later works. It is also one of the most illuminating.

In a letter to J. Alan White, Lewis admitted that to appreciate it fully, his earlier works would have to be known, 'otherwise the reader of *Rude Assignment* would half the time be at sea, and in a rough sea at that....'[6] This may be true, in a sense, for the work is a spirited defence of his critical and polemical standpoint over the years—that being in greater need of defence, he feels, than his purely creative work which could be left to speak for itself. In its review of his political writings, adjustments are made in the light of later opinions, and some admissions are made as to wrong judgments. In many cases, these footnotings have been considered in the course of this study. But there is a great deal in *Rude Assignment* which expands and reinforces earlier argument in a new way; and this, together with the original thinking which it devotes to the problems of peace, make the book of the first importance as Lewis's final statement on subjects which had preoccupied him throughout his writing life.

The work is divided into three parts again, of which the first is given over to the 'Three Fatalities' which had been instrumental in shaping his career: the ambivalent position of the intellectual in the modern world; the nature of satire; and the overriding influence of politics in contemporary thought. Part Two supplies something of the personal background to his career; and Part Three examines the various books that he has written and clarifies what he calls *A Pattern of Thinking*. In this he defends and develops the ideas put forward in *The Art of Being Ruled* in the light of twenty-five more years' experience of the process.

The Foreword to Part Three contains a highly significant remark in explanation of the unfortunate line in foreign affairs which he had pursued during the thirties. The fact that the Cold War had by now turned many former 'Pinks' and 'fellow-travellers' into hard-line critics of Soviet imperialism had not escaped his attention. But as a result of their new political alignment, he did not find them in any way sympathetic to the anti-Soviet line which he had pioneered almost on his own. Their argument, of course, was that *circumstances* had changed, rather than their allegiances. After all, '*time* for them is still and always the reality: and a thing that is true today was not necessarily true yesterday. There are fashions in politics as there are in hats.'[7] But for his own part, Lewis shows no disposition to accept his one-time critics as latter-day allies—even had they been so disposed to accept him. For the political outlawry which he felt that he had been made to suffer unfairly is something which he is not prepared to forget:

First of all, the harm has been done, and a change of fashion will not undo it. I have been pushed into a position where I should remain, even if the pretext for driving me there could no longer today be resorted to. Secondly, these people are all too deeply committed ever to change anything but their labels. They are not interested, it must be remembered, in an objective truth: they inhabit a verbal world, of labels and slogans. However they may modify the terms of their political ritual, or I may in the future modify my views in detail, the antagonism must remain, even if for the moment our policies happened to be identical.[8]

That Lewis firmly believed he had been 'pushed' or 'driven' into the position he had come to adopt during the thirties is clear enough. But one might be excused for wondering whether in fact he had not accepted it—however fortuitously—of his own free will. As a protagonist of classical 'order', he had become interested in the idea of authoritarian government, this being, in his view, the form of government probably most propitious for the encouragement of the creative artist.[9] Observing the emergence of an undoubtedly authoritarian ruler in the person of Adolf Hitler, he had examined—more optimistically than he might have done—the political philosophy that he supposed Hitler to represent. Promptly attacked for 'advocating' Nazism —which he had never done—he had automatically begun to defend his point of view. And as Left-wing opinion in Britain was uncompromisingly hostile to both Nazism and Fascism, he had quickly persuaded himself that Britain was being stampeded by the Left into a holy war against both in the interests of Communism. Convinced that war was the ultimate evil; that Britain would only ruin herself by becoming involved in war; and that only Wall Street and the Kremlin could hope to benefit by it—he had attempted to arrest what he regarded as a disastrous trend. In the course of doing this, he had allowed himself to adopt the role of apologist for both Fascist aggression and Nazi militarism—so long as neither appeared to endanger British interests. While denouncing what he called British 'interference' in Europe, he was also constrained to seek justification for the acts that were inviting it. Only when Hitler himself had finally disillusioned him, did Lewis abandon his belief that Germany's aims were peaceful and her ambitions limited to righting the acknowledged wrongs inflicted by the Versailles Treaty.

This tactical exercise might well result in *retirement* into a position: but did it really amount to being 'pushed' into that position? That, at any rate, was how it appeared to Lewis himself. On the other hand, how would it have appeared to him if events had proved that he had been *right* in the line which he had followed? As it was, he is forced to the plain admission:

'assuming the impossible, that one's own countrymen could have been persuaded to renounce war as an instrument of policy, there would have remained in Germany a demented military adventurer, namely Herr Hitler, whom nothing would deter from wholesale "patriotic" bloodshed. Had we behaved with the most exemplary restraint and magnanimity, the result would have been just the same.'[10] Yet to many people it seemed— thanks to the policy of appeasement—that indeed Britain *had* 'behaved with the most exemplary restraint and magnanimity', and that World War II had been the direct consequence.

At least Lewis could claim that he had been right in his long distrust of Stalinism. That, far from being an experiment in enlightened government, it represented a political tyranny of the harshest kind, most of his earlier critics were prepared to concede by 1950. Six years later, the fact was to be admitted even by the Soviet Communist Party in Moscow at its Twentieth Congress. For as Lewis was to point out in a later story,[11] economic and constitutional rights amount to very little without actual *political* rights: and with its single-party structure, the Soviet system under Stalin or anyone else, amounts to a complete denial of the latter.

Lewis's old distrust of multi-party democracy in Britain during the twenties and thirties had been based upon his contention that there was no real conflict between the policies of the three parties involved. British democracy had therefore amounted to little more than a single-party system itself—but this he no longer finds to be the case in the late forties. For the first time, with the post-war triumph of an effective Labour Party dedicated to the introduction of Socialism, he can recognize 'a genuine cleavage between the two main Parties'. And as he makes it clear enough in *Rude Assignment*, his own sympathies are still with Socialism.

For one thing, Socialism stands by its very nature for the Internationalism to which he is again committed. But he is sadly forced to admit that there seems no immediate likelihood of Britain's implementation of the one leading on to a cosmic triumph of the other. For while the idea of a World State has 'no open enemies' that he knows of, 'it has the quietest set of friends and supporters of any doctrine in history'.[12] Since the death of Wells in 1946, in fact, very little had been written or urged on its behalf. Admittedly, a half-hearted attempt had been made at the Hague in 1948 to explore the possibilities of setting up some form of a World Government, but this had been supported only by the Western powers and had got nowhere. It had not even won the official support of the Labour Party, though the Conservatives, under Churchill's leadership, had approved the idea in principle. But the obvious intention of the Soviet Union to build up a counter-coalition in its own likeness had quickly brought the idea to a dead end. It is worth remembering, furthermore, that Bertrand Russell—who had been, along with Wells, the greatest advocate of World Government—had been at the time in favour of the United States threatening the Soviet Union with a nuclear attack, by way of persuading them to accept worldwide nuclear disarmament! Perhaps it is not surprising that Lewis himself was prepared to accept that World Government could probably be promoted by no other means.

Not that he is in favour, it should be added, of any such lunacy:

> I am no longer interested in war as a thing to talk about as if it could be isolated—I shall certainly never again take my garden hose to extinguish a volcano—but as to Russia let me say this. I hope we shall not be quite so foolish as to go to war. At least do not let us busily discover that Russian communism is *bad*—having formerly busily persuaded ourselves during a quarter of a century that it was *good*—so as to have an excuse for war. I have always regarded it as most imperfect, illiberal and autocratic, myself. But happily I am not subject to these violent reversals of opinion.[13]

With all due respect, the last assertion might be questioned—at least so far as it concerns the virtues or otherwise of national sovereignty. Also, as regards the rightness of the Soviet Union's policy of 'absorbing' its neighbours, Lewis had quickly qualified the opinion expressed in *The Cosmic Uniform of Peace*. Where he had originally suggested that it should be 'a matter of general satisfaction', the passage was altered in *America and Cosmic Man* to agree that it was 'justly a subject of reproach' —if only on the grounds of 'the coercive methods employed'.[14] Even so, in *Rude Assignment* he still views the matter of Soviet expansionism with mixed feelings. As an Internationalist, he realizes that national sovereignty will never be surrendered voluntarily: the smaller nations must therefore be prepared to 'lose it in some other way'.[15] That they would do so, after all, had been implicitly guaranteed by the compacts made with the Soviet Union at Teheran, Yalta and Potsdam—which add up, as Lewis sees them, to one more 'ill-favoured peace'. Even so, 'seeing that they *were* made, would it not be better to accept the inevitable, and get along on that basis—we with our customary tact and diplomatic finesse trying to make our lot of Germans into democrats like ourselves, and the Russians, on their side of the "iron curtain", naturally busy stalinizing their lot?'[16]

As for Stalinization itself, even this, apparently, had its acceptable sides. The 'certain coolness' which Lewis reported in 1941 as having existed between Stalin and himself had begun to thaw with the Nazi invasion of Russia. In a letter dated 20 August 1944, he had even gone so far as to admit that whatever the Trotskyists might say, 'Stalin has a working state-system, with the air purged of humbug'. Indeed, he confesses that he 'cannot share the horror and discouragement felt by the "Partisan" at the sight of Uncle Joe'.[17] And leaving Sir Alexander Cadogan out of it—with the Red Army crushing the very guts of the *Wehrmacht*, many of the English news-papers were saying much the same thing at the time.

Whether he chose to admit it or not, in fact, Lewis's thoughts upon day-to-day political matters, like those of everyone else, were apt to be subjective and dictated by the course of events. After all, this is only in line with his later belief that complete objectivity, however desirable in criticism of the arts, is politically impossible. Even if it were not, a strictly rational approach to politics ('which would be the correct one elsewhere') would be sure to land the political commentator in difficulties. In support of this view, he quotes Philip Rahv: 'objectivity, in the usual sense of that term, is unattainable in a serious political struggle: in politics knowledge is the product of participation and involvement.'[18] It was precisely because Lewis was *not* involved in politics, but insisted upon his right to study them as 'objectively' as he could, that his political pronouncements are so unreliable—and often so contradictory. As for his occasional indulgence in political prophecy, he would have been well advised to realize that this is as inexact a science as long-range weather forecasting: there are far too many imponderables involved in both. For as Sir George Thomson once observed, the weather in London next month may well be dependent on a man in Upper Quebec either throwing away or stubbing out a lighted cigarette tomorrow evening....

Lewis is far nearer the truth than he had been sometimes when he declares in *Rude Assignment* that 'Politics are something flexible, vivid, various, not cut and dried'. He is equally right when he suggests that a man's politics are far more implicit in his behaviour than in the way he votes. He has a perfectly sound case when he complains bitterly of having been branded as a Fascist by a generation of 'Pinks' merely because he had been anti-Communist. By the same token, he had been wrong himself in assuming that all who were anti-Fascist must necessarily be Communists or fellow-travellers. But Zimri, of course, was hardly alone in his preference for extreme opinions. And the simple fact remains that, like Ramsay MacDonald, Stanley Baldwin, Neville Chamberlain, Winston Churchill, Stafford Cripps, Waldron Smithers, Frederick Voight and J. L. Garvin, Lewis had been middle-of-the-road in his political behaviour throughout his life. He had been middle-of-the-road no less in his refusal to support the party of Sir Oswald Mosley in the later thirties, than in his refusal to join the party of Lenin in the earlier twenties. Desperate diseases may sometimes appear to call for desperate remedies; and spectacular reforms have sometimes been achieved by dictatorships. But Lewis's judgment is probably rightest of all when he confesses that—like most of us, and everything taken into consideration—he would 'rather muddle along with the democratic rulers of the West'.[19] For like Sartre's Mathieu, he would surely have hated a *perfect* political system of any complexion: it would have deprived him of the right to say No.

Such a system he had once done his best to define in *The Art of Being Ruled*. Unfortunately, he had promptly made the mistake of supposing that Italian Fascism bore some relation to such a system. Being careful to make no such mistake again, *Rude Assignment* includes a clear re-statement of his political philosophy, and it is for its chapter *Advice to the Inmates of the Power House* that the book is most valuable. Lewis is now prepared to allow (apologetically) that in *The Art of Being Ruled* there is 'a tincture of intolerence here and there regarding the backward, slothful, obstructive majority'.[20] He is also ready to admit that the work is 'difficult' in that, 'inspired by the Hegelian dialectic', it had sought to debate both sides of too many questions that it raised. This ambivalence, and the misunderstanding to which it appeared to have given rise, *Rude Assignment* attempts to correct.

He points out that in 1925 he had still not emancipated himself from 'tribal, or national, superstition': he was still obsessed, furthermore, by the wish to defend the ideals of a western civilization which had since collapsed. Realizing that it was already in course of being replaced by something different, he had attempted to find an acceptable way out of the chaos.

One thing had been clear enough to everyone: the First World War had completely disrupted the society which had itself given rise to it. The poor, needless to say, were mainly concerned with the business of staying alive: they could barely subsist on what they earned, let alone the reduced wages with which the middle-twenties were threatening them. On the other hand, the rich had lost a great deal of what they had once possessed to the business interests which had been raised by the war-boom to new heights of wealth and power. 'A society has premonitions of its end,' says Lewis. 'This one began burning up the rest of its money, before "they" took it away from them. Mortification already set in at the edges. They began to stink. I have recorded that stink.'[21]

Not that the mortification had been confined to Britain alone: as Lewis saw it, the whole of the western world had grown sick. Germany and the old Austro-Hungarian rump-of-empire were bankrupt. France was powerful, but greedily—and therefore dangerously—vindictive. The new nations created by Versailles were unstable agglomerations of mutually hostile peoples. Italy had found its own solution for stemming industrial disorder. But to the east, Eliot's 'hooded hordes' had hardly ceased their swarming over the 'endless plains'. For Lewis also, the towers were falling from Vienna to London—only for him, the prospect was anything but 'unreal'. Something, he had felt, would have to be done about it, over and above the Sanskrit insistence on giving and sympathizing. Control appeared to be the operative word—and control, in terms of society as distinct from the individual, was a matter of effective government.

As Lewis was consistently to point out, government is never a *good* thing: but it is at all times, for social man, a *necessary* thing. As he had again expressed it in *America and Cosmic Man*, 'Government is man's badge of servitude'. But the social contract by which men agreed to be governed was the only contract which could guarantee them what they needed if they were to enjoy a civilized status—'libraries, laboratories, studios, concert-halls, and theatres'. The very nature of Lewis's listing makes it plain that so far as he is concerned, civilization implies culture and the arts first and foremost. (His inclusion of 'laboratories', one feels, is almost accidental: there is certainly no mention of schools or universities!) But given his concept of civilization, the question naturally arises: what form of government will be *best* for culture?

He reminds us that in primitive and patriarchal societies, it is the Elders who are the leaders: it is upon them that the business of government devolves. But in the post-war society of the twenties, the business of government was being disputed with the Elders. It was being disputed most notably by the business interests which had been mainly responsible for the late war, and whose power was dependent upon continuance of the free-for-all which amounted, in point of fact, almost to the abnegation of government. It was very much the concern of such interests—Big Business, as Lewis chose to call them—that the majority of the governed became less of a militant electorate than a quiescent market. And by this general process of anaesthesia, government itself stood to benefit: a truculent proletariat was the last thing wanted by those who would have been the first victims of revolutionary change. Quiescence, therefore, was induced by every technique that indoctrination, publicity, market research and even plain resourcefulness could command. The principle of dividing and ruling was once more pressed into service: the 'class-wars' of age, sex, intellect, sport and the rest, were promoted on all sides, with the sole aim of reducing the public to the state of unthinking, irresponsible children. As such, they became ideal material for exploitation and rule. The sex-war and the age-war had the added advantage of recruiting a cheaper labour-force for industry. All of which, as we have seen, it had been Lewis's business to point out at the time.

The tendency of the average man to *lend* himself to this kind of classification, his willingness to allow the strength of his numbers to be dissipated by calculated sub-division, was a point that Lewis had underlined from the start. It was all very much a part of the average man's impulse to associate with his immediate neighbours, to club together and coalesce into mutually exclusive groups or gangs or crafts or orders. And as Lewis was never tired of warning, it is a tendency which makes exploitation unusually easy. Most men wish to lose themselves in the group, to submit themselves to group-responses, and to find strength and reassurance within a group-rhythm. It is therefore only too easy for their energies to be channelled. As Lewis puts it: 'They have to cease to be conscious of all the other things they are, outside that particular category' to which they have been encouraged to belong. In that way their energies can easily be directed. 'Thus the "proletarian" should forget that he is *also* a Catholic, or vice versa—a Catholic that he is a member of the working class.'[22] If it were not so tragic, it would be amusing to see how convincingly the proletariat of Northern Ireland have recently been proving Lewis's thesis....

Not that this malleability of the majority is anything that Lewis hails with enthusiasm. Though he observes and analyses it, in no sense does he rejoice in it. If the herd instinct makes people all the easier to manipulate politically, it is of no consequence to him, since he has no desire to take advantage of the fact. He certainly has no intention of *inciting* people to abrogate their liberties: he is merely concerned to protect his own. That society should be so insect-like is something which he never ceases to deplore. Indeed, the theory put forward by *The Art of Being Ruled* was an open invitation to the intelligent to escape exploitation by cultivating their individualities. If they refused to accept the challenge, then there was no more to be said: herded and manipulated they would continue to be—but not by Lewis.

Once again in *Rude Assignment*, this time a little more urgently, the fact is hammered home that true freedom can be equated only with individuality. Though he had coined the phrase, it is far from Lewis's view that freedom and irresponsibility *should* be accepted as 'commutative terms'. That sort of freedom—the freedom to opt out of one's responsibilities to oneself—is the very reverse of freedom as he values it. Reduced to its ultimate absurdity, it is merely a freedom *not* to be free.

Yet the fact remains that the evasion of responsibility is highly agreeable to most people. Lewis cites the example of soldiers he had met after the Second World War who told him that they had been only too happy to take orders, being thus relieved of all necessity to take painful decisions for themselves. He admits that none of them, apparently, had been in action: they had merely enjoyed the good luck to take life easily in some military back-water. But what of that? he asks. Often enough, 'people would rather be told to go to their death than not to be told to go *somewhere* and to do *something*'.[23]

It is not the right of such people to live their lives in the way they prefer to do which Lewis is questioning. It is merely the advisability of allowing them by so doing to put a brake upon the development of those with greater initiative. The time wasted by enlightened agencies, e.g. the post-war educational system, in trying to fit them for ways of life and thought which they dislike, is a misuse of resources which could be better employed in other ways. Indeed, there is a significant shift in emphasis between what Lewis was advocating in *The Art of Being Ruled* and what he is advocating in *Rude Assignment*. This is only to be expected, insofar as the unregulated society of the twenties had been replaced in the later forties by an austerity-ridden society ruled in an entirely different manner. Though human nature had remained unchanged, the nature of government had altered very much in the way that Lewis had hoped that it would: a planned State-Socialism was being tried where a policy of Conservative *laissez-faire* had signally failed. Unluckily, the economy to which it was being applied had been almost ruined before the experiment could be put into effect.

One of the recurrent complaints in *The Art of Being Ruled* had been that a systematic 'vulgarization' of the arts and sciences had been connived at by government, business interests and the media. The standards of the masses had been accepted as the operative standards because they were demonstrably the most lucrative to meet. This, Lewis had protested, effectually deprived the creative artist and the experimental scientist of their functional roles in society. Unless they conformed to standards which they despised, or turned their talents to serving demands which they deplored, there was little that they could do to keep themselves alive. The creative artist's plight had been further complicated by the cult of the Amateur: the spectator had been turned into the actor, and every man into his own artist. Such a trend could only result in the final extinction of all creative achievement—by which alone a culture was to be judged.

In *Rude Assignment*, very little is said on the subject of vulgarization: the fact is taken for granted. The vast increase in the popularity of the media—most notably, perhaps, the sudden eruption of television—had so conditioned the public taste that Lewis may well have felt no more could be done about it. But he is still very much concerned about the possibility of a 'limited separation' between 'creative man and his backward fellow'. Only by such protection—a sort of intellectual quarantine—can creativity be given a chance to develop its full potential. Once again, in fact, he is complaining of the way that the intellectual is being sacrificed in the interests of the admass. 'The teacher exhausts himself on the unwilling scholar; the creative writer has to waste all but a fraction of his life in wresting from society the physical means to create; the man of science sees his discoveries misused by that violent moron monopolizing wealth and power, whose unintelligence is only matched by his destructiveness.'[24]

When first put forward, this plea of Lewis's for 'limited separation' had been roundly condemned by some critics as an attempt to create an intellectual *élite*, if not to build up a new doctrine of *Übermenschlichkeit* on the old Nietzschean pattern. Once again, in *Rude Assignment*, Lewis protests that his plea for 'a partitioned-off *area of creative development*' implied no such thing. It certainly implied no creation of a ruling caste, though this had been forecast in *The Art of Being Ruled*, and was now—in an age ruled by the technocrat and the planner—already in being, for all practical purposes. It is merely an insistence that certain crafts have certain peculiar needs, which a simple re-ordering of the hierarchic structure of society could easily meet. In the 'new hierarchic-occupational pagoda' which he is advocating, all men would be enabled to work in the way for which they were best suited. He does not regard this as amounting to any new 'theory of the State': it would merely be making it possible for the State to get the best out of the various creative and intellectual resources at its disposal. It would involve no assumption of social superiority on the part of the intellectual, or the imposition of any social stigma upon the rest. In philosophical terms, it would merely involve a recognition by the State that while all men are perfectible, some are more perfectible than others....

It might be supposed that such an idea would have small chance of being adopted by a Socialist society bent upon achieving full egalitarianism. In such a society, it might be thought, any form of privilege would be expected to disappear. But Lewis is certainly not of that opinion. As he sees it, Socialism is the one system under which such a husbanding and encouragement of intellectual potential would be practicable. The attainment of social equality under Socialism, he asserts, means little more than the elimination of the boss-class. What it clearly does *not* dispute is 'the fundamental inequality of Prof. Einstein and Sir Waldron Smithers', on the one hand, 'or the physical inequality of Joe Louis and Professor Laski'.

The Socialism of post-war Britain, he notes with approval, is 'hard-boiled'. It is already 'apt to be very fussy about people keeping where they belong'. Labour itself is being directed into channels where it can most usefully be employed. In a fully planned economy it could scarcely be otherwise:

> This is therefore a particularly favourable moment for considering proposals for the elimination of friction between the backward and the enlightened, seeing that there is no sentimental obstruction, of a kind that would always favour the stupid as against the intelligent, the idle and irresponsible as against the diligent and conscientious, the destructive as against the creative. A tough public mind is taking the place of a soft one.[25]

Whether this reading of the national mood was correct or not, it is interesting that Lewis should think the times more propitious for his ideas than they had been. He is careful once again to stress that the sort of 'hierarchic-occupational pagoda' that he has in mind would present equal opportunities of development to all and sundry. The only test for sponsorship would be proved and outstanding ability. It would be no harder for the son of a miner to become a brilliant composer than for the son of a brilliant scientist to find himself returned to more congenial market-gardening. But once his aptitude had been recognized, it should be made easy for the ballet-dancer to dance, the writer to create literature, and the artist to paint whatever he chooses.

Though Lewis appears to have overlooked the fact, such a system of vocational sponsorship by the State had long been operating in the Soviet Union—as any Communist might have reminded him. What most Communists might *not* have reminded him is that no better system could be devised for ensuring adherence to an ideological Party Line. The Soviet writer is indeed free to write what he chooses, provided that it is what his Commissar wants to read. And if Lewis had lived to see how the Soviet system has been operated against Solzhenitsyn, Sinyavsky, Yuli Daniel and the rest, it might have convinced him that even a hierarchic-occupational pagoda is liable to have its drawbacks.

Of one thing we can be reasonably certain: the sort of critical sniping to which Lewis subjected bureaucratic incompetence and official bloody-mindedness in the stories of *Rotting Hill* would not have been likely to earn him thanks in any pagoda administered from Whitehall. Even in *Rude Assignment* it is clear enough that the post-war Britain to which he had returned was far from being to his liking. Though long predisposed to State Socialism in theory, he soon found the everyday reality— hobbled as it was by war-shortages, war-controls, war-psychology and plain war-weariness—a twilight world in which he could feel small joy. It was as though the war had drained everyone of the desire to assert himself, the will to protest and the ability to demand. The queues had become a symbol of national resignation and national apathy. There was no more debate, no argument and no outspoken criticism. Since the Second World War had 'not been a money-war but ideological', everything which it had brought in its wake had been silently accepted. Once wartime censorship had been lifted, the British had listlessly begun to censor themselves:

An obvious danger is to be discerned in this changed mood. In

England it is as if no one dared to listen to anything against war *itself*. That is out of bounds, as a subject: it is as if the war were still in progress, with its censorships and disciplines. Sentiment of the 'We can take it' type has made war taboo. Worst symptom of all is to be found in reactions to the Atomic Bomb. Or, rather, there is no reaction. Its mention is resented, as if it were a rival to the doodlebug and blockbuster, but an unfair and unsportsmanlike one (as might be expected, seeing that it is American, the Briton would growl). It arouses no interest, and is disliked.[26]

It was not in Lewis's nature to march off to Aldermaston, or sit down in protest in Trafalgar Square like Bertrand Russell (once the Bomb was also in Russian supply). But the Bomb was very much in his thoughts during the late forties, as has already been shown. He viewed its threat with 'mixed feelings', as he did the creation of the Soviet power bloc. For more than ever he was convinced of the necessity of achieving world peace by means of a single-state World Government, and to that end the threat inherent in the Bomb appeared the only likely means. Or perhaps one should say peace for whatever was left of the world if the Bomb were ever resorted to, as Lewis was now persuaded that it would be.

As he believed, the day of the small, independent nation was long since passed: the concept of national sovereignty had outlived its viability, nor was there anything observable in the skirmishing at the United Nations Organization which reassured him to the contrary. In a world so obviously dominated by power blocs, sooner or later the small nations would have to align themselves or quietly be 'absorbed'. If he, Lewis, were to advocate that Britain should seek to merge its economy with America's—or, alternatively, merge it with Europe's, which would ultimately mean with Russia's—it would imply no preference on his part for the political system of either country. It would merely mean that it seemed to him 'the best course for a ruined country to take'. Being enthusiastic about neither Capitalism nor Communism, he simply believes that 'one of those two choices has to be made'.[27] He carefully refrains from making any overt choice himself, though his declared fondness for America can leave little doubt as to which his choice would be.

But would any such alignment for Britain or any other small

country offer a reasonable guarantee of peace? Obviously not, since both Russia and America appear to him quite ready to push the world into final catastrophe. He does not, apparently, consider the possibility of the uncommitted powers combining into a third bloc of declared neutrality, such as the Afro–Asian countries were later to attempt. Nor does the idea of a European bloc, such as we are now entering, seem any effective defence against Russian aggression, should Russia decide to become aggressive.

Nor does he believe it will be possible, by mutual agreement, to outlaw the use of nuclear weapons. The mere fact of their existence precludes the likelihood that they will remain unused for long. At the time he was writing *Rude Assignment*, America still enjoyed a monopoly of the Bomb: before the book was published, the Russians had a Bomb of their own. Lewis is only the more confirmed in his belief that however limited at the outbreak the next war may appear to be, 'at the first threat of defeat, at the first serious reverse, out it will come—Gilda, the Queen of Battles'![28] As we now know, only the personal intervention of President Truman was to keep Gilda safely in wraps two years later in Korea.

So far as our own hindsight goes (and a few more years may radically change it) Lewis's attitude was unduly pessimistic. War was avoided in Europe at the time of the Berlin airlift, while *Rude Assignment* was still being written. War in Korea came very soon afterwards, and ended short of cosmic disaster. War came later still in Vietnam, and at last seems likely to peter out in its turn. War has come in the Near East and the Indian sub-continent—with what final results perhaps we have still not seen. The Bomb has been tested many hundred times, but it has still been used only twice. The realization may even have been accepted that a third time would *not* be lucky....

As the thirties amply demonstrated, Lewis was not at his best in the role of prophet. His guesses could be woefully wrong— as indeed could many other people's, with far more facts at their disposal. But to have been wrong once or twice does not mean that one will be wrong invariably. Are we justified, therefore, in ignoring his warning that almost inevitably the Bomb will be pressed into service again? Is the Third World War, which he felt to be coming, still in wait for us before the end of the century? There is little that we can do about it, perhaps, but if it should be, Lewis has his own idea as to what the outcome will be. And the final statement of that idea in *Rude Assignment* provides a notable close to his whole political testament:

> The death-roll would make all former wars seem ladylike little catastrophes, unquestionably. But Professor Einstein's estimate that not more than half the population of the earth would be killed is doubtless correct.
>
> Quiet people, like myself, cannot be expected to look forward to such an event. But an atomic war—if it is *necessary*—will do no great harm. All the corpses whose arms and legs had shed their skins like discarded gloves (and other anatomical novelties for which our new toy is responsible) would be disposed of, the insane would be put under restraint, the hospitals jammed with the cancerous wrecks, the ruined towns tidied up. Things would start up again, the human scene just as civilized as it was before.
>
> But here is what interests *me*. In spite of the hearty 'business as usual' attitude—and a very firm hand with those who suggest that there is anything odd or screwy about it all: for all the 'I can-take-it' bursting gamely from blue and swollen lips, and the 'brave smiles' fading only upon mortification on the faces of the cheerful radioactive dead—for all the well-known capacity to 'keep smiling' long after there was any conceivable thing to smile about—a miracle would happen. An *idea* would steal apologetically into the minds of a number of those still sound in wind and limb whose intellective apparatus (though sluggish and clogged with slogans and soggy uplift) still functioned. The idea would take the form of a leading question: 'Are we all right in the upper storey?'
>
> But the deciding factor will be that men have entered upon the era of super-states: then, under the eliminatory impact of this new device for wiping out life—this monstrous blast, like the breath of an outraged god—the time must rapidly come when only *one* battered entity, calling itself a 'nation', will be there. And that will be that.
>
> My restrained optimism is, then, a by-product of atomic energy. One or two more wars it seems necessary to allow for—alas. Then the great climacteric in life on earth should come: the day on which man will resign himself to Peace.[29]

If this 'restrained optimism' seems rather like a note of inverted pessimism, it is the note on which Lewis's political testament may be said to end.

NOTES

1. *A C M*, p.170.
2. *Letters of W M*, p.343.
3. Ibid., p.374.
4. Ibid., p.391.
5. *R A*, p.172.
6. *Letters of W L*, p.528.
7. *R A*, p.143.
8. Ibid., pp.142-3.
9. 'With me the first incentive to so unattractive a study was a selfish, or at least a personal one: namely a wish to find out under what kind of system learning and the arts were likely to fare best. A craft interest, that is to say. Of course later my intellectual zeal transcended this limited and specialist enquiry.' *R A*, p.64.
10. *R A*, p.209.
11. *R H*, p.84.
12. *R A*, p.94.
13. Ibid., p.81.
14. *A C M*, p.157.
15. *R A*, p.67.
16. Ibid., p.84.
17. *Letters of W L*, pp.378-9.
18. *Quoted in R A*, p.63.
19. *R A*, p.165.
20. Ibid., p.188.
21. Ibid., p.171.
22. Ibid., p.177.
23. Ibid., p.180.
24. Ibid., p.183. As regards the 'unwilling scholar', it is not without relevance that the question of compulsorily raising the school-leaving age should once again be in serious debate. Apart from its temporary easing of the unemployment problem, it remains to be seen how many teachers will succumb to the strain of trying to teach an age-group which is in active rebellion against being taught any longer.
25. Ibid., p.186.
26. Ibid., p.172.
27. Ibid., p.221.
28. Ibid., p.96.
29. Ibid., pp.96-7.

The Dark and the Afterglow

Lewis was to publish six more books before his death in March 1957, in all of which there are political echoes or overtones. But they add little more than occasional qualification to the ideas that had taken final shape in *Rude Assignment*. The first of them, *Rotting Hill*, which appeared in December 1951, Lewis describes as no more political than 'some of Charles Dickens' books, and all by Mr. Shaw'. If all the characters in its ten stories and sketches are obsessed by politics, he explains, 'it is because today our lives are saturated by them'.

But there is one very noticeable difference about Lewis's treatment of politics in *Rotting Hill*: for the first time, they are discussed as something that is happening to Lewis himself no less than to his readers. In his earlier books, while allying himself by sympathy with the ruled, he always appears to be writing from the privileged viewpoint of his 'outsideness'. In *Rotting Hill*, on the other hand, he is one of those to whom things are being done: it is more than a matter of mere empathy—it is a case of his finally becoming *identified* with the ruled. And it is perfectly clear that Lewis is not enjoying the experience. For what is happening to him, under post-war Socialism, he feels to be more than an assault upon his individuality: it amounts to what he regards as the extinction of a way of life. That the way of life should never have been enjoyed by more than a few— himself among them—he is the first to agree. Nor does he deny that for most of his fellow-countrymen (the seventy per cent whose part he had taken many times before), England had become 'a brighter rather than a darker place'. That the work-ing class should at last be savouring the joys of emancipation is something about which he is prepared to enthuse. He merely wonders whether it is necessary for Socialism to turn his world into an assembly-line, and 'to reproduce the atmosphere of the factory in every part of human life, from the dentist's chair to the marriage bed'.

Quite clearly, post-war Socialism in Britain was far from being the efficient and enlightened form of government for which he had so long hoped. This he does not impute to any fault of the Labour Party: the bankrupt economy they had inherited, post-war confusion and lack of amenities, all the prob-lems of reorganization and redeployment in industry—these would have overtaxed the energies of any political party. But it is not so much the difficulties posed by such understandable factors which bother him: it is far more the post-war psychology of the British people themselves. As Lewis sees it, Socialism is being hamstrung by 'the phenomenon of working-class slack-ness': those for whom the Welfare State had been created were refusing to pay with their labour and goodwill for the benefits which it had ensured for them. Traditional distrust of capitalism and management had been bred in the labouring classes over the years, and was now being turned against the anti-capitalistic government that they themselves had returned to power. 'Decades of ca' canny and the ingrained habit of go-slow, pro-ducing a population of the laziest workmen in Europe, has proved the arch-enemy of socialism.'[1] And where the country as a whole had hoped for a new social order, it was merely find-ing anarchy. Even Aneurin Bevan, says Lewis, had conceded that 'he personally had never greatly believed in the possibility of ruling without coercion'.[2]

Rotting Hill, it must be admitted, is far from being Lewis's most objective book. Indeed, it is his one exasperated incursion into unashamed *sub*jectivity: he allows himself every petulance to which personal discomfort can give rise. He suffers every-thing from the shrinkage of a button-hole and unfunctional nail-scissors to truculent contractors and the horseplay of a team of plasterers. The rot that he finds at work in society grows out of the rot that is literally in his studio woodwork; and the irri-tations and inconveniences of life in post-war London seem to have been even more irksome to him than wartime hardship in the limbo of Momaco!

But even if the British Worker had been doing more to oblige him, there is something about the whole nature of Socialism in action which Lewis mistrusts. Where he had once been insistent upon the need for a planned economy, he now fears that too much power is being made over to the planner, since the planner now has the authority to impose his plans on all and sundry. Or perhaps it was merely that he felt the authority had been made over to the *wrong* planners. But as he argues with one of his characters: 'There was too little planning formerly: our chaotic cities bear witness to that. But an over-planned life is at least as bad as no plan at all.'[3] That way, he fears, lies the loss of *all* liberties—even those which exist under a system where freedom is so largely illusory! With the best of intentions, in fact, the Attlee Government appears to be forging for itself a dangerous instrument of oppression. Admittedly, like the Bomb, this may never actually be used against us. 'But there is so slender a chance that some evil man will not be forthcoming to use such an instrument as the total power involved in state-socialism oppressively that we really may dismiss the idea.'[4] The one-time authoritarian poacher had indeed turned democratic gamekeeper!

Whether or not one agrees that Socialism encroaches upon the liberty of the individual—and many people certainly would —it is perhaps more debatable 'how absolutely impossible' Socialism would have been without the foundations laid for it by Christianity. 'A long process of religious conditioning ... has led us to a point at which we empower the State to deprive us of practically everything. This,' he adds ironically, 'is the work of Jesus.'[5] It might equally be argued that only with the *collapse* of Christian belief had Socialism been made possible. While the Victorian God was in his heaven, all had indeed seemed right with the world: to have suggested otherwise would have bordered upon impiety. It was only with the emergence of scepticism that the social system began to be studied and ways of perfecting it to be sought. For once they had off-loaded their belief in original sin, men had begun to seem perfectible in themselves. Lewis did not appear to share T. E. Hulme's weakness for original sin as such. But at least he is now persuaded that without Christianity as its mainstay, Socialism may become a dangerous doctrine:

> The natural twentieth century drift must be towards the eventual repudiation of Christianity, or its sentimental political puritan hang-over. We see that occurring everywhere, do we not? In a word, the danger is that in its hour of triumph socialism will forget, ignore, or violently discard, the ethics by means of which it was able to gain acceptance and to mount to power: indeed that it may strip away all our civilized Christian freedoms and thrust us back into a system of villeinage and worse. Socialism without ethics is a terrible thing.[6]

There, at least, it is easy enough to agree with Lewis. But ethics are not peculiar to the Christian faith, and there is the little matter of Christian belief which has to be confronted. Socialism and Christianity may indeed run parallel courses towards the idea of social justice. But the ideal of redemption is not shared by them in common; and for only one of them is social justice an end in itself. It seems clear, as one reads through his political works, that Lewis could never quite bring himself to accept completely the beliefs of either doctrine. For him, belief was emphatically *not* the same as Truth. On the other hand, Truth was all too frequently for him a matter of what he personally believed. This paradox was responsible for many of the contradictions to be found in his political thinking. It might also be held responsible for many of his wrong judgments.

The Writer and the Absolute, published six months after *Rotting Hill*, in July 1952, is a far more considerable work and contains some of Lewis's most scintillating literary criticism. It is concerned, once again, with the writer's place in a society which has become more or less dominated by politics. 'Freedom of the writer to speculate, to criticize, to create: such is the ultimate desideratum of the writer a man-of-letters', Lewis declares. But such freedom is becoming ever more circumscribed, as political opinion hardens into the absolute that we now know. Political absolutes having replaced religious absolutes, the writer who has no party behind him to give his opinions currency is in a dangerously exposed position. In France, even such a fashionable Left-wing writer as Sartre is forced to admit that by his refusal to join the Communist Party, he has found himself rejected by a doctrinaire audience for whom he represents anti-Communist heresy! Though avidly read in Left-wing circles from Tel Aviv to New York, he blames the Communist Party for 'locking away from him the public of his choice: for not handing over the proletariat to *him* and themselves going out of business'.[7]

Curiously enough (since he himself had always refused allegiance to any political party) Lewis tends to blame Sartre for his non-acceptance of the Communist Party line, while still availing himself of Marxist attitudes to which—as a heretic—he has no right. This Lewis puts down to the reason suggested by Sartre himself—*le snobisme révolutionnaire*. Despite his intellectual integrity, he feels that Sartre has only himself to blame for the anomalous position in which he finds himself. In the thirties, he had 'drifted fashionably into the *front populaire* watershed, was the French equivalent of a fellow-traveller'. The path which he had chosen, Lewis concludes, 'leads either to communism, or to nothing. It was "le Néant" that he chose'.[8]

Himself a pluralist rather than an absolutist, Lewis prefers what he calls 'a various world', where he is not squeezed by one extreme or the other—in French terms, Communism or the Catholic–Fascism which he would probably (later) have identified with Gaullism. Yet in an age where political pressures have become so strong, an attempt at objectivity has come to represent a greater threat to political orthodoxy than extremism of an opposite kind. As Lewis feels that he has proved by his own example:

> If a writer desires an easy life, he should be an extremist: if one could be mathematically at the point farthest from both extremes, which is of course impossible, one would be entirely alone. And any position near to this imaginary absolute of objectivity cannot but be an exceedingly uncomfortable one, for there is another extremism of the Middle of a much realer kind than the more usual extremes such as those of Left and Right.[9]

An anti-extremist of the Middle—that is probably as near as we shall ever get to defining Lewis's political standpoint accurately. As the pressures from either side increased, that hypothetical point where he chose to take his stand would be forced over towards either Left or Right. In a decade like the thirties, where political sympathies in Britain lay mainly with the Left, it was towards the Right that he automatically tended to move. But always on that see-saw of political opinion, he strove to maintain his precarious balance where he felt that the fulcrum lay.

That absolute mean may indeed have been impossible to establish, but in his refusal to accept any position dictated to him by the political interests in his time, Lewis might fairly claim to have approached a political mean on occasion, even if objectivity were still not to be found there.

It is certainly true that 'By their nature human beings wish everyone to think exactly as they do'; and Lewis himself had been no exception to that general rule. He had done his best to influence political opinion; and for the most part he had signally failed. His failure, furthermore, had led to a serious misunderstanding of his motives, for which he had been made to pay heavily. As he drily observed at the end of the game, 'philosophers and poets have always touched politics at their peril'. Even his friend Ezra Pound, 'in some moment of poetic frenzy', had been misguided enough to mistake 'the clownish Duce for Thomas Jefferson....'[10]

Yet the philosophical turn of Lewis's thought, however unapt for political involvement, could still serve him brilliantly when applied to its proper subjects. His analysis of the existentialism of Sartre in *The Writer and the Absolute* is worthy to stand beside the best of the criticism in *Men Without Art*. Here once more, Lewis can hunt out the ubiquitous quarry of Bergsonism with his old relish. Heidegger, and even Marx himself, can be pressed into service and help him lay bare the unhealthiness of the existentialist withdrawal and all its fashionable *angoisse*. Both, he finds, are 'militantly irrational'; while the nihilist's 'escape through action' from the *néant* which he has created for himself is one more example of Lewis's old anathema— 'intuitive extremism'. Nor is Sartre alone in being put under the knife: Camus, Malraux and even Orwell provide so many extra scalps for his belt as The Enemy rides again. Each in his turn is used to illustrate Lewis's thesis that politics and literature must always remain irreconcilable, since literature 'depends altogether upon unobstructed access to the true'—and any such access it is the business of politics to limit or prevent. 'Naturally,' says

Lewis in his conclusion, 'the ability to *perceive* the true—which is under everybody's nose but not seen by everybody—is confined to people of considerable intelligence.'[11]

Alas, there was a tragic irony behind that apparently bland assumption. For even before the publication of *Rotting Hill*, Lewis was already virtually blind. 'Pushed into an unlighted room, the door banged and locked forever', there was precious little left on earth that his critical painter's eye could perceive any more. As he calmly announced in one of the most objective—and certainly the most moving—of all his published articles, he would be forced 'to light a lamp of aggressive voltage' in his mind from then on 'to keep at bay the night'.[12]

It was that unearthly light which was to cast its glaring refulgence over the boulevards and piazzas of Third City, and the more sinister canyons of Metapolis in *The Human Age*.

Even the after-life, it would seem, is not without its infernal politics. . . .

On the surface at this particular time, politics (and the course of world events which they dictate) do not appear to have followed the direction mapped out for them by Lewis. Only in the Soviet bloc and in China has authoritarian government entrenched itself—unless we choose to dignify with that name the forms of arrested development observable in Spain and Portugal. Independence as a concept, if not as an economic reality, has been bestowed upon most of the one-time colonial territories of the world, which now enjoy their own versions of it in reasonable facsimiles of western democracy. National sovereignty, outside of the Soviet bloc, has been given a new lease of life (if that is the phrase) and operates triumphantly (again, if that is the phrase) in the councils of the United Nations. Perhaps we should say that the free-for-all continues.

Internationalism, as envisaged by Russell, Wells and Lewis, appears to be more of a pipe-dream than ever; and what was once offered to men of good will everywhere as an 'Open Conspiracy' has thus far achieved nothing whatever. The rapid advancement of world communications appears to have resulted in a growing national competitiveness: we expect the day when Andorra and Liechtenstein will each have its international airline contesting world markets with Aeroflot, B.O.A.C., Air France and Pan-American....

Freedom, which Lewis decided was wanted by almost nobody, has now become something of a fashionable cult. At least it has provided an excuse for exhilarating circuses and demonstrations the world over. It has become a rallying cry for dissident high spirits among all the minorities, in the universities and even in the class-room. Punitive measures of many sorts have been renounced as an infringement of basic human rights and replaced by weaker forms of non-aversive control. The exercise of authority is resented on all sides, not least of all by those who might be expected to benefit from it. Freedom is a word upon everybody's lips—whatever it means to anyone individually.

It would seem that society, rather than submitting indifferently to its rulers, is pushing its way into new areas of permissiveness. Insofar as this merely makes it easier to control politically, the tendency of the rulers is clearly to encourage society in the trend. The slackening of social restraints, after all, is itself a convenience to law and order, since it releases restrictive forces for use in more politically useful ways. In itself, permissiveness may even be felt to offer some sort of palliative to the continuance of high unemployment—which appears to be necessary to the operations of free enterprise as at present understood. Or so Lewis might perhaps have argued.

So far as his theory of the 'class-wars' is concerned—if direction of these ever really *was* vested in the rulers, priorities and strategy appear to be changing. The sex-war in particular has entered upon an entirely new phase, and the concept of rule as a strictly male prerogative may soon have to be abandoned. National decisions on peace or war and the suppression of revolt, which are of vital importance to the world at large, have already been taken by women-rulers in India, Israel and Ceylon. In two of those countries, women for the most part are still liable to strong religious pressures. But in the West at least, women are rapidly winning acceptance of the principle of full sex-equality, whatever use they choose to make of it. They cannot be thought of for very much longer as a convenient source of cheap labour.

Far more importantly, the Pill and the legalization of abortion have given women a far greater control over the functioning of their bodies—which in turn has given them a far wider sexual circulation. They may still remain the sort of sex-machines that they always appeared to Lewis, but at least the machines are becoming largely self-propelled. Even if some of them are induced to discard their bras—and whatever next—they still represent an expanding consumer market for those who are interested in encouraging tendencies. The fuller enjoyment of sex can be just as profitable to business interests as the wider use of cosmetics proved, back in the twenties.

Homosexuality, as might be expected, shows no sign of decreasing as a social phenomenon—or perhaps one should now be thinking in terms of optional bi-sexuality. Whichever way, it is clearly ceasing to carry any social stigma: indeed, in certain professions and occupations, it is coming to have a distinct edge in marketability. Once again, of course, it represents a new opportunity for the manufacturer: the average homosexual spends considerably more on his clothes and general appearance than the average heterosexual. As for the *cause* of homosexuality, quite apart from environmental and psychological factors, this is becoming recognized as a simple matter of biochemistry: it will soon be correctible by pre-natal medication—or even inducible, if this is ever accepted as a way of counteracting the population explosion.

The age-war, no less than the sex-war, has been stepped-up into new intensities, and has proved yet another bonanza for the exploiter and the hidden persuader. (On the other hand, it may soon be growing into a militant threat to the property rights of the higher age-groups.) Perhaps the manipulatable weaknesses of the young are most clearly to be seen in the spread of the drugs habit—the 'habit' having been methodically inculcated. The new reaction against the whole idea of authority has also been good for business in this area, as has the generally applauded 'flight from reality'. Hallucinatory narcotics, after all, are the easiest means of escape from the classical contour and the hard outline; and Lewis could hardly have asked for a clearer indication of what he had diagnosed as the chief ailment of the times. Not even the Bergsonian flux could rival the sensory excitements of a psychedelic trip.

But there are many other aspects of the age-war which Lewis would have been interested to analyse. One of the most notable, perhaps, is the emergence of the anti-social drop-out, with the strangely disciplined uniformity of his clothes and hair-style. Only a so-called affluent society could ever have given rise to such an eccentric, since it is necessary for the convinced hippy to be able to drop out of *something*—in this case, the affluence which he despises, or to which he feels that he will be unable to attain in a competitive society. It may simply be a case of the discipline of conformity engendering a contrary discipline of *non*-conformity. But whatever the cause, it seems likely that further rises in unemployment may well rob non-conformity of its charm: hippidom will have lost any glamour it may have had, once dropping-out becomes an involuntary process.

Hippidom, in any case, is already on the decline, having long since been out-publicized by the greater turbulence of yippidom. This form of political activism has the general advantage of being outside the older political disciplines—including that of the Communist Party. The ideological differences between Moscow and Peking have greatly strengthened the influence of the self-styled Maoists, who seem to be displacing the Trot-skyists in the further purlieus of Left-wing unorthodoxy. But it is the sudden re-emergence of the Anarchists and the Anarcho-Syndicalists which would probably have interested Lewis the most. By all the laws of objective analysis, it had seemed to him that Anarchism was on the way out: in a world domin-ated by power, he had felt, 'no outstanding thinker' was ever likely to identify himself with any such anti-power movement. It is still true that no 'outstanding' thinker has much to say for Anarchism, but the whole idea of decentralization and decision by local committee ('soviet' is no longer the fashionable word) has found new support at the universities, where the concept of 'student power' has given Anarchism a new dignity.

It should be added that the politics of the student have little to do with the politics of the people—least of all, with the politics of the working class. A student is by definition a privileged person—not to say a subsidized person—and as such tends to be resented unheard by organized labour, privileged by organ-ization as it is itself. In the Paris street-fighting of the sixties, it was amusing to note how *rapprochement* between the Sorbonne and the Renault workers completely failed to materialize, despite the social solidarity insisted upon by the students.

Perhaps the most interesting aspect of 'student power' (abroad if not yet here in Britain) has been the use which it makes of violence as an instrument of political persuasion. For as Gandhi's image gives place to that of Che Guevara, the tendency to resist passively has already changed to a habit of resisting rather more militantly with petrol-bombs and high explosives. While no more than a foreseeable aspect of life in the so-called Violent Society—the Vicious Society as it was called by the discoverer of the Jehu Syndrome—this will certainly have an eventual influence over public thinking in regard to politics as a whole. Politics, in short, will come to be thought of as a form of violence in themselves—and once that has been accepted, the way to Fascism via the blacklash will be wide open. While the public may not necessarily desire freedom—whatever it appears to be demonstrating about—it undoubtedly desires security. For the word to have any meaning at all, that can only imply the security of the majority, and the elementary safeguards which possession of property by the individual requires.

Lewis had regarded the break-up of the family as not only assured by the evolution of the socialized state, but also as a good thing in itself. And here at least he appears to have been right: the break-up is already becoming apparent. There are many obvious reasons for this, though most of them had not been there for him to take into account when he made his prophecy. The educational jungle, with its early inducement to accept the group-rhythms of the gang; the general decline in standards of family-mindedness in an age of permissiveness; the influence of television (whose compulsive hold upon the child gives way to a post-pubic reaction against the habit of family viewing); the group-rhythms of organized sport and trade unionism; the greater opportunities for sexual experimentation; rootlessness on the American pattern; the sensational glamourization of crime by the media; the growing need for direction of labour; the opening of new frontiers by cheap holiday travel; the ending of insularity which will follow upon Britain's entry into the Common Market—all will have their part to play in the gradual supercession of the family as an effective social unit. Just how far the process has gone already can be clearly understood if we remember the recent escalation in the provision of geriatric care. The old are becoming increasingly dependent upon the State for their maintenance and creature comforts: they are regarded less and less as the responsibility of their families.

As to Lewis's contention that it is a conscious policy of government to encourage the individual to lose himself within the group—this may have to be looked at rather more carefully. As we can clearly see, it has not always resulted in effective rule by calculated division. It is, after all, the basis of all successful trade unionism. As such, it has countered industrial exploitation to the point where some new method of smoothing relations between labour and management has become an urgent national priority. As Rousseau himself could have reminded Lewis, the group will always be stronger than the individual politically—a fact which the Confederation of British Industries has recognized on its own side of the negotiating table. Indeed, Lewis himself had come to realize this obvious fact by the fifties. He would probably have realized it all along, if the power of the unions had not suffered such a disastrous setback as a result of the General Strike. It was not until after the Second World War that they found themselves able once more to bargain from a position of strength.

On the cultural front, the trend has been altogether away from the classicism which Lewis had begun his pamphleteering to defend. So far as the visual arts are concerned, his confident assertion in the thirties that abstraction was already a spent force has hardly been borne out. The post-war vogue of abstract expressionism is still very much with us, though the latest indications would seem to suggest that the bottom is dropping out of that fashionable and lucrative market. Nor does one have to catalogue all the pops and ops and isms and schisms with which art promotion has tried to shore itself up over the last few years. That Lewis's own art should have increased its following so steadily at the same time is perhaps a sign that the *Zeitgeist* is beginning to change its course again. Like a shift in the Gulf Stream, this may well be bringing a change of climate in due time.

The primitivism which Lewis attacked in *Paleface*, however, is now more popular in its appeal than ever. This is partly due, perhaps, to the cheaper convenience of air travel, which has brought Mexico and Tahiti into accessibility only exceeded by that of the Costa Brava. Ethnology itself is a vastly more popular subject for study than it was in the twenties; and the excellence of modern colour reproduction has turned many a scholarly text-book into coffee-table reading. Certainly, the primitive has lost all appearance of the exotic, and may therefore ultimately lose its fashionable appeal. But will that necessarily do very much for the classicism upon which Lewis took his stand? It might well be argued that art can never be classical for long, since deviation from the norm will always have its romantic appeal—and strict adherence to any norm will end by being no art at all.

So far as his preference for 'outsideness' goes, here again, at first sight, Lewis appears to have fought a losing battle. The hard outline—the carapace—is now far more the concern of the scientist than ever it was of the creative artist. Even so, the soft inside has long outrivalled it as a subject for scientific and aesthetic study, if only because we know so much less about it. Whatever one says about art, for every new science that is exact, there are a score that are inexact—until our knowledge of them is adequate. Computerization is making new sense out of much data that once held little meaning for us. Indeed, the computer is something which Lewis clearly left out of his calculations. Its power of analysis is all that he hoped his own might be—utterly logical and dispassionate.

As an instrument of rule and control, needless to say, the computer is infinitely adaptable. To some extent it may already be said to be replacing the technocrat and the bureaucrat, though still dependent for its effectiveness upon the programming of both. In the military field, as in most other fields, it has already taken over a great deal of decision-making. It is not too fanciful to suppose that it may one day replace both judge and jury in the court of law, where the weighing of evidence is still a subjective process. Certainly it could be used to establish a new form of government by instant referendum, thereby dispensing with most of the oratory at Westminster. But whatever Lewis came to feel about the referendum as the one true voice of democracy, it seems highly unlikely that it will regularly be resorted to as the deciding factor by any government worthy of respect.

Leadership, after all, is a quality which can *not* be found in computerization—even if Lewis had looked for it there, which no respect for science would ever have persuaded him to do. It is unfortunate that his own thoughts on the subject were so sadly compromised by his tendency to mistake *effective* leadership for *good* leadership. That the two may be anything but synonymous is clear enough; but for anyone appreciative of leadership in itself, perhaps no era in history could have proved the point so disconcertingly. We can accept Lewis's assurance that at no time was he 'in the least danger of falling in love with a political Star, or becoming excited about a Party'.[13] He was far too exacting and critical for any such form of indulgence. But he was none the less convinced of the *need* for political leadership, and only unlucky in the way that leadership in his time was evilly perverted by those of whom he had better hopes.

Even so, Lewis was never convinced that a sound principle was to be rejected because of a bad example. As he put it in *The Cosmic Uniform of Peace*: 'Because a warcrazed politico in a prostrate Germany, ruined by war and inflation, called himself a Leader, it is sincerely to be hoped that *all* leadership will not forever after be looked at askance.'[14] And whether or not one shares his own mistrust of the shiftlessness and irresponsibility of the average man, some quality of leadership is obviously called for if politics are to have any meaning at all.

The question therefore arises, is the current trend towards or away from authoritarian government as Lewis felt that it should become? Does the acceptance of firm political leadership (which need not call for a political Star) imply the acceptance of despotic rule—or may it, alternatively, be our only safeguard against it? To be able to answer that question responsibly, one would have to be a far better political prophet than Lewis—or any other political commentator that one can call to mind. Despotism is at large in the world: it successfully controls at the moment nearly half the population of the world. Leadership, of one order or another, is in control of the rest. But whether leadership in the democratic sense will be able to prevail against the despotism to which it is ideologically opposed remains to be seen.

If it ever came to a shooting war between Communism and the West, as Lewis feared, the question would be resolved (for any survivors) in a reasonably short while. But perhaps we shall not be pushed into quite so decisive a solution of the matter. Gilda may well grow obsolete in her wraps.

Whatever one thinks about the chances of an eventual showdown with Communism (which I, for one, do not expect) the fact remains that democratic government itself is plainly in need of radical overhaul. The monetary system from which we have suffered since the sudden acceleration of technology is manifestly unfit for our needs: new and unorthodox reforms are being called for even in the most orthodox economic circles. Quite apart from the short-sighted clash between labour and management already noticed, there is a deplorable failure on the part of most countries to make the most of their available resources. The first principles of ecology are still not being applied to the saving of what remains healthy in our environment: the end of the century may see it damaged almost beyond repair.

On the social front, there is an alarming deterioration in the standards of behaviour, which will sooner or later have to be halted. The rising incidence of crime is far too dangerous to the prestige and efficiency of government for us to tolerate it indefinitely. Violence is gradually becoming a way of life, and if the State is unwilling or unable to protect it against crime and force, the law-abiding majority may one day decide to take measures in protection of its own interests. More force may then have to be put into containing the backlash than might have been necessary to remove its cause. It need hardly be added that this applies no less in the field of race-relations than in those of criminal or anti-social activities.

It may well be that the society of the future will decide that our cherished ideal of the rights of the individual may have to be modified in itself. This has already been suggested by one of the leading behaviourists, whose opinion is that if our culture 'continues to take freedom or dignity, rather than its own survival, as its principal value, then it is possible that some other culture will make a greater contribution to the future'.[15] It may be that some recrudescence of the Christian Humanism advocated back in the twenties by Irving Babbitt will seek to establish its own priorities, under which society will be thought of more in terms of duties than of rights. Or it may be that a stricter, more authoritarian form of Socialism may finally declare the supremacy of the State and an end to individual rights altogether.

But whatever the final outcome may be, it seems likely that the nature of democratic government as we know it may have to be revised, if only to adjust to the requirements of new and even more revolutionary technologies. What the needs of the new society may be, we have no means of knowing. But it is precisely because it can be improved, as Lewis pointed out, that democratic government stands a probable chance of surviving.

During the Second World War, Britain evolved for herself a form of democratic collectivism which was a match for both Fascism and Communism. The vigorous productivity of the war years, if repeated today by national consent, could raise our standard of living far above any yet known in Europe. Given the common purpose, there is no reason to suppose that democratic government and democratic resolve could not be equally effective in peacetime as under threat of invasion. The undoubted efficiency of Soviet Communism, together with its now incontestably superior military potential, might seem a sufficient reason for proving as much.

In terms of government, war is the ultimate admission of *inefficiency*, for nothing could ever be a fraction so wasteful of everything that government was instituted to preserve. It should not be necessary for threats of war or invasion—which now means war and likely annihilation—to teach us the way to live. In both Europe and America we see society in process of changing its essential pattern and character. A quiet revolution is in progress everywhere—a quiet revolution which bodes nothing but good for the future, provided its energies are directed *towards* the future and are not allowed to turn inwards upon itself. For the problems that can be thrown up by 'quiet' revolutions (such as the Industrial Revolution) can be no less dangerous than those which spark off revolutions far more noisy. It is during such periods of revolutionary change, as Lewis insisted, that the stability of good and efficient government is most necessary; for completion of the revolution will bring government of a new kind automatically. But failure to govern well while the quiet revolution is in progress can only lead to frustration and misery.

It was in the interests of efficient government that *The Art of*

Being Ruled was written in the mid-twenties. And as it sought to prove, the art of being ruled consists—above all—in ensuring that we are being ruled well. Our chances of being so will be greatly enhanced by reminding ourselves just what the aims of government should be; just what the anomalies of government as we know it are; and just what practical steps can be taken by all of us to remove those anomalies.

If Lewis concerned himself *mainly* with the anomalies of democratic government in his time, at least he did his time some service. For nobody could have turned a more brilliant spotlight on the various ways in which the worst in all of us can be flattered and used and directed to defeat the best in us. It was in its encouragement and happy acceptance of that technique that he found democracy to be most at fault. By insisting upon the paramountcy of the admass, it was denying its individual minds the chance of leading the way to those better things implicit in individual freedom. And despite the misuse which he felt had been made of the word, freedom was what—as individual and as intellectual—Lewis valued most on earth:

> The life of the intelligence is the very incarnation of freedom: where it is dogmatic and harsh it is impure; where it is too political it is impure: its disciplines are less arbitrary and less *political* than those of religion: and it is the most inveterate enemy of unjust despotic power. In its operation it is less violent and more beneficent than religion, with its customary intolerance of emotional extremes. It does not exercise power by terror or by romantic pictures of the vast machinery of Judgment and Destruction. It is more humane than are the programmes of the theological justiciary. And its servants are not a sect nor an organized caste, like the priest or the hereditary aristocrat, but individuals possessing no concerted and lawless power, coming indifferently from all classes, and living simply among other people. And their pride, if they have it, is because of something inside themselves which has been won at no one else's expense, and that no one can give them or remove from them.[16]

If that is the ultimate ideal of freedom, only under the most enlightened form of government can we ever hope to attain it. And as Lewis himself was persuaded in his later years, that government will surely be democratic—and perfected by our own efforts.

NOTES

1. *R H*, p.ix.
2. Ibid., p.228.
3. Ibid., p.285.
4. Ibid.. p.241.
5. Ibid., p.xii.
6. Ibid., p.60.
7. *W and A*, p.115.
8. Ibid., p.120.
9. Ibid., p.195.
10. Ibid., p.41.
11. Ibid., p.198.
12. *The Sea Mists of the Winter*, published in *The Listener*, 10.5.51.
13. *R A*, p.64.
14. *The Sewanee Review*, Autumn 1945, p.524.
15. *Beyond Freedom and Dignity*, by B. F. Skinner, p.181. In view of Lewis's contempt for behaviourism, it is amusing to find this book re-arguing points first made in *The Art of Being Ruled*!
16. *A of B R*, pp.432-3.

Abbreviations Used in the Notes

for books by Wyndham Lewis which are quoted in the text
(for fuller descriptions see the Select Bibliography)

A C M	*America and Cosmic Man*
A I P	*America, I Presume*
Anglosaxony	*Anglosaxony : A League that Works*
A of B R	*The Art of Being Ruled*
As of G	*The Apes of God*
B and B	*Blasting and Bombardiering*
C Y D	*Count Your Dead : They Are Alive!*
D of Y	*Doom of Youth*
D P and D S	*The Diabolical Principle and The Dithyrambic Spectator*
Hitler	*Hitler*
L and F	*The Lion and the Fox*
Letters of W L	*The Letters of Wyndham Lewis, edited by W. K. Rose*
L W o E	*Left Wings over Europe*
Mr Bull	*The Mysterious Mr Bull*
M W A	*Men Without Art*
O G and N G	*The Old Gang and the New Gang*
O-W S	*One-Way Song*
Paleface	*Paleface : The Philosophy of the 'Melting-pot*
R A	*Rude Assignment*
R H	*Rotting Hill*
The Jews	*The Jews, Are They Human?*
The H C	*The Hitler Cult, and How it will End*
T and W M	*Time and Western Man*
W and A	*The Writer and the Absolute*

Select Bibliography

A. Books by Wyndham Lewis published during his lifetime

1913   *Timon of Athens.* (Portfolio of drawings: no text.) The Cube Press, London.

1914   *BLAST, No. 1. Review of the Great English Vortex*, edited by Wyndham Lewis. The Bodley Head, London.

1915   *BLAST No. 2. Review of the Great English Vortex*, edited by Wyndham Lewis. The Bodley Head, London.

1917   *The Ideal Giant, The Code of a Herdsman, Cantelman's Spring-Mate.* Privately printed for the London Office of the *Little Review*.

1918   *Tarr.* The Egoist Ltd, London.

1919   *Fifteen Drawings.* (250 sets: no text.) The Ovid Press, London.
       The Caliph's Design: Architects! Where is your Vortex? The Egoist Ltd, London.

1921   *The Tyro, No. 1. A Review of the Arts of Painting, Sculpture and Design.* Edited by Wyndham Lewis. The Egoist Press, London.

1922   *The Tyro, No. 2. A Review of the Arts of Painting, Sculpture and Design.* Edited by Wyndham Lewis. The Egoist Press, London.

1926   *The Art of Being Ruled.* Chatto and Windus, London.

1927   *The Lion and the Fox: The Rôle of the Hero in the Plays of Shakespeare.* Grant Richards, London.
       The Enemy, No. 1. A Review of Art and Literature. Editor: Wyndham Lewis. The Arthur Press, London.
       The Enemy, No. 2. A Review of Art and Literature. Editor: Wyndham Lewis. The Arthur Press, London.
       Time and Western Man. Chatto and Windus, London.
       The Wild Body: A Soldier of Humour and Other Stories. Chatto and Windus, London.

1928   *The Childermass: Section 1.* Chatto and Windus, London.
       Tarr. (Revised version.) The Phoenix Library, Chatto and Windus, London.

1929   *The Enemy, No. 3. A Review of Art and Literature.* Editor: Wyndham Lewis. The Arthur Press, London.
       Paleface: The Philosophy of the 'Melting-pot'. Chatto and Windus, London.

1930   *The Apes of God.* (750 signed copies.) The Arthur Press, London.

Satire and Fiction. Enemy Pamphlet No. 1. The Arthur Press, London.
1931 Hitler. Chatto and Windus, London.
The Diabolical Principle and the Dithyrambic Spectator. Chatto and Windus, London.
1932 Filibusters in Barbary (Record of a Visit to the Sous). Grayson and Grayson, London. (Withdrawn after publication.)
Doom of Youth. Chatto and Windus, London. (Withdrawn after publication.)
The Enemy of the Stars. (Revised version of the play first printed in BLAST, No. 1.) Desmond Harmsworth, London.
Snooty Baronet. Cassell, London.
Thirty Personalities and a Self-Portrait. (Portfolio of drawings, with a foreword. 200 sets, signed.) Desmond Harmsworth, London.
1933 The Old Gang and the New Gang. Desmond Harmsworth, London.
One-Way Song. Faber and Faber, London.
1934 Men Without Art. Cassell, London.
1935 Beyond this Limit: Pictures by Wyndham Lewis and Words by Naomi Mitchison. Jonathan Cape, London.
1936 Left Wings over Europe: or, How to Make a War About Nothing. Jonathan Cape, London.
The Roaring Queen. Jonathan Cape, London. (Withdrawn before publication.)
1937 Count Your Dead: They Are Alive! or A New War in the Making. Lovat Dickson, London.
The Revenge for Love. Cassell, London.
Blasting and Bombardiering. Eyre and Spottiswoode, London.
1938 The Mysterious Mr Bull. Robert Hale, London.
1939 The Jews, Are They Human? Allen and Unwin, London.
Wyndham Lewis the Artist, from 'Blast' to Burlington House. Laidlaw and Laidlaw, London.
The Hitler Cult and How it will End. Dent, London.
1940 America, I Presume. Howell Soskin, New York.
1941 The Vulgar Streak. Robert Hale, London.
Anglosaxony: A League that Works. The Ryerson Press, Toronto.
1948 America and Cosmic Man. Nicolson and Watson, London.
1950 Rude Assignment: A narrative of my career up-to-date. Hutchinson, London.
1951 Rotting Hill. Methuen, London.
1952 The Writer and the Absolute. Methuen, London.
1954 Self Condemned. Methuen, London.
The Demon of Progress in the Arts. Methuen, London.
1955 The Human Age. Book Two: Monstre Gai. Book Three: Malign Fiesta. Methuen, London.
1956 The Red Priest. Methuen, London.
The Human Age. Book One: The Childermass. (Slightly revised version.) Methuen, London.

B. Selections of Lewis's work published since his death

1963 The Letters of Wyndham Lewis. Edited by W. K. Rose. Methuen, London.

1966 *Wyndham Lewis: A Soldier of Humor and Selected Writings.* Edited, with an Introduction, by Raymond Rosenthal. A Signet Classic. The New American Library, New York; The New English Library, London.

1969 *Wyndham Lewis: An Anthology of his Prose.* Edited with an Introduction by E. W. F. Tomlin. Methuen, London.

1971 *Wyndham Lewis on Art: Collected Writings 1913–1956.* Edited and introduced by Walter Michel and C. J. Fox. Thames and Hudson, London.

1972 *Wyndham Lewis,* by William Pritchard. Profiles in Literature. Routledge and Kegan Paul, London.

C. Main critical studies and symposia on Lewis and his works

1932 *Apes, Japes and Hitlerism,* by John Gawsworth. The Unicorn Press, London.

1932 *Wyndham Lewis: A Discursive Exposition,* by Hugh Gordon Porteus. Desmond Harmsworth, London.

1937 *Twentieth Century Verse: Wyndham Lewis Double Number,* edited by Julian Symons. No. 6/7, Nov./Dec., 1937.

1951 *A Master of Our Time: A Study of Wyndham Lewis,* by Geoffrey Grigson. Methuen, London.

   The Art of Wyndham Lewis, edited with an essay and notes by Charles Handley-Read, and a critical evaluation by Eric Newton. Faber and Faber, London.

1954 *Wyndham Lewis,* by Hugh Kenner. The Makers of Modern Literature. Methuen, London.

1955 *Wyndham Lewis,* by E. W. F. Tomlin. Writers and Their Work: No. 64. Published for the British Council and the National Book League by Longmans, Green, London.

1957 *Wyndham Lewis: A Portrait of the Artist as the Enemy,* by Geoffrey Wagner. Routledge and Kegan Paul, London.

1961 *Wyndham Lewis at Cornell: A Review of the Lewis Papers presented to the University by William G. Mennen.* By W. K. Rose. Cornell University Library, Ithaca, New York.

1968 *Canadian Literature No. 35: Wyndham Lewis in Canada,* edited by George Woodcock. University of British Columbia, Vancouver. Winter 1968.

1969 *Wyndham Lewis,* by William H. Pritchard. Twaine, New York.

1970 *Agenda: Wyndham Lewis Special Issue,* edited by William Cookson. Vol. 7 No. 3–Vol. 8 No. 1 (3 issues). Autumn–Winter 1969–1970.

1971 *Wyndham Lewis in Canada,* edited by George Woodcock, with an introduction by Julian Symons. Canadian Literature Series, No. 2. University of British Columbia, Vancouver. (Reprinted from *Canadian Literature No. 35* above, with additional material.)

   Wyndham Lewis: Paintings and Drawings. Text and Catalogue by Walter Michel, with an introductory essay by Hugh Kenner. Thames and Hudson, London.

To appear:

   Les Cahiers de l'Herne, No. ?: Wyndham Lewis, dirigé par Bernard Lafourcade. Editions de l'Herne, Paris.

D. Short selection of works relating to the social and political events written about by Wyndham Lewis

ARENDT, HANNAH. *The Origins of Totalitarianism.* New York. 1951. (2nd edition, enlarged, Allen and Unwin, London. 1958.)

BABBITT, IRVING. *Democracy and Leadership.* Constable, London. 1924.

BARTLETT, VERNON. *Nazi Germany Explained.* Gollancz, London. 1933.

BASSETT, REGINALD. *Democracy and Foreign Policy. A Case History: the Sino-Japanese Dispute, 1931–33.* Longmans, Green, London. 1952.

——*Nineteen Thirty-One: Political Crisis.* Macmillan, London. 1958.

BULLOCK, ALAN. *Hitler: A Study in Tyranny.* Odhams, London. 1952. (Revised edition, 1964.)

BURNHAM, JAMES. *The Managerial Revolution.* Putnam, London. 1942.

BUTLER, R. D'OLIER. *The Roots of National Socialism.* Faber and Faber, London. 1941.

CARR, EDWARD HALLETT. *The Twenty Years' Crisis, 1919–1939.* Macmillan, London. 1939.

CARR, RAYMOND. *Spain, 1808–1939.* Oxford History of Modern Europe. Clarendon Press, Oxford. 1966.

"CATO". *Guilty Men.* Gollancz, London. 1940.

CHURCHILL, WINSTON S. *Great Contemporaries.* Thornton Butterworth, London. 1937. (Enlarged edition, Macmillan, London. 1942.)

——*Step by Step.* Thornton Butterworth, London. 1939.

——*The Second World War.* 6 vols. Cassell, London. 1948–54.

CROSS, COLIN. *The Fascists in Britain.* Barrie and Rockliff, London. 1961.

FOOT, M. D. R. *British Foreign Police Since 1898.* Hutchinson's University Library, London. 1956.

GANNON, FRANKLIN REID. *The British Press and Germany, 1936–1939.* Clarendon Press, Oxford. 1971.

GEDYE, G. E. R. *Fallen Bastions: The Central European Tragedy.* Gollancz, London. 1939.

GILBERT, BENTLEY B. *Britain Since 1918.* Batsford, London. 1967.

GILBERT, MARTIN. *Britain and Germany Between the Wars.* Problems and Perspectives in History. Longmans, Green, London. 1964.

——*The Roots of Appeasement.* Weidenfeld and Nicolson, London, 1966.

GILBERT, MARTIN AND GOTT, RICHARD. *The Appeasers.* Weidenfeld and Nicolson, London. 1963.

GRAVES, ROBERT AND HODGE, ALAN. *The Long Week-End: A Social History of Great Britain, 1918–1939.* Faber and Faber, London. 1940.

HADLEY, W. W. *Munich, Before and After.* Cassell, London, 1944.

HAMILTON, ALASTAIR. *The Appeal of Fascism: A Study of Intellectuals and Fascism, 1919–1945.* Anthony Blond, London. 1971.

HARRISON, JOHN R. *The Reactionaries.* Gollancz, London. 1966.

HIRTH, FRÉDÉRIC. *Hitler, ou Le Guerrier Déchâiné.* Éditions du Tambourin, Paris. 1930.

HITLER, ADOLF. *Mein Kampf.* Unexpurgated edition, translated by James Murphy. Hurst and Blackett, London. 1939.

JORDAN, W. M. *Great Britain, France, and the German Problem, 1918–1939: A Study of Anglo-French Relations in the Making and Maintenance of The Versailles Settlement.* Oxford University Press, London. 1943.

KEYNES, JOHN MAYNARD. *The Economic Consequences of the Peace.* Macmillan, London. 1919.

MONTGOMERY, JOHN. *The Twenties: An Informal Social History*. Allen and Unwin, London. 1957.

MOSLEY, SIR OSWALD. *My Life*. Nelson, London. 1970.

MOWAT, CHARLES LOCH. *Britain Between the Wars, 1918–1940*. Methuen, London. 1955.

MUGGERIDGE, MALCOLM. *The Thirties: 1930–1940 in Great Britain*. Hamish Hamilton, London. 1940.

NAMIER, LEWIS B. *Europe in Decay: A Study in Disintegration, 1936–1940*. Macmillan, London. 1950.

PRICE, G. WARD. *I Know These Dictators*. Harrap, London. 1937.

REED, DOUGLAS. *Insanity Fair*. Jonathan Cape, London. 1938.

——*Disgrace Abounding*. Jonathan Cape, London. 1939.

ROTHERMERE, VISCOUNT. *Warnings and Predictions*. Eyre and Spottiswoode, London. 1939.

RUSSELL, BERTRAND. *The Practice and Theory of Bolshevism*. Allen and Unwin, London. 1920.

——*A History of Western Philosophy, and its Connection with Political and Social Circumstances from the Earliest Times to the Present Day*. Allen and Unwin, London. 1946.

——*The Autobiography of Bertrand Russell*. 3 vols. Allen and Unwin, London. 1967–69.

SELDES, GILBERT. *Sawdust Caesar*. Arthur Barker, London. 1936.

SETON-WATSON, R. W. *Britain and the Dictators: A Survey of Post-War British Policy*. University Press, Cambridge. 1938.

——*From Munich to Danzig*. Methuen, London. 1939.

SHIRER, WILLIAM L. *The Rise and Fall of the Third Reich: A History of Nazi Germany*. Secker and Warburg, London. 1960.

SKINNER, B. F. *Beyond Freedom and Dignity*. Alfred A. Knopf, New York. 1971.

SYMONS, JULIAN. *The General Strike*. Cresset Press, London. 1957.

TAYLOR, A. J. P. *The Origins of the Second World War*. Hamish Hamilton, London. 1961.

——*English History, 1914–1945*. The Oxford History of England. Clarendon Press, Oxford. 1965.

THOMAS, HUGH. *The Spanish Civil War*. Eyre and Spottiswoode, London, 1961. (Revised edition, Penguin Books, London. 1965.)

THOMPSON, NEVILLE. *The Anti-Appeasers: Conservative Opposition to Appeasement in the 1930s*. Clarendon Press, Oxford. 1971.

VOIGHT, FREDERICK A. *Unto Caesar*. Constable, London. 1938.

WATKINS, K. W. *Britain Divided: The Effects of the Spanish Civil War on British Political Opinion*. Nelson, London. 1963.

WELLS, H. G. *The Open Conspiracy: Blue Prints For a World Revolution*. Gollancz, London. 1928.

——*The Work, Wealth and Happiness of Mankind*. Heinemann, London. 1932.

WHEELER-BENNETT, J. W. *Munich: Prologue to Tragedy*. Macmillan, London. 1948.

WISKEMANN, ELIZABETH. *The Rome–Berlin Axis: A History of the Relations between Hitler and Mussolini*. Oxford University Press, London. 1949.

——*Europe of the Dictators, 1919–1945*. The Fontana History of Europe. Collins, London. 1966.

——*Fascism in Italy: Its Development and Influence*. The Making of the Twentieth Century. Macmillan, London. 1969.

WOOD, NEAL. *Communism and British Intellectuals*. Gollancz, London. 1959.

Index

© Cassell & Co. Ltd 1972